More praise for
THE SUM OF SMALL THINGS

"What makes Currid-Halkett's argument powerful is that she mines the data to prove that the members of this group are passing on their privilege to their children in just as pernicious a way as the old aristocrats passed on their estates and titles."

—HARRY WALLOP, *Times*

"A key companion to Robert Putnam's survey of dwindling US social mobility, *Our Kids*."

—BARBARA KISER, *Nature*

"The aspirational class gets a kick in the quinoa courtesy of Elizabeth Currid-Halkett's *The Sum of Small Things*."

—SLOANE CROSLEY, *Vanity Fair*

"*The Sum of Small Things* . . . looks at the consumer side of proximity and inequality. Kicking off from Thorstein Veblen's idea of conspicuous consumption, in which the leisure class of the 19th century displayed its inherited wealth through material goods, she posits a new 'aspirational class.'"

—DYLAN REID, *Literary Review of Canada*

"Anatomises [the 'aspirational class'] using fascinating American consumption data."

—SIMON KUPER, *Financial Times*

"There are a lot of good data in this book."

—DANNY DORLING, *Times Higher Education*

"Currid-Halkett's biting, often humorous commentary is not just a send up of the so-called 'coastal elites.' It's a trenchant analysis that combines economic and sociological evidence to describe major trends."

—DAN KOPF, *Quartz*

"[Elizabeth Currid-Halkett] paints a remarkably fine-grained portrait of how the spending habits of Americans have evolved over the decades."

—*ECONOMIST*

"There is a lot to learn here about the contemporary face of income inequality."

"What are the status consumption habits of the twenty-first century? In *The Sum of Small Things*, Elizabeth Currid-Halkett blends social science and keen observation to present the new, best guide to this topic of never-ending interest, for the status-conscious in all of us."

"'Organic,' 'artisanal,' 'boutique'—these are the catchwords of what has become, in Elizabeth Currid-Halkett's view, a new self-regarding social class, grounded less in money than in elite education, and inured to the problems of those less fortunate. This is a timely, original, and disquieting analysis of contemporary American society."

"Exploring how the consumer choices of today's 'aspirational class' express identity and values yet reinforce social exclusivity and economic status, Elizabeth Currid-Halkett's lively book offers a thoroughly researched and fair-minded update to Veblen's classic look at the leisure class. Eschewing mockery and polemics, *The Sum of Small Things* challenges readers to think hard about culture and consumption in a postscarcity economy."

"Just as Thorstein Veblen captured his time with the phrase 'conspicuous consumption,' Elizabeth Currid-Halkett nails the contemporary rise of a subtler but no less materialist inconspicuous consumption. This book is a must-read for anyone who wants to understand modern cities or culture today."

"*The Sum of Small Things* crackles with original insights about consumer goods and the individuals who choose them. Currid-Halkett's concepts of 'the aspirational class' and 'conspicuous production' advance consumption studies and provide fresh news about the search for distinction. Fast-paced, well-told, and unfailingly interesting, this book is an intellectual treat across the board."

"This book takes readers on a tour of contemporary U.S. inequality—in particular the classes who occupy its highest strata—via characteristic patterns of consumption behavior. Revealing polarizing patterns of class behavior, this engaging and thought-provoking work will attract a substantial readership and generate discussion."

ELIZABETH CURRID-HALKET

Elizabeth Currid-Halkett is the James Irvine Chair in Urban and Regional Planning and professor of public policy at the University of Southern California. She is the author of *The Warhol Economy* and *Starstruck*. Her work has been featured in the *Los Angeles Times*, the *New York Times*, the *New Yorker*, and the *Wall Street Journal*. She lives in Los Angeles with her husband and their two sons. Find her online at http://www.elizabethcurridhalkett.com/.

The
SUM
of
SMALL
THINGS

The
SUM
of
SMALL
THINGS

A Theory of the Aspirational Class

Elizabeth Currid-Halkett

PRINCETON UNIVERSITY PRESS

Princeton and Oxford

Requests for permission to reproduce material from this work should be sent to Permissions, Princeton University Press

Published by Princeton University Press, 41 William Street, Princeton, New Jersey 08540

In the United Kingdom: Princeton University Press, 6 Oxford Street, Woodstock, Oxfordshire OX20 1TR
press.princeton.edu

Cover design by Karl Spurzem

First paperback printing, 2018
Paper ISBN: 9780691183176
Cloth ISBN: 9780691162737

Library of Congress Control Number: 2018948352

Data source for tables: Consumer Expenditure Survey, Bureau of Labor Statistics

British Library Cataloging-in-Publication Data is available

This book has been composed in Minion Pro and Bauer Bodoni Std 1

Printed on acid-free paper. ∞

Printed in the United States of America

Oliver. Ezra. Richard.
The sum of my everything.

CONTENTS

ACKNOWLEDGMENTS

Thank you so very much to the following lovely human beings....

My literary agent and dear friend, David Halpern from the Robbins Office on whom I rely to put one metaphorical foot in front of the other. Whatever writing block or distress I may be relaying to him, David's voice is a blanket of cashmere calm and he makes me laugh, always. Thank you to the rest of the Robbins Office for chapter reads, editorial suggestions, and various other triage support.

Princeton University Press: Meagan Levinson, my editor who worked closely with me to organize the concepts and arguments as cogently as possible (any lapses are my own). Seth Ditchik, who acquired this book at Princeton before leaving for Yale University Press, and whom I appreciate for investing in my ideas from their nascent stages and for his intellectual contributions to early drafts of the manuscript. My copy-editor, Karen Verde, who taught me the appropriate use of gerunds and commas. Sara Lerner and Samantha Nader, Julia Haav, Caroline Priday, and the entire publicity team at Princeton, all of whom are enthusiastic, hardworking, and so creative—you dazzle me every time.

My lecture agent, friend, and kindred spirit, Lucy Blumenfeld. To many more joint manicure/book strategy sessions.

My colleagues at USC who have read draft chapters, helped with data and methods, and engaged with my ideas. I'm so lucky to have you just down the hall. The same for my dean, Jack Knott, who always supports my research and whatever direction it takes so long as I work hard and try my best. My doctoral students Hyojung Lee and Soyoon Choo have been indispensable and offer an attention to detail and freshness that this book (and I) have been so lucky to receive. In particular, Hyojung, soon to be a post-doctoral scholar at the Joint Center for Housing Studies at Harvard University, has been my cerebral comrade for much of the study of the Consumer Expenditure Survey. Very early on, Hyojung believed in the ideas underpinning this book and he set off on the journey with me in search of the evidence.

Thank you to USC's Lusk Center for Real Estate for the research funding support, particularly the chapters using the Bureau of Labor Statistics' Consumer Expenditure Survey.

Thank you to the kind people I interviewed for this book for giving me your time, thoughtfulness, and wisdom, all of which shine through in these pages.

My intellectual heroes: Harvey Molotch, Allen Scott, Saskia Sassen, Michael Storper, Susan Fainstein, Jerold Kayden.

My favorite people: Brooke Cutler, Cara Esposito, Marisa Christian, Eric Lovecchio, Sloane Crosley, Michelle Dean, Tess Mordan, Dave Auckland, James Brookes, Michael Storper (also see: intellectual hero), Elizabeth Price, Quintin Price, Eyal Ben-Isaac, Joan Halkett, Bill Halkett, my sister Sarah, my brother Evan, my sister-in-law Gabriela, my nephew Liam. Mom and Dad. I wish I could show each and every one of you an x-ray of my heart so you could see how much of it you fill.

Ezra, Oliver, Richard: You are the sum of my everything.

The
SUM
of
SMALL
THINGS

CHAPTER 1

The Twenty-first-Century
"Leisure" Class

A hand-wrought silver spoon, of a commercial value of some ten to twenty dollars, is not ordinarily more serviceable—in the first sense of the word—than a machine-made spoon of the same material. It may not even be more serviceable ... One of the chief uses, if not the chief use, of the costlier spoon is ignored; the hand-wrought spoon gratifies our taste, our sense of the beautiful ... the material of the hand-wrought spoon is some one hundred times more valuable than the baser metal, without very greatly excelling the latter in intrinsic beauty of grain or color, and without being in any appreciable degree superior in point of mechanical serviceability.

—Thorstein Veblen, *The Theory of the Leisure Class* (1899)

In the 1920s, Muriel Bristol attended a summer's afternoon tea party in Cambridge, UK. A number of professors and their spouses were also in attendance. On this particular occasion, the host poured Bristol a cup of tea and poured in the milk thereafter. Bristol protested, explaining that she liked her "milk in first," as the tea tasted better that way. Despite skeptical resistance from those in attendance, Bristol insisted she could tell the difference. Ronald Alymer Fischer, one of those present, who would later go on to become "Sir Fischer" and the godfather of modern empirical statistics with his famous book *The Design of Experiments*, had an idea. Surely, if eight cups of tea were poured, four with "milk in first" and the other four with tea in first, and the lady identified them correctly then she would be proven right (her chances of merely guessing by chance would be 1 in 70). Fischer, like everyone else present, believed Bristol would likely fail the test. In other words, they believed

Bristol's belief in her tea acumen was embedded in a false sense of aesthetics and taste rather than reality. As it turns out, Bristol correctly determined the order of tea and milk in each of the eight cups.

Fischer's experiment, which went on to transform statistics and modern science (it became the foundation for testing the "null hypothesis"),[1] would not have been possible if not for the embedded status and its accompanying aesthetics in how one drinks one's tea. Milk in first or last has been a sign of status since the Victorian era, as the choice of one or the other implies one's class position.

In fact, the difference boils down to the materials from which one's dishware is made. In the Victorian era, materials used to make lesser-quality teacups would often crack if hot tea were poured into them. Pouring milk in first mitigated the chances of cracking one's cup. However, those with money could afford the fine china that could withstand the heat of tea, thus milk in later was a signal of one's elevated economic position.[2] Even when the order of milk and tea was primarily a practical matter, it revealed class more than taste. After all, those owning fine china would put the milk in last to demonstrate this luxury. As the butler in the famous British drama of the same time period, *Upstairs, Downstairs*, remarked, "Those of us downstairs put the milk in first, while those upstairs put the milk in last."

Even in more contemporary times, when the quality of almost all dishware is strong enough to withstand hot tea, milk in first remained a sign of social class. The twentieth-century English novelist, Nancy Mitford, employed the term "M.I.F." to describe the lower classes, and the turn of phrase is still used satirically in popular media to describe the working classes or those without refined social skills. Today, the famous English tea purveyor Fortnum & Mason characterizes the choice as a "thorny question," devoting an entire essay on its website to how to drink tea.

How did such a prosaic choice of action, so subtle and ostensibly innocuous, become an amplified sign of class? Throughout time, matters of seeming practicality have evolved into symbols of status. In Victorian England, the displaying of medicines in the parlor was a sign that one could afford to see a doctor and buy medicine. In pre-Revolutionary Paris, the use of candles was rare and expensive, yet even when access to light (and later electricity) became more democratized, the lighting of candles at dinnertime remained a sign of taste and breeding.[3] The same is true for the use of cloth napkins when paper napkins would do (and eliminate the hassle of laundering).

Everything we do has social meaning. Our childhood, family life, income bracket, and concurrent social circles teach us how to go about our lives and interact with the world in big and small ways. Through both behaviors and material goods, we disclose our socioeconomic position, whether we like it or not. As the famous sociologist Pierre Bourdieu observed in his book *Distinction*, status emerges from prosaic cultural forms and signs, and most fundamentally, from how we live.

Status has always consumed us. This observation has been made by many before me, and perhaps best by the great British anthropologist Dame Mary Douglas, and more recently by Daniel Miller in his book *Consumption and Its Consequences*. Often the things we acquire and how we use them demonstrate this status to the world. There are obvious big-ticket items—large homes in the right zip codes, sports cars, fine china, and expensive watches. Yet, even manners convey a certain upbringing or way of life—sending handwritten notes rather than email, the way we place our utensils upon finishing a meal, having fresh flowers delivered to our beloved and so forth. Almost all of these behaviors suggest social position and rely on the use of visible goods and the skills for how to employ them in a particular way. Or, as Douglas observed in her book *The World of Goods*, "The goods are both the hardware and the software, so to speak, of an information system ... Goods that minister to physical needs—food and drink—are no less carriers of meaning than ballet or poetry."[4]

Similarly, our consumption of goods for status should not be taken lightly or merely as superficial posturing. Consumption is a part of how we define ourselves as individuals and vis-à-vis social groups (as members and outsiders and sometimes both at the same time). We need to see our consumption of goods as an intricate part of humanity's social system. Just as our work or family structure cultivates who we are, so does what we buy and the norms of behavior we learn. We must see consumption as appropriated to signal things much deeper than what is simply visible.[5]

4 • CHAPTER 1

THE THEORY OF THE LEISURE CLASS

Perhaps no one captured and articulated the social significance of consumption better than the social critic and economist Thorstein Veblen.
Written in the late 1800s, Veblen's polemic treatise *The Theory of the
Leisure Class* is the defining text that precisely expresses the relationship
between material goods and status. At the peak of the Gilded Age, and
in the wake of the triumphs of the Industrial Revolution, Veblen's work
was very much a sign of the times he lived in. He became a leading
thinker and popular critic during the Progressive Era, deriding profits
and the consumption and wastefulness that came along with the wealth
of capitalism. Veblen is most famous for his concept of "conspicuous
consumption," the use of particular goods through which status is revealed. Veblen directed most of his critique toward the "leisure class," a
wealthy and idle group who vainly and incessantly demonstrated their
social and economic position through material goods, many of which
were useless and nonfunctional items.[6]

Veblen's theories were met with outrage—he vilified an entire stratum
of society as useless and superficial and accused them of almost exclusively responding to social rank and cues. As H. L. Mencken rejoined,
"Do I enjoy a decent bath because I know that John Smith cannot afford
one—or because I delight in being clean? Do I admire Beethoven's Fifth
Symphony because it is incomprehensible to Congressmen and Meth-
odists—or because I genuinely love music? Do I prefer kissing a pretty
girl to a charwoman because even a janitor can kiss a charwoman—or
because the pretty girl looks better, smells better and kisses better?"[7]

The Theory of the Leisure Class scathingly critiqued the upper classes
of society and challenged orthodox economic theories embedded in the
idea that people spent to maximize utility of their money.[8] Veblen confronted conventional notions of how we spend, arguing that emulation
and imitation motivated consumer habits, much of which were irratio-
nal and wasteful. Veblen's famous example of leisure-class conspicuous
consumption is the use of a hand-wrought silver spoon. While, of course,
flatware made of other materials or machine-made would be perfectly
acceptable and did not look any different from their pricey counterpart,
the use of silver flatware would demonstrate to others a particular rank in
society. Veblen also snidely observed the use of gratuitous canes (which

implied a man did not need to use his hands for labor) and corsets which, as they were so constraining, meant a woman could not possibly work. Only those of the leisure class were able to acquire and actually use such goods. This particular critique is what made Veblen famous and infamous—and still relevant more than one hundred years later.[9] *The Theory of the Leisure Class* remains one of the most important books on economic thought written in the past two centuries.[10]

While Veblen is most known for his critique of conspicuous consumption, his study of status was far more complicated and in-depth than the conventional shorthand given to his theories.[11] Veblen's overarching thesis is that the recognition of social division and stratification is central to understanding modern society. One's social position was more important than any value or usefulness a person gave to the world. Ironically, the demonstration of high social position (through consumption, leisure, and nonpecuniary practices) often manifested itself through the *uselessness* of objects and activity. Veblen also observed the phenomenon of "conspicuous leisure"—reading classics at Oxford, traveling abroad, participating in sports and doing nonfunctional things with one's time, and "conspicuous waste"—gratuitous service workers or help around the house. The ability to use time for something with no obvious productive purpose was an option only for the upper classes. The lack of one's own utility or the uselessness of one's goods was the most salient marker of status. In Veblen's worldview, the silver spoons and signaling of one's lack of use through canes or corsets suggested that appearance matters more than real happiness or comfort. Like Karl Marx, Veblen saw the economy as a dominant part of the social reality of his time.[12] He believed that the economy provided the fundamental structural framework from which all of society emerged, formed, and interacted. Thus what we consumed, what we had the economic means to consume, and what others observed us consuming, determined our place in society.

One hundred years later, the term conspicuous consumption is still used to capture this particular type of economic and social behavior. But society and the economy have changed dramatically since Veblen's time and new forms of consumption and behavior have emerged to reveal social position. A century after Veblen wrote *The Theory of the Leisure Class*, massive changes in technology and globalization have changed how we work, live, and consume. The Industrial Revolution and the sophistication of manufacturing both created a middle class and reduced the cost of material goods such that conspicuous consumption has become a mainstream behavior. Simultaneously, the leisure class has been replaced by a new elite, grounded in meritocracy, the acquisition of knowledge and culture, and less clearly defined by their economic position. With this new group comes a new set of norms and values. They work longer hours and for the most part, their meritocracy and cultural values are prized over birthright. As modern capitalism opened the floodgates to material consumption, it has also brought about increasing inequality.[13] But the distance across classes is not simply defined by the stuff people own. These changes have transformed the dynamics of work, leisure, how we consume, and how our consumption is linked to status. Despite the seeming "democratization of luxury," to quote Daniel Boorstin, the twenty-first century has brought greater socioeconomic inequality than ever before, further distancing the elites from the rest.

All of these various changes in society and the economy challenge and change the meaning and attainment of status and consumption in the twenty-first century. What does consumption look like today and how has it changed over the past several decades? How do our gender, race, profession, and where we live impact what we buy? If acquisition of material goods is now fairly accessible to all, how do wealthy elites maintain their status? And if Veblen stepped into the twenty-first century, what would he say? This book is about those changes and how they have impacted the way we spend money, the way we spend time, and how we reveal our status in big and small ways.

But first, let's look at how status has always been central to human civilization.

CONSPICUOUS CONSUMPTION
THROUGHOUT HISTORY

While conspicuous consumption may feel like a truly capitalist, post-Industrial Revolution spectacle, humans have been engaging in the status wars since the beginning of human civilization. Veblen believed that much of what he observed at the turn of the twentieth century emerged in prehistoric times.[14]

Andrew Wallace-Hadrill's study of ancient Roman society demonstrates that conspicuous consumption was alive and well prior to AD 79. The less well-off emulated the higher social class, many thousands of years before the arrival of flat screen TVs and cheap monthly car payments that obfuscate current class lines. In his archeological study of early Pompeii and Herculaneum homes, ranging in size and number of rooms, he finds that "the same status markers that are found in the grandest homes also occur, albeit more rarely, in quite small units."[15] For example, Wallace-Hadrill points out that decoration, a very basic symbol of status, was displayed by the wealthy in their homes and imitated by the poor, even when they had little space or means to do so. Later, during the Roman Empire or the Imperial period, as Rome became wealthier and more powerful, the prevalence of decoration was greater and more democratic. The habits of the rich were imitated more consciously by aspirational plebeians. And yet, at the same time, Wallace-Hadrill observes that as the lower classes attained access to forms of decoration, the differences in quality between that which the elites and the less wealthy displayed became much greater, suggesting that the elites used rare materials or unusual methods as a way to establish their standing, as conspicuous goods on their own would no longer signify status. For example, mosaics were difficult to create, impossible to fake, and arduous to execute without the right skills and materials, and thus remained a rare marker of elite status. The use of glass windows such as bay windows and stained glass in Victorian England's upper-class houses also exemplifies the use of scarcity to reveal status.[16] These upper-class homes drew their architectural aesthetics from England's grand estate mansions.

The use of decoration to suggest and imitate status continued throughout Europe in the seventeenth century. Under the Dutch Empire, two-thirds of Delft households possessed at least one painted canvas—a decoration that initially marked elite status and was then imitated by the less wealthy. In pre-Revolutionary France, the middle class emulated the aristocrats by using wallpaper designed to look like palace tapestries,[17] stucco employed to mimic marble, and porcelain disguised as gold. One could even pretend to have a library by installing fake book spirals on the wall.[18] Women imitated Marie Antoinette's hairstyle as an effort to be closer to royalty.[19] Almost a century later, Victorian England's courtiers' silk stockings were quickly imitated by the working class in the form of worsted stockings—again, using cheaper materials but with the same effect.[20]

Undoubtedly all of these examples demonstrate imitation in the aspirational sense—lesser quality versions of the elite's goods intended to communicate status. In these historical cases as in those of the current day, whether knockoff Louis Vuitton or fake wood floors, the difference is barely discernable to the naked eye. The observation of AD 79 remains the same as it was in Veblen's time and today: "Of course, there is a great gulf between the luxury of the elite houses and the simpler aspirations of the small," writes Wallace-Hadrill. "But what matters is to understand that they do not belong to different cultural universes."[21] (Today, one can even get linoleum that mimics marble, not a far cry from stucco's purpose in pre-Revolutionary France.) In short, from the beginnings of documented human civilization, a desire to demonstrate status, or to imitate and assimilate with high social classes, is evident. Or, as Wallace-Hadrill remarked to me in an interview, "We can utterly confirm that conspicuous consumption occurred in pre-capitalist society. It's quite a quaint point of view to see it as capitalist."

CONSPICUOUS CONSUMPTION GOES MAINSTREAM: MASS PRODUCTION AND THE MIDDLE CLASS

While capitalism may not be responsible for conspicuous consumption, it is true that the Industrial Revolution opened the floodgates of consumption to the common man. The prosperity brought by the Industrial Revolution was seemingly egalitarian, offering wealth to a whole new stratum of society—a middle class. While it took almost a millennium and a half for world income to double prior to the eighteenth century, the Industrial Revolution and modern capitalism brought that same doubling in just 70 years in the nineteenth century and then again in just 35 years in the twentieth century.[22]

Prior to the Industrial Revolution and the creation of the steam engine, many objects were only affordable for the truly wealthy. Items like sewing machines and typewriters (Victorian versions of electronics) were still unavailable for the masses. London's Great Exhibition of 1851 displayed many of the luxury objects of the burgeoning industrial world, such as Morris wallpaper and pianos, but they were relegated to the wealthy.[23] As mechanization and specialization enabled the production of a great number of goods, it became possible to distribute authentic consumer items to this growing middle class. Imitation was no longer the only conduit by which to get closer to the elite. Instead, through both mass production and fast credit (a development from the latter half of the twentieth century), many more people began to consume the same products as elites.

In Veblen's time the elite leisure class owned property, and controlled the means of production and the means to acquire material goods. The Industrial Revolution brought massive economic restructuring and the introduction of a middle class of businessmen and workers. These new workers were unlike the landless proletariats before them who were oppressed under the noble class. In the ensuing decades, the middle class, not just the upper tiers of society, acquired property, and generated wealth and disposable income that allowed them to purchase status through consumption. By the early twentieth century the middle class bought cars thanks to the constantly growing American automobile industry (first the Model-T, then Chevys and Cadillacs). By the 1950s, many owned suburban homes through the GI Bill and Federal Housing Authority. New technologies and rapid production manufacturing techniques allowed this middle class to acquire TVs, air conditioning units, and stereos as they were all being produced at greater speed and lower cost.

Today, conspicuous consumption is so commonplace that it has become synonymous with overly showy goods, whether BMWs or Louis Vuitton handbags, that convey a sense of wealth and higher social position. The nouveau riche are particular culprits, but so are the rising upper middle classes and oligarchs of Russia and China. Some scholars even argue that the poor engage in the practice more than the rich.[24] In *The Affluent Society*, John Kenneth Galbraith himself observed that because so many people could afford luxury expenditures, such goods were no longer a mark of distinction. In fact, the display of wealth was deemed "passé" to a point that conspicuous consumption was no longer associated with the very wealthy, but rather with everyone else. Indeed, in *The Power Elite*, Galbraith's contemporary C. Wright Mills observed that the absence of an American aristocracy meant that possessors of money—"sheer, naked, vulgar"—were given entrance everywhere, thus forcing the truly elite to find more implicit marks of status than wealth and consumption habits.

Another force at work in the proliferation of contemporary conspicuous consumption is the increased awareness of the lifestyle of elites. In the early nineteenth century, Queen Victoria and Prince Albert were photographed in their homes amidst their household goods. The rise of advertising in the late 1800s further spread the images of lifestyles to aspire to, and thereby cultivated a new middle-class consumer economy.[25] In the latter half of the twentieth century, Princess Diana's luxury lifestyle was on display throughout numerous magazines worldwide.

In America, which has always had a democratic view of its rich, the wealthy were often thought of as accessible, rags-to-riches Horatio Alger types. Even old East Coast society, while shrouded in more mystery than its Californian counterparts, paraded about New York and Boston, as captured by the writings of Edith Wharton, Dominick Dunne, Truman Capote, and Tom Wolfe. Today, our media and celebrity tabloids document every house, pair of shoes, diamond ring, and restaurant of our Hollywood aristocracy. After all, American high society has never comprised aristocrats or hundreds of years of birthright social position, thus making its superiority mainly one of wealth. The access to information about elite lifestyle made the average man hungry for more (and instilled the belief he could attain it). This entrée coupled with cheaper consumer goods made it possible. Conspicuous consumption was no longer confined to the echelons of the elite.

THE DEMOCRATIZATION OF CONSPICUOUS CONSUMPTION

The label-consciousness of the late nineties and early noughties is perhaps best captured by one of the era's most popular television programs, *Sex and the City*, which documented a time when a gleaming Rolex watch, or a pair of Louboutin shoes, identifiable by their signature red soles and pencil-thin stiletto heels, signaled a certain position in society. Similarly, wealth was displayed through the luxury markets of Armani, Ralph Lauren, and Oscar de la Renta, and the masses emulated through the purchase of knockoff Gucci sweatshirts from New York City's Times Square. The signature charging polo player embroidered on a golf shirt or crisp white button-down shirt signaled that the wearer had spent quite a lot of money on a commonplace good that was *clearly* of superior quality—a twenty-first-century example of Veblen's silver flatware. Sure, the fake Prada handbags would, at times, fool even the most discerning eye, but real luxury—the actual luxury handbags, Lauren golf shirts, and Armani dresses—was still out of reach of the masses, both in terms of cost and exclusiveness. Their status rested on the aggressive logos emblazoned across the item, the bigger the better. You knew it was a Prada handbag because the shiny black and silver triangle placed overtly on every bag said it was so. The luxury logo was the leitmotif for the era's over-the-top glamour, the rise of Wall Street money, and nouveau riche.

But these earlier eras of logos and luxury excess undoubtedly created a hunger among the masses—and it was slowly being satiated. In just a few years between the mid-1990s and the 2000s, a number of brands established what are called "diffusion lines"—that is, authentic clothing and accessories produced by the fashion house at a much lower and affordable price point. The most prominent of these brands emerged in a flurry—Armani's Armani Exchange (A/X) (1991), Ralph Lauren's Polo (1993), and Marc by Marc Jacobs (2001). While linens and housewares were also being produced by diffusion lines (Laura Ashley, Ralph Lauren), clothing was particularly pivotal in this transformation and democratization of conspicuous consumption. To that end, mass-produced luxury clothing of a different sort began appearing in shopping malls and downtown centers—Banana Republic was purchased by Gap in 1983 and rebranded as upscale classic clothing. J.Crew, formally a clothing catalogue company known as Popular Club Plan, renamed itself and opened a retail store in 1989, positioning itself as a less expensive version of Ralph Lauren. These efforts to bring luxury to the mass market have been met with unabashed demand: A/X boasts 270 stores in 31 countries, while J.Crew has 287 stores and $2.5 billion in revenue. Ralph Lauren has 460 stores and $7.4 billion in sales, and The Gap has opened 3,700 stores worldwide.[26]

By global standards, these diffusion lines and mainstream luxury clothing lines are still expensive. One is not likely to spend less than $100 (and often much more) on a single item at Banana Republic. Yet, the cost of these clothing items is significantly less than the original luxury lines and they convey very similar aesthetics—the crisp blue-blood look of Ralph Lauren or quirky preppiness of Kate Spade is easily imitated by Banana Republic or J.Crew. Marc by Marc Jacobs products may not be made with the same tailoring or quality of materials as the flagship brand, but they do capture the bohemianism and subversiveness that has made the designer so celebrated and revered.

The increase in online shopping has also had a profound impact on consumer access to coveted brands. Once upon a time, if you lived in small-town Kansas or Missouri you needed to visit a major city to obtain high-end fashion. Today, a simple click on Sak's Fifth Avenue's website will send a pair of Manolo Blahnik's "BB" shoes to any woman in the country, provided she's willing to spend $600 for the privilege. Additionally, the web enables luxury brands to distribute items from their past seasons to various discount fashion sites. Apparel and shoes websites such as Bluefly (1998), Zappos (1999), Overstock.com (1999), and of course the original bargain-hunting virtual mecca, Ebay (1995), allow mainstream consumers to engage in conspicuous consumption at blue-light special prices. Some more recent additions to this group include Gilt (2007) and Rue La La (2007), which offer luxury goods from Cartier watches to Chanel handbags at shockingly reduced prices through their "flash sales," in which an Hermès handbag will be reduced from $20,000 to $10,000 and La Perla lingerie is 60% off for a limited time (sometimes hours or a day or so). Admittedly these are not inexpensive items, irrespective of the sale. Rent-the-Runway, established in 2009 by two Harvard wunderkinds, allows women to rent high-end designer dresses for a fraction of the price, the price of which includes a free back-up size shipped with compliments. Although just a temporary fix, this company provides women luxury items for the events that matter, even if most could never afford to actually purchase the gowns.

The desire for branded goods has created an expanded market that extends beyond the upper class for which it was intended. Target now teams up with high-end designers to create affordable Missoni, Lily Pulitzer, and Proenza Schouler, while Kohls, Macy's, and Kmart sell celebrity brands meant to imbue the consumer with a sense of Kim Kardashian, Jessica Simpson (or some other celebrity's) style. Rolex's Tudor line is a more affordable version of the watch (only available in Europe). As cars go, the Volkswagen Group is the master at creating different price points for versions of the same thing. Or, as one car aficionado remarked, "The Lamborghini Gallardo was basically the Audi R8. The Audi A3 is the Golf which is the Seat Leon. VW Group has become very smart at identifying the things that make a difference to their customers … so Audi people will pay for a 'Golf in a frock' because they don't see it as that. They [The consumers] like better plastics, polished aluminum, etc."

Globalization, mass marketing, mass production, and knockoffs have created a conspicuous consumption profile for many more people. This deluge of material goods would suggest that the barriers to entry into upper-class conspicuous consumption have been all but eradicated. The "stuff" once associated with a wealthy lifestyle—cars, multiple handbags, closets full of clothes—is seemingly accessible to mainstream society. At first blush, conspicuous consumption has been democratized.

THE BACKLASH

This is not to say there hasn't been a backlash to the democratization of conspicuous consumption. In the late 1990s, in an effort to gain more market share, Burberry's famous checked plaid, found on the inside of its tailored but old school trench coats, began to appear on many other goods, including umbrellas, wallets, and cell phone cases. The newfound ubiquity of the plaid (dubbed "chav check," a pejorative) reduced Burberry from the uniform of English aristocrats to an ironic, reinterpreted badge of youth subculture. Emblazoned across scarfs, ties, and hats, counterfeit versions began showing up on the black market and being coopted by "chavs," an insulting term used to describe the working-class youths of Britain who had a penchant for knockoff designer logo-tastic goods, or whom the *Economist* called "the stereotypical white working-class delinquent looking for trouble."[27] The re-appropriating of Burberry's status by this group caused a public relations nightmare for the company by alienating their core consumer base, who enjoyed the staid subtleness from which the company had not deviated since the mid-1800s. Only in the 2000s, when Rosie Marie Bravo and Angela Ahrendts (the former CEOs, respectively) and current CEO and chief creative officer Christopher Bailey took the helm and re-envisioned the brand (less plaid, more military references) did Burberry finally recover its lost sales.[28] Not only did Burberry scale back on all that plaid, but Bailey created magnificently tailored clothing using unique materials and design that were both incredibly expensive in their own right but also very difficult to imitate. For example, Bailey's multi-thousand-dollar Warrior bag, replete with large metal armor and studs, would be almost impossible to successfully knock off.

In a world where almost everything (except perhaps a Burberry Warrior bag) can be imitated or accessed for a lesser price, how has the status game shifted for the new elites? Without question, even in the aftermath of the Great Recession, wealthy people are getting richer all the time, and they use this wealth to buy things that are not even possible to imitate. Simon Kuper, who writes about some of these questions for the *Financial Times*, recently explained to me that the upper class now maintains its exclusivity by attaining limited edition versions of goods. Whether artisanal cheeses or limited vintages of wine or Ferraris—regardless of the price point—the item in question accrues status by virtue of simply being scarce rather than merely expensive. In Europe, where manufacturers are having trouble selling mass-market $15,000 cars, Ferraris, starting at $275,000 are going like gangbusters.[29]

THE EROSION OF THE LEISURE CLASS, THE RISE OF THE ASPIRATIONAL CLASS

Not only has the democratization of conspicuous consumption changed the landscape, so too has the erosion of the leisure class. Other than the odd trust fund playboy or oligarch's debutante, the leisure class no longer exists. Many of the individuals who are spending hundreds of thousands of dollars on designer goods have made their own money—many through legitimate hard work (and, admittedly, others less so). The disappearance of a wealthy, idle aristocracy and the rise of an educated, self-made elite (what some call a meritocratic elite) means that "leisure" is no longer synonymous with our upper classes. But there is a cost to this more egalitarian version of status. According to work done by Cornell University economist Robert Frank, there is a measurable decline in leisure and happiness among the wealthy. "In fact, while income inequality may be growing, 'leisure inequality'—time spent on enjoyment—is growing as a mirror image" writes Frank, "with the low earners gaining leisure and the high earners losing."[30] From 1985 to 2003, wealthy men lost leisure hours, decreasing from 34.4 to 33.2 hours per week, while less wealthy men saw an increase from 36.6 to 39.1 over the same time period. While the same pattern is consistent for women, high-earning women lost even more leisure time—a 2-hour decline over the study period.[31] In his book *Changing Times: Work and Leisure in Postindustrial Society*, Jonathan Gershuny observes that, unlike in Veblen's time, the top socioeconomic groups have less time, not more, and these two variables, work and leisure, have a "reciprocal relationship"— time is influenced by production and the work required for these new forms of highly valued production. Today abundance of leisure no longer indicates higher status.[32]

These statistics might imply choice, but the larger economic restructuring of the global economy from Veblen's time to the present day suggests much less agency on the part of both the rich and the poor. The manufacturing economy provided a means by which social mobility could be acquired through income rather than birthright or landownership. In fact, the income derived from factory jobs, particularly in the middle of the twentieth century, enabled a broad swath of the population to acquire property and houses of their own, along with the consumer items, whether armchairs or curtains, with which to fill them. Through the 1960s, many middle-class families were able to live materially prosperous lives derived from their relatively highly paid factory and management jobs. In many instances, college degrees (let alone professional or graduate degrees) were not required to do economically well. In 1950, for example, only 7.3% of all males had a college degree. By 1962, the rate was just higher than 11% of all males (female rates were lower in both instances). Contrast these statistics with 2014, when almost a third of both men and women had college degrees.[33] In the mid-twentieth century, social and economic mobility was significantly tied to individuals' loyalty to their institutions. During this era, institutional loyalty (e.g., working 40 years for Ford Motor Company or General Electric) was associated with ongoing promotion, raises, and the compensation to support a middle-class consumer lifestyle. People were valued, not for their Ivy League degree or desirability by competitors, but rather for their steady devotion to the institutions for which they worked and which supported them—the military, the government, companies, and unions. C. Wright Mills's conception of the "power elite" draws heavily from the fact that these institutions were the nexus of control in the economic and social landscape. Significant critique of this economic structure emerged during the 1950s and 1960s, most famously William Whyte's *The Organization Man* (1956) which found the collective, group think of corporate America a stifling attack against individualism and creativity. Workers' ties to their organizations triumphed over their own ideas and ambitions, and yet, to Mills's point, this loyalty was rewarded and it paved a path for ongoing mobility. The classic film *The Man in the Gray Flannel Suit* (1956) and more recently the TV series *Mad Men*, were popular mainstream depictions of how this relationship played out.

The collapse of the manufacturing economy changed the currency of social and economic mobility quite considerably. Deindustrialization of Western economies (particularly within the United States and Great Britain) is largely explained by three key forces: oversaturation of the market (there are only so many dishwashers a household can buy), technology and automation (machines are low-cost and faster than people when it comes to factory lines), and globalization (labor costs are cheaper elsewhere and technologies in transport along with computers make it possible to outsource production to Southeast Asia or South America).[34] As a result, those well-paying factory jobs that defined the good life in the United States disappeared quickly. In 1970, a quarter of the American workforce was employed by the manufacturing sector. By 2005, that figure had dropped to 10%.[35] The numbers are not just statistically surprising; embedded in the reduction of manufacturing is the social and economic contract made with the middle class. These jobs were well-paid but relatively unskilled, thus many members of America's middle class achieved prosperity, material comfort, and economic and social security without birthright, and, antithetical to the current formula for upward mobility, without a college degree. The hemorrhaging of these factory jobs to developing countries and the closing up of factory shops meant that this stable middle class had lost its means for survival. Deindustrialization brought erosion to major urban centers (where many factories were located) and joblessness throughout huge swaths of the country.[36]

In manufacturing's place came the rise of the service economy, a truly bifurcated economic structure. Globalization manifested itself in the outsourcing of cheap labor for manufacturing but also through the emergence of elite "global cities," to use Saskia Sassen's term. Global cities became the sites for the new economic means of production—information and financial capital. The labor market elites responsible for the greatest profit-making were found in professional sectors—accountancy, finance, law, and medicine, or what Sassen calls "high level producer services." Another account of this economic restructuring offers a similar but simpler explanation: The global economy had moved from producing widgets to producing ideas—those who were responsible for generating those ideas, what Robert Reich has called "symbolic analysts"[37] or Richard Florida has termed the "creative class"—are the winners in the new economy.[38]

While a college degree is not an explicit measure of membership to Sassen's, Reich's, or Florida's categorization, it certainly helps and most members do possess one. Thus the rise of an economy dependent on innovation and knowledge is also one dependent on professional skills, many of which are acquired through education. Mobility into the top echelon of the new world order is reliant on acquisition of knowledge, not birthright, not property held for generations, and not, sadly for many, loyalty to one's work institution. But these new elites are not simply members of an economic group tied to one another by their financial success. They are not plutocrats or necessarily on top of the economic pyramid. Many who have acquired education and prize knowledge are indeed affluent labor market elites, but plenty are not. For this new class of people, knowledge is prized independently of its economic function. For bankers, lawyers, or engineers in this group, their education and specialized knowledge have enabled them to attain upward mobility in the world economy. But in general, those who have obtained knowledge—those with creative writing degrees from Yale, screenwriters who have yet to sell a screenplay, musicians and Teach for America volunteers—

are also members of this new cultural and social formation. Instead of income level, this new group is tied by a *shared set of cultural practices and social norms*. The unifying characteristic shared by members of this new elite cultural formation is their acquisition and valuing of knowledge, rather than their income level. They use knowledge to attain a higher social, environmental, and cultural awareness. The process by which they obtain knowledge and subsequently form values is what reveals social position. This new group is thus defined, more than anything else, through its shared cultural capital—they speak the same language, acquire similar bodies of knowledge, and share the same values, all of which embody their collective consciousness. Reading cultural commentary, being up-to-date on the news (preferably via the *New York Times*, *Wall Street Journal*, or *Financial Times*), and eating organic food are but a number of ways by which they connect with one another irrespective of their economic means. And there is a well-intentioned goal behind these efforts: The knowledge and cultural capital are used to make informed decisions around what to eat, how to treat the environment, and how to be better parents, more productive workers, and more informed consumers.

This new, dominant cultural elite can be called, quite simply, the *aspirational class*. While their symbolic position sometimes manifests itself through material goods, mostly they reveal their class position through cultural signifiers that convey their acquisition of knowledge and value system—dinner party conversation around opinion pieces, bumper stickers that express political views and support for Greenpeace, and showing up at farmer's markets. These behaviors and signifiers imply aspirational class values and also suggest the knowledge acquired to form them. Today's aspirational class prizes ideas, cultural and social awareness, and the acquisition of knowledge in forming ideas and making choices ranging from their careers to the type of sliced bread they purchase at the grocery store. In each of these decisions, big and small, they strive to feel informed and legitimate in their belief that they have made the right and reasonable decision based on facts (whether regarding the merit of organic food, breast-feeding, or electric cars). In short, unlike Veblen's leisure class or David Brooks's "bobos," this new elite is not defined by economics. Rather, the aspirational class is formed through a collective consciousness upheld by specific values and acquired knowledge and the rarified social and cultural processes necessary to acquire them.

In *Bobos in Paradise*, David Brooks chronicled the cognitive dissonance of "bobos" (bohemian bourgeois) who grew up in the counterculture 1960s and felt a deep discomfort around their adulthood wealth. This group is also an economically based elite, or what Brooks called "the new upper class." The uneasiness many bobos felt in reconciling their hippy, nonmaterialistic earlier years and their newfound wealth resulted in consumer habits that were still expensive but ultimately attempted to distance themselves from money. In an attempt to transcend materialism, the rich bobos buy Subzero brand fridges and remodel their bathrooms with slate walls and a Zen aesthetic (but they still need to have a lot of money to do so). "It's virtuous to spend $25,000 on your bathroom, but it's vulgar to spend $15,000 on a sound system and a wide-screen TV. It's decadent to spend $10,000 on an outdoor Jacuzzi but if you're not spending twice that much on an oversized slate shower stall, it's a sign that you probably haven't learned to appreciate the simple rhythms of life ... if your furniture is distressed, your conscience needn't be."[39]

Today's aspirational class lacks such self-consciousness, and many members lack bobos' financial means. The aspirational class is motivated by self-confident values and is actively choosing its way of life through an extensive process of information gathering and forming opinions and values, some of which involve money but many of which rest on cultural capital instead. They distance themselves from conventional material goods not because they are uncomfortable with wealth (bobos) but rather because material goods are no longer a clear signal of social position or a good conduit to reveal cultural capital or knowledge. Rich oligarchs and the middle class both can acquire "stuff," but, for the aspirational class, it is members' eagerness to acquire knowledge and to use this information to form socially and environmentally conscious values that sets them apart from everyone else—which is why a $2 heirloom tomato purchased from a farmer's market is so symbolically weighty of aspirational class consumption and a white Range Rover is not. Aspirational class consumption acts as a signal of its members' philosophy of life and their value system. Of course, within this new elite cultural formation there is an economic gradient. There are wealthy aspirational class members—perhaps a partner in a law firm—who are amply spending on nannies, Ivy League tuition, and organic strawberries. Others within this group, such as an unemployed screenwriter or Rhode Island School of Design (RISD) trained artist, are barely able to economically participate in this world but use their insubstantial means to signify membership. The screenwriter too reads the *New York Times* and (perhaps irrationally and to his own economic detriment) also buys his organic strawberries at Whole Foods. He carries a canvas tote that displays a political or literary statement as another signal of his cultural knowledge and engagement with the intellectual current of the moment. In short, this new cultural and social formation is elite by virtue of the material and symbolic trappings required to be a member, but ultimately those who are members of this new cultural and social formation *aspire* to be their version of better humans in all aspects of their lives, with their economic position taking a back seat.

If knowledge is what drives the world economy, it is also the currency by which this new elite group defines itself and acquires the status signals of its position—whether material or symbolic. Thus, the attainment of information and knowledge becomes valued not simply in the new economic world order but in all matters of life. Social norms and goods of the aspirational class reflect an implicit knowledge and procurement of knowledge that informs their consumption practices. Aspirational class leisure, whether reading the *Economist*, listening to NPR, or taking a yoga class, is imbued with knowledge and productivity in the same spirit as work. Motherhood practices of the aspirational class suggest not simply money but extensive research into the perfect way to feed, console, and educate the under-three set. The material goods and practices become the signifiers of this knowledge and thus in turn show membership within this rarified group.

REVISITING VEBLEN

Despite radical changes in the global economy and the means by which we obtain social and economic mobility, much of Veblen's framework for how to understand the signifiers of class position hold true today, albeit in unusual and complicated ways. In the 100-plus years since Veblen's book was first published, his theories apply more today than ever before, and they apply to all of us. Veblen might wonder where all the silver spoons and members of the idle leisure class went, but in their place he would find the aspirational class and their Chemex pour-over coffee. Just as in the 1800s, in the twenty-first century, our desire to reveal status is in keeping with the current economic and social world order.

In the tradition of Veblen's work, *The Sum of Small Things* looks at how society and class are signified and embodied through the lens of consumption and social practices. As Frank Trentmann writes in *Empire of Things*, his history of consumption from the fifteenth century to the present day, "Here, consumption is relational rather than an individual preference (rational or not), part of a social positioning system that tells people where they stand."[40] Conspicuous consumption is still a very significant means to reveal social position, but those in the twenty-first-century aspirational class have found new means to show their status. In this book I argue that three simultaneous consumption patterns are occurring. First, the democratization of conspicuous consumption has provided many more material goods to the middle class, but this change is to their detriment. As they spend more on material status symbols, they are spending less on those things that would pave the way to greater intergenerational upward mobility. Second, as a result of the mainstreaming of conspicuous consumption, the aspirational class's means of displaying its social position has become more complicated. Its members have found new means of identifying themselves and they do so through spending on behaviors and goods that are not necessarily conspicuous at all and not always material. These new elites are consuming fewer conventional conspicuous consumption items, and instead look to more subtle status markers that come through the forms of conspicuous production and inconspicuous consumption. The wealthier members of the aspirational class devote their financial resources to making their lives easier and more efficient. Inconspicuous consumption also describes the aspirational class's appropriation of certain behaviors and goods that don't cost a lot and are not ostentatious but are becoming equally crucial to signaling social position. The choices to practice yoga, take kids to hockey rather than soccer, drink almond milk instead of regular milk, and reuse grocery bags every week are all signifiers of position that are not inherently more expensive than their alternatives but thought to be more informed. By turn, these behaviors become markers of status. Finally, many of the behaviors that were what Veblen called "conspicuous leisure"—for example, college degrees and playing sports—are now essential to upward mobility. Much of leisure, for the aspirational class, has become productive.

When Veblen wrote his treatise on the leisure class, the practice of conspicuous consumption was relegated to a very marginal stratum of society. Yes, all social classes practiced conspicuous consumption to some extent, but the leisure class was the only group with the means to use material goods to reveal status. Today, material goods are plentiful but their ability to reveal or enable social mobility is increasingly limited. There is no longer a dominant leisure class; in its place the aspirational class is rewriting the patterns of consumption while simultaneously disengaging in conventional material conspicuous consumption. They reveal their social position through much more subtle behaviors and goods that are not necessarily expensive but imply a rich cultural and social capital relegated to aspirational class membership. The members of the aspirational class are not the villains of Wall Street, Russian oligarchs buying up London and Manhattan, they are not plutocrats on private jets. They are no leisure class. Not all of them make enormous amounts of money, but they are educated and they prize knowledge and engage in consumer practices that reflect these values and cultural capital. Yet, these positive attributes may make the aspirational class even more pernicious than the superrich who are vilified in the media or the leisure class of the nineteenth century. There are not many billionaires and oil titans in the world, but the aspirational class is a big and powerful cultural formation. Most importantly, through their subtle and increasingly inconspicuous choices in how to spend, how to behave, and what to value, they shore up their and their children's distinct sociocultural (and often economic) position of privilege, leaving everyone else out. The aspirational class members' self-assurance with their decisions and seeming deservedness of their social position allows them to ignore the growing inequality all around them. At the very least, they do not see themselves to blame. Because of the nature of the data and research undertaken, this book reports on the patterns of consumption in America. But without question, the observations regarding class, social positioning, and the emergence of the aspirational class are witnessed in geographies far beyond America's boundaries. In fact, the emergence of the new immaterial means to status—inconspicuous consumption, conspicuous production, and motherhood practices—can be seen across Western affluent countries. A walk through Notting Hill reveals the same consumption habits as those found in San Francisco or Park Slope, Brooklyn. *The Sum of Small Things* attempts to unpack the consumption habits of the twenty-first century, how they have changed, how contemporary consumption patterns reflect our social and economic positions in big and small ways, and the implications of these choices and practices for our communities, our cities, and our society as a whole.

CHAPTER 2

Conspicuous Consumption in the Twenty-first Century

It is from our disposition to *admire*, and consequently to imitate, the rich and the great, that they are enabled to set, or to lead what is called the fashion. Their dress is the fashionable dress; the language of their conversation, the fashionable style; their air and deportment, the fashionable behaviour. Even their vices and follies are fashionable.
—Adam Smith *The Theory of Moral Sentiments* (1790)

In *The Theory of the Leisure Class*, Thorstein Veblen observed that conspicuous consumption was also practiced among those outside of the rich, or what he called the "impecunious classes." These poorer strata of society spent on nonessentials—maybe not as much as the leisure class with their silver spoons and games of croquet, but as he pointed out, from hunter and gatherer societies to the present day, most human beings have a desire to fit in and we often rely on social constructs to do so. Veblen, scorned as he was for his writings on class and consumption, has perpetuated as a person of interest for writers and scholars in the decades thereafter and to the present day. He pinpointed an important truth: Material goods define who we are and where we stand in the social order.

Fifty years later, in his book *The Affluent Society*, John Kenneth Galbraith observed a wide swath of society engaging in gratuitous consumption or what he called "consumer-demand creation."[1] Galbraith did not believe that much of what we bought was necessary, or "organic," as he put it. The rise of "private demand" and the consumer economy occurred at the expense of the public good. In his 1957 book, *The*

Hidden Persuaders, Vance Packard argued that the rush of consumer goods meant advertisers, marketers, and promoters needed to create consumer desire, perpetuating a cycle of materialism.[2] Galbraith found this cycle disconcerting because as society became more absorbed by materialism, the superficial differences between the rich and the rest seemed much less distinct. The ostensible democratization of consumerism obfuscated inequality and essentially lulled society into thinking everyone had a slice of the pie and would mask real issues of wealth disparity.

The consumption of socially visible material goods to convey socioeconomic status has been in place for thousands of years. Even before the deluge of cheap goods that the latter half of the twentieth century provided, the historian Paul Johnson observed that the Victorian and Edwardian English working class wore "Sunday best" (or placed ornaments on their working clothes if they could not afford the former) and spent extravagantly on beach vacations or what the English call "sun holidays"—much to the consternation of the middle class, who believed this behavior was wasteful and useless. Yet the working classes were doing what the middle class and leisure class practiced in their own socioeconomic universes, albeit employing different means to demonstrate status. As Johnson himself remarks, because the middle class was not a part of the working-class cultural world, they could not understand the intergroup dynamics that made these efforts important means of assimilation and status marking. The working classes found their own conduits to suggest social position, just as the middle and upper classes did within their own groups.[3] On the other hand, the rising bourgeoisie, as an economic juggernaut independent of the aristocracy, bought big houses and decorated them ornately to identify themselves as a part of this new middle class. After all, the middle classes were increasingly upwardly mobile without the benefit of birthright.[4] Veblen believed the proliferation of conspicuous consumption would increase as society became more and more industrialized, paving the way for overall rising incomes and a flood of new consumer goods. In his Pulitzer Prize–winning work, *The Americans: A Democratic Experience*, the University of Chicago historian Daniel Boorstin described the relationship between America's built environment and its development as a society. One of

Boorstin's lasting observations is that of the emergence of department stores and their display of lavish goods as one of the first instances of the "democratization of luxury" for the masses.

This book focuses primarily on the habits, norms, and consumer patterns of the twenty-first-century aspirational class. Yet, this cultural formation could not exist without what has come before it. To understand how the aspirational class consumes requires understanding how Americans in general consume and how this has changed over time. Like all groups, aspirational class identification is part differentiation and part assimilation, and often both at once. This chapter will look at how America consumes across income levels and over time and how these spending habits are influenced by our race, gender, profession, location, and income level. Only then do the habits and practices of the aspirational class make sense as a part of the wider context of American consumer culture in the twenty-first century.

Over the past several decades, there has been an increase in three important macro trends in American spending behavior. First, the rich and upper middle class—that is, those in the top 1% and those in the top 5% and 10% income brackets—spend less as a percentage of their expenditures on conspicuous consumption relative to what the US average spends on the same goods, while the middle class—the 40th–60th percentiles—spends more. Second, as a share of their expenditures, the middle class is spending more on conspicuous consumption relative to their income while the wealthy (and the very poor) are spending less. Third, conspicuous consumption among the rich has been replaced by "inconspicuous consumption"—spending on nonvisible, highly expensive goods and services that give people more time and, in the long term, shape life chances. These include education, health care, child care, and labor-intensive services like nannies, gardeners, and housekeepers. This chapter will deal with the first of these two trends and briefly discuss the third; I will devote chapter 3 to inconspicuous consumption. For now, let's look at how America spends and in particular the role of conspicuous consumption in those spending patterns.

How do we know such specific details about how America spends? In order to get at macro consumer trends, my doctoral student Hyojung Lee and I analyzed a unique and largely unstudied dataset called the Consumer Expenditure Survey. For decades, the Consumer Expenditure

Survey (CE) has been interviewing and surveying American households on their consumption habits, documenting everything from the units of cornflakes the average Minnesotan consumes to how much money a New Yorker spends on shoes, child care, rent, or silver flatware. Administered by the government's Bureau of Labor Statistics, the CE gathers this data through two channels: diary data recorded by households over two one-week periods, and quarterly interviews with households conducted by the Bureau of Labor Statistics. The diary data allow for the tracking of small, frequent purchases associated with day-to-day life, from bags of potato chips to cups of coffee. The interview data capture bigger expenditures like mortgages, car payments, and new televisions. The integrated data thus deliver an overall picture of how America spends its money. Using this information, we have been studying macro changes in American consumption habits over the past 20 years. The nature of the data allows us to study consumption habits by race, education, gender, geographic location, and myriad other demographic and socioeconomic characteristics. When we first discovered this dataset we were specifically interested in the seemingly "gratuitous" expenditures that were made to suggest status. But the data also allow us to analyze the general patterns in how we consume and how consumption has changed over time. Thus our study provides a portrait of conspicuous consumption, but also uncovers broad trends in where we live, where we work, our age, our race, and our marital status shape our consumer habits in surprising ways.

A PORTRAIT OF AMERICA'S CONSUMPTION

Remarkably, our consumption habits as a society have remained roughly constant decade after decade, which is to say that despite the ebbs and flows in the items that serve as markers of status (kale vs. spinach, BMWs vs. Cadillacs, dishware, and where to go on vacation), there are predictable patterns in the proportions of food, housing, alcohol, entertainment, personal insurance, and pensions that we consume.

For example, in 1996, we devoted 14.2% of our total expenditures to food; in 2014, our total expenditure in this category was 15%.[5] Alcohol is similarly constant, hovering at just less than 1% of total expenditures,

Table 2.1. General consumer expenditure patterns (all income groups) by share of annual total expenditures (%, selected years)

	1996	2000	2004	2008	2012	2014
Annual total expenditures	100.0	100.0	100.0	100.0	100.0	100.0
Food	14.2	13.6	13.7	14.8	15.0	15.0
Alcoholic beverages	0.9	0.8	0.8	0.7	0.7	0.8
Housing	30.3	30.9	32.0	33.3	32.2	33.0
Apparel and services	4.1	3.7	3.0	2.5	2.3	2.2
Transportation	19.7	20.0	19.0	17.3	17.8	16.9
Health care	5.1	5.3	5.9	5.9	6.8	8.1
Entertainment	5.2	4.9	5.1	5.1	4.6	4.6
Personal care products and services	0.9	0.8	0.7	0.6	0.6	0.6
Reading	0.5	0.4	0.3	0.2	0.2	0.2
Education	1.4	1.5	2.0	2.1	2.3	2.1
Tobacco products and smoking supplies	0.8	0.9	0.7	0.7	0.7	0.6
Miscellaneous	2.5	2.0	1.6	1.6	1.6	1.1
Cash contributions	3.3	3.6	3.5	3.6	3.9	3.5
Personal insurance and pensions	11.2	11.5	11.9	11.6	11.3	11.2

as is tobacco, which remains static (surprisingly so, given the huge anti-smoking campaigns of the past 15–20 years). We spend the same on personal insurance and pensions (roughly 11% of total expenditures), and housing (slightly more than 30%). These findings suggest that basic household needs and expenses remain persistent—housing and buying groceries. In a few instances, we spend notably less: apparel (from 4.1% of total expenditures in 1996 to 2.2% in 2014) and transportation (19.7% in 1996 and 16.9% in 2014), both of which reflect globalization's cheaper cars and cheaper clothes. There are two categories where we spend more: health care (up from 5.1% to 8.1%) and education (up from 1.4% to 2.1%). (See table 2.1.)

As a society, we all eat out more, we all drink out more, and we all buy more stuff for our houses, whether fridges, furniture, textiles, or clocks. Our spending on these goods is linearly related to our income: The more we make, the more we spend on such items. Most people, except for the very poor, spend roughly the same share of their expenditures on these items. One exception to note: China, dishware, and those silver spoons are significantly less of a status marker today than in 1996. Every income group spends less on dining accoutrements, both in absolute dollars andas a share of expenditures. Take the top 1%: In 1996, they spent at least 0.1% of their expenditures on these classic Veblen status goods; by 2014, they spent almost zero percent of their total expenditures on them.

At first blush, as a society we seem to look more or less the same as we did almost 20 years ago. But if we parse out consumer patterns by income groups, a more nuanced story emerges which suggests Veblen's and Galbraith's concerns about conspicuous and material consumption were just the tip of the iceberg when it comes to massive differences across income and class. I will elaborate on this finding in the coming pages.

For example, overall, while education expenditures have increased 60% since 1996, the top 1%, 5%, and 10% income fractiles have increased their share of education expenditures by almost 300% during this same time period. Conversely, education expenditure shares have remained almost flat for the other groups, which suggests that top groups drove the uptick in education spending. Housing holds roughly the same share of total expenditures for the wealthy over the past 18 years, but it is 3–4% more of total expenditures for the middle class and lower income group. Food has become a greater share of expenditures for the third and fourth quintiles (those in the 40th–60th percentile and 60th–80th percentile of income distribution), while remaining flat for everyone else. Do these increases in basic costs of living for our middle classes decrease their spending power on education, cash contributions, and pensions—expenditures that have notably increased for the higher income groups, and tend to be expenditures that can shape the future, rather than just offer immediate gratification? The top 1% has increased the share of expenditure on personal insurance and pensions by 25% since 1996 and cash contributions by 28% since 1996, while those for average consumers have remained flat. (The top 5% and 10% have increased expenditures in cash contributions and education but not personal insurance.) The increased consumption shares of these expenditures in the top income groups suggest genuinely different trajectories for the future in a number of ways. The children who benefit from increased investment in education go on to obtain better jobs, higher incomes, and a better future for their families. Those who can afford it devote more to their pensions and insurance, have a better retirement (and in fact, *can* retire), better medical care, and better quality of life. These types of investments offer meaningfully different outcomes for those able to spend compared to everyone else.

CONSPICUOUS CONSUMPTION AND "VEBLEN GOODS"

The late Princeton economist Harvey Leibenstein coined the term "Veblen goods" or "Veblen effects" to describe the goods that are used for conspicuous consumption. Examining consumption patterns by income also shows differences across society in how we conspicuously consume those classic Veblen goods. Let's look at the first emerging trend I mentioned at the beginning of this chapter: The rich are spending less on goods that demonstrate wealth. In 1996,[6] the top 1% spent almost four times more than everyone else on conspicuous consumption—apparel, watches, jewelry, cars, and other socially visible goods. This is not an entirely surprising finding given that they were earning more than five times more than the national average—there's a significant amount of excess money. But today, still making more than six times more than everyone else in income (and that's an average, never mind those making ten or twenty times more), they are spending only three times more than everyone else on conspicuous consumption.

The important relationship here is the *income to conspicuous consumption ratio*,[7] which enables us to approximate what their income essentially allows them to spend on conspicuous consumption as compared to the nation as a whole. If the ratio is 1.00, then they are spending on conspicuous goods what would be expected given their income level (or 100%). By this measure, the top income groups are spending just 65–80% of what their income to conspicuous consumption ratio allows. Further, for the top 1% and 5%, this ratio has decreased 18 and 12 percentage points respectively since 1996 (it's gone down 10 percentage points for the top 10%). The exception is clothing and accessories: The top 5% and 10% still spend significantly less than their income to consumption ratio would allow, but they spend more than they did in 1996, while the middle class and low-income groups still spend more than they should in this category but the same or less than they did in 1996.

Table 2.2. Conspicuous consumption to income ratio in 1996 and 2014 (selected items)

	Overall		Clothing and accessories		Vehicles		TV and audio equipment	
	1996	2014	1996	2014	1996	2014	1996	2014
All households	1.00	1.00	1.00	1.00	1.00	1.00	1.00	1.00
Top 1%	0.65	0.47	0.61	1.06	0.58	0.31	0.77	0.44
Top 5%	0.76	0.64	0.80	0.91	0.69	0.58	0.62	0.62
Top 10%	0.80	0.70	0.86	0.90	0.75	0.67	0.71	0.70
60th–89th percentile	0.99	1.03	0.97	0.97	0.98	1.04	1.01	0.95
40th–59th percentile	1.19	1.35	1.11	1.11	1.28	1.46	1.18	1.42
0–39th percentile	1.47	1.51	1.46	1.38	1.50	1.38	1.68	1.78

These other groups, along with the low-income group (0 to 39th percentile), often spend more on conspicuous consumption than their income-consumption ratio would advise. For the poor, the basic expenses are a greater share of their income, so they have less, if any, funds available for conspicuous consumption. Since 1996, the spending on conspicuous consumption by those in the low-income group has declined for clothing and cars, but their overall ratio has mostly increased.

Middle-class income groups, however, demonstrate the opposite trend, capitalizing on the flood of affordable consumer goods coming from around the world. For the middle class (those in the 40th to 59th percentile), their income to consumption ratio has gone up by 16 percentage points. During this time period, clothing and accessories have become cheaper overall as a result of globalized manufacturing and new technologies, yet the middle class still spends 35% more on conspicuous consumption than their income would suggest they should, and 16 percentage points more than they did in 1996 (see table 2.2).[8] The same trend holds true for specific types of conspicuous goods such as clothing and accessories, and vehicles, TVs, and audio equipment: In 2014, the top 1% spent less on TVs than they did in 1996, and the magnitude of decline in this consumption category was greatest within this income group. According to the income-consumption ratio, the top 1% spend less than half of what would be expected, while the middle class spends over 40% more than expected for both cars and television (see table 2.2).

But to be clear, the rich are not suddenly consuming less all around. In fact, as a share of their total expenditures, the top 5% or top 10% spend just about on par with the other income groups on conspicuous goods—it's just that their income would allow them to spend even more. In 2014, 17% of their total expenditures went to conspicuous consumption versus the middle class, who spent 18.1%. The closeness in their share of conspicuous consumption expenditures suggests that while having more money may give you more opportunities to spend on conspicuous consumption, the consumption of visible, material goods tends to be a universal practice across all income groups. What Veblen observed more than a century ago still holds true today.

GILDED CONSPICUOUS CONSUMPTION

Because many conspicuous goods are now accessible to every income group, the wealthy do not distinguish themselves through goods that are widely available and increasingly affordable to the middle class (even if only through finance plans and credit for the latter). The conventional items of conspicuous consumption have become part and parcel of many Americans' lives, and so the rich now disproportionately spend on fancy watches and jewelry and boats—luxury items with tremendous price tags that are impossible for the average American to afford. These are the new status items for the rich. Looking at the data, the top 1% spent significantly more money on watches and jewelry than everyone else in absolute dollars and as share of total expenditures. In 2014, the top 1% spent more than double even what the top 5% spent and significantly more as a share of total expenditures compared to the national average. The same is true for repairs for those expensive watches and jewelry: The rich have always spent more for high-end repairs, but today the top 1% spends more than eight times the national average in absolute dollars, while the top 10% class spends half of the national average. Of course, this trend makes sense because the wealthy own watches and jewelry worth repairing, and those repairs cost real money. The "servicing" of a Rolex or its ilk will cost anywhere from $500 to $1,000, which is significantly more than an average person would spend on a watch in the first place. The same finding holds true for car repairs and

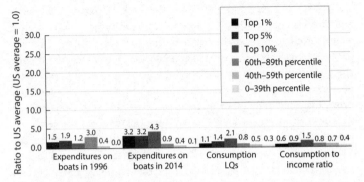

Figure 2.1. Boats: Share of total expenditures, consumption as compared to national average and consumption to income ratio. Data source: Consumer Expenditure Survey, Bureau of Labor Statistics.

service clubs, where the top 10% spends almost double the national average and the middle class spends less than the national average.

Unsurprisingly, boats are a conspicuous item among the twenty-first-century gilded set, with an even greater deviation from the average household's consumption. In 2014, the top 1% spent three times more than the national average. As a share of their total expenditures, the top earners tend to spend more than the national average, as shown in the consumption LQs (1.1 to 2.1 in the LQs), ranging from 6% to 100% more. Unsurprisingly, middle-class and lower income groups spend much less on boats than everyone else on this item, just 50% and 26% of the national average, respectively (shown as 0.8 and 0.3 in the LQs) (see figure 2.1).

One final observation on conspicuous consumption: A notable expenditure item for lower income families is funerals. Since 1996, low-income families consistently rank as the highest spenders on funerals relative to their total expenditures, while the rich spend less than the national average on them for most of the years studied. In 2014, the top 1% spent significantly less on funerals than everyone else even in absolute dollars, while the poor spend a 26% greater share of total expenditures than the national average and the middle class conform to national trends. Throughout time, this pattern bears out and we can turn to historians for some explanation. Paul Johnson remarked that funerals were an important display of status among the working class of Edwardian and Victorian England, while they were shunned by the bourgeois (who would have had myriad alternative outlets to display status). In comparison to the rich, who host and attend museum galas, charity events, and endless dinner parties, the poor are relatively limited in their avenues to engage in conspicuous consumption. Or, as David Sloane, the urban historian and author of *The Last Great Necessity: Cemeteries in American History*, explained, "For working class families the death, especially of a child or a breadwinner, traditionally has immense impacts. Also, poorer communities often have very high levels of social capital, and are reliant on that social capital for their survival. Most families spend considerable amounts of money on the performative aspects of the funeral—a necessary expense to show respect—as well as on the community aspect of the funeral—[for example] the Irish wake." Sloane continued, "In addition, wealthier families ... have a different attitude towards death, the dead, and funerals.... many keep it very private, and thus lower their expenses. They may have a memorial service with a reception, but the costs may be limited. Finally, the richer one is, the more educated one is, the more likely they are to cremate. Many working class families are more likely to bury, while wealthier families are much more likely to cremate—which isn't always but should mostly be cheaper."[9]

VEBLEN EFFECTS: HOW RACE, EDUCATION, AND MARITAL STATUS AFFECT HOW WE SPEND

Income—high or low—affects how we spend, and not just how much we spend on conspicuous consumption, but the peculiarities and idiosyncrasies in what we choose to spend on as well, whether funerals or watches. Income influences spending on conspicuous consumption, but many other factors influence our desire for material goods. How we respond to and are motivated by socially visible goods, what economists call "Veblen effects," is also determined by our age, profession, race, and marital status—even where we live.

Two academic papers have made significant inroads into understanding the economic, social, and demographic variables that shape our conspicuous consumption practices, looking beyond simply how much money one makes. Writing in 2007, University of Chicago and Wharton School economists Kerwin Charles, Erik Hurst, and Nikolai Roussanov sought to explore the role of race in status purchasing. Using the Consumer Expenditure Survey, they find that across all races, as people become wealthier and more educated, they spend more in absolute dollars on conspicuous consumption. Controlling for all other factors and just looking at the effect of race, Charles and his colleagues find that blacks and Hispanics spend more of their income on conspicuous consumption than whites within the same income and education groups. Charles speculates that this finding is a result of discrimination: These minority groups are under greater pressure to visibly display their social position than whites or Asians. By demonstrating that they own a nice car, dress well, and so forth, they are able to signal their class. For minority groups with a history of being discriminated against, conspicuous consumption becomes a means through which they can efficiently demonstrate their social and economic position before being prejudged.[10] This finding is almost the opposite of what has been observed of upper-class WASP culture: With an absence of any discrimination and oppression, this group has been able to comfortably downplay material goods, with the assumption that their social position will be assumed by the color of their skin.

Others who study conspicuous consumption have tried to study the role of specific material goods in relationship to a variety of demographic characteristics. Ori Heffetz, a Cornell University economist, views conspicuous consumption as those goods that are "culturally visible," that is, they are consumed in particular socioeconomic contexts, rather than simply being a necessity that everyone needs (such as water or a loaf of bread). Heffetz, like Charles and his colleagues, finds that the wealthier people are, the more they spend (in absolute dollars) on visible goods (regardless of race or ethnic background). Even though lower income groups may be devoting more of their income to conspicuous consumption, Heffetz would argue that the rich get a greater impact from whatever funds they devote to conspicuous spending.[11] This observation may seem like a contradiction to the earlier point that top income groups are devoting less of their expenditures to conspicuous consumption. There are two points to keep in mind here. First, even if it is true that wealthier individuals spend more in absolute dollars on conspicuous goods, these goods have less of an impact on their overall net income. So, a Rolex watch may cost $10,000, but if you're very rich, that $10,000 may be the equivalent of $50 to a middle-class family. The important distinction is that conspicuous consumption costs the rich less, irrespective of absolute dollars spent. Second, controlling for all other things, a higher income person will spend more (in absolute dollars, not in share of expenditures) on conspicuous consumption, but this observation is not in contradiction with the wider pattern that top income groups tend to spend less of their overall income on conspicuous consumption. These wider patterns are not isolating income as the only determining variable; instead, they are looking at the whole population of wealthy people, taking into account demographics, professions, and age. Through studying the rich collectively, it is clear they are spending less on conspicuous consumption and more on inconspicuous consumption.

In our studies on conspicuous consumption, Hyojung and I draw from the work of Charles, Heffetz, and their colleagues, but update and expand the data to the present decade (along with adding previous years and more variables). We present a more detailed and up-to-date portrait of what affects our consumption patterns. Our work considers the interplay of education, race, age, geography, city size, household size, home-ownership, marital status, and income elasticity. In each of these instances, we isolate a particular variable (such as education) and study its individual effect on spending. For example, considering race, we are looking at heads of households who are identical by every measure above, other than their race. These individuals attained the same education level, make the same amount of money, have the same number of children and so forth. This allows us to pinpoint the exact effect of race (or income, education, or some other chosen variable) on how someone spends. We also add another component central to twenty-first-century spending patterns: Understanding new forms of consumption that reveal status and socioeconomic position. Given the increase in conspicuous consumption across society, how do different groups distinguish themselves from one another? In the beginning of the chapter, I highlighted a new trend among the wealthy: the rise of inconspicuous consumption. That is, consumption that is not intended to be socially or culturally visible but reveals class position, such as the hiring of gardeners, nannies, or car services, or funneling money into education and retirement plans. None of these goods are material or used for status, but reveal wealth through the fact that one can afford to use them. I will devote the next chapter to the role of inconspicuous consumption within the new elite. Here, however, I consider the different variables that impact our choice to spend on conspicuous and inconspicuous consumption or to not spend on either.

Our results suggest that who we are, demographically speaking, has a profound impact on how we spend. On the subject of age: Controlling for all other demographic and socioeconomic factors, the younger one is the more one spends on both conspicuous and inconspicuous consumption. Although, with regard to inconspicuous consumption, the differences by age are less dramatic. The least likely to spend on conspicuous consumption are those ages 45–54 and those 75 years or older. This finding makes sense: Those in the 18–24 age range have fewer obligations than those in the older age groups. Those in the 45–54 age range are in the prime of their spending on household and children upkeep (whether mortgages, children's clothing, or school fees), and thus spend less on conspicuous consumption. However, when it comes to inconspicuous consumption, those beyond 75 years old spend almost as much as those in the 16–24-year age bracket, while those aged 34–54 spend the least. For the 75 and older group, they likely now depend to a greater extent on labor-intensive services, whether that is at-home care or a housekeeper.

In our analysis, race is also a significant factor in how people spend. Our results corroborate the earlier work by Kerwin Charles and his colleagues and the role of conspicuous consumption for minorities. Our results show that Hispanics are the most likely to spend on conspicuous consumption: 4.4% more than non-Hispanic whites, 15% more than blacks, and almost 20% more than Asians, though next to Asians, Hispanics are the least likely to spend on inconspicuous consumption. Non-Hispanic whites are the biggest spenders on inconspicuous consumption, followed by blacks. Controlling for all other factors, Asians spend the least on both conspicuous and inconspicuous consumption (see tables 2.3 and 2.4).

Married people spend the most on conspicuous consumption, and widowers the least. The never-married spend almost 18% less than the

Table 2.3. Ratio of consumption by age of householder (16 to 24 = 100.0)

	Conspicuous	Inconspicuous	Other expenditures
16–24	100	100	100
25–34	88	83	122
35–44	75	78	126
45–54	69	78	128
55–64	61	82	124
65–74	52	91	113
75 and older	19	95	104

married, a surprising finding given they would seem to be the ones with fewer home obligations and more free time and money. Then again, married people may have regular "obligations" such as birthdays, Christmas, and other holidays that influence their spending on their spouse, along with similar holidays for their children. Homeowners spend more on conspicuous consumption than renters, likely as a result of the uptick in spending on both home furnishings and vehicles—both of which are more frequent expenditures for those who own a home, perhaps because they are in a different part of the life cycle than those who rent.[12]

Just like Heffetz and Charles, we find that the more affluent individuals are, the more they spend in absolute dollars on conspicuous consumption (but again, lower income groups are devoting greater shares of income to socially visible spending).[13] More interesting, however, higher income is more closely associated with spending on inconspicuous consumption than conspicuous consumption. Using our income elasticity measure, we generated Engel curves for conspicuous consumption, inconspicuous consumption, and other expenditures. An Engel curve allows us to see how spending on particular items varies by income level and changes in income. The most famous example, which Ernst Engel found himself, is that lower income families tend to spend a

Table 2.4. Ratio of consumption by race/ethnicity of householder (non-Hispanic white = 100.0)

	Conspicuous	Inconspicuous	Other expenditures
Non-Hispanic white	100	100	100
African American	89	82	95
Asian and Pacific Islander	86	68	94
Hispanic	104	69	96
Other	98	86	98

greater share of their household budget on food, and as a household acquires more income, their food budget does not increase in lockstep. Because food is essential, regardless of income, a household must devote a certain amount of money toward acquiring it. Yet, we only need a certain amount of food, thus we don't start spending significantly more just because we become richer. Even if we start buying organic produce or imported foods, luxury food items compared to basic groceries does not present the same price disparity as that between other goods, like that between a Porsche and a Honda. Our study of household expenditures on basic necessities (e.g., housing and food) corroborates Engel's initial finding. For our Engel curves, we were interested in what a particular income group would do if they received a 1% increase in income. We find that the greatest income elasticities occur in the top 1% group, but that they are most likely to devote greater amounts of money to inconspicuous goods than to visible, status goods. For the top 1%, a one percent increase in income results in a 0.23% increase in conspicuous spending and a 0.24% increase in inconspicuous spending (along with a 0.21% increase in expenditures overall). In this example, the top 1% has little need to spend on other expenditures, say extra food, utilities, and so forth that a lower income family might pay for with extra income. Thus, for a top 1% household, increases in income enable more gratuitous rather than necessity spending. If basic needs are already met, why not buy the new car/watch/boat/etc. or hire a babysitter for longer hours or a gardener to do some more landscaping? These percentages may seem small, but they have a big impact for the already well off. People in top income brackets often get much more substantial raises (or bonuses, more likely) than a 1% increase, so for example, a 4% increase in income results in a 1% increase in both conspicuous and inconspicuous spending.

Contrast these results with that of those in the 20th percentile: For every 1% increase in income, they spend a very small, almost negligible amount on additional conspicuous or inconspicuous consumption (0.09%) but almost 0.14% more on other expenditures like food and shelter. In fact, until we arrive at the top 10%, 5%, and 1%, all income groups who receive an increase in income spend more on other expenditures that are not inconspicuous or conspicuous, but more essential (see figure 2.2).

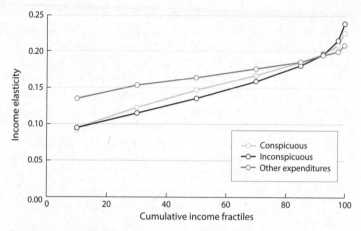

Figure 2.2. Income elasticity by income group. Data source: Consumer Expenditure Survey, Bureau of Labor Statistics.

We also find that for most income groups, income elasticity follows a predictable and linear line, except at the top, where small increases in income result in more dramatic increases in non-necessity spending. This finding suggests that for most income groups, small increases are helpful for day-to-day bills and cost-of-living expenses but do not suddenly move them into more gratuitous spending—for the rich, these marginal increases can be immediately channeled into extra holidays, shoes, or landscaping, and other goods or services that are not fulfilling a basic need (figure 2.2). A poorer family might use that same 1% income increase to buy more groceries or pay off a bill. Heffetz found similar results in his Engel curves looking at a variety of different consumer goods, specifically cars, air travel, education, and jewelry, all of which are purchased at disproportionately high rates for those in the top income groups.

Outside of income level, education is the biggest predictor of conspicuous and inconspicuous spending. Those with a bachelor's or master's degree or higher (e.g., MD, JD, or PhD) spend 35% more on conspicuous goods than high school dropouts, almost 20% more than high school graduates, and 5% more than those with some college and/or an associate's degree. Because this analysis controls for income, the story is not simply one of education providing the income for such spending

Table 2.5. Ratio of consumption by educational attainment of householder (high school dropouts = 100.0)

	Conspicuous	Inconspicuous	Other expenditures
High school dropout	100	100	100
High school graduate	118	132	105
Some college and associate's degree	129	163	108
Bachelor's degree	135	188	114
Master's degree or higher	135	204	116

patterns. Rather, as Heffetz suggests, those with particular education backgrounds may be in social contexts that value conspicuous spending more, and education is a good proxy for "permanent income," that is, what they should expect to make ongoing for their lives. This latter point explains why more highly educated people might spend more on a car, house, or a new watch—their economic situation looks generally more stable. Even more profound, the more education one has, the more one spends on inconspicuous goods. Those with a master's degree spend over 100% more than high school dropouts and about 15% more than those with just a bachelor's degree. The increases in spending in these groups are leaps rather than increments (while other expenditures increase more linearly). Even by just finishing high school, one spends 32% more on inconspicuous consumption than if one drops out (see table 2.5 and figure 2.3). I speculate that underpinning these spending patterns is not just social contexts where visible goods matter but also the nature of jobs associated with higher education levels. A medical doctor, lawyer, or consultant (for example) may work longer hours, and thus the investment in a housekeeper, gardener, nanny, or any other good or service makes home life easier. They work long hours and often get paid handsomely for doing so, which allows them to outsource housework. (Contrast their 60-hour weeks with those of a service worker who works just as many hours but at a fraction of the income level and thus doesn't have the option of hiring a housekeeper or gardener.) Embedded in these occupations is higher permanent income (doctors and lawyers are rarely in the constant state of concern as to whether they will be fired or not, and while financiers do run that risk, they tend to get paid enough to offset such concerns). Thus, the combination of higher income with increased hours may influence these types of spending patterns.

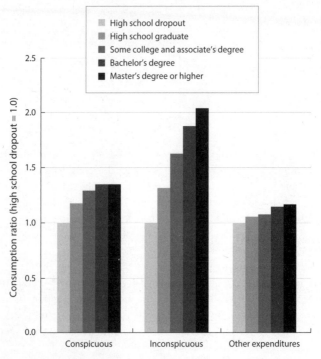

Figure 2.3. Educational attainment of householder. Data source: Consumer Expenditure Survey, Bureau of Labor Statistics.

Where we live, in terms of geographic region and city size, and whether we live in a city or not, also influences how we spend. I will delve into the specific distinctions across cities in a later chapter, but broadly speaking, those who live in the northeast are the least likely to spend on conspicuous items and those in the south and west are the most likely to spend on status goods (see table 2.6). Those who live in western states (such as Arizona, California, Nevada, New Mexico) spend the most in both categories (in actual dollars), and also on other expenditures. In certain parts of all of these states, housing prices are much lower than on the East Coast, which suggests people may have extra income to devote to spending in other areas. People in these regions also prioritize conspicuous consumption more generally than those in other

Table 2.6. Ratio of consumption by Census region (South = 100.0)

	Conspicuous	Inconspicuous	Other expenditures
Northeast	93	102	102
Midwest	99	106	99
South	100	100	100
West	100	119	108

parts of the country. City size also matters: People living in bigger cities tend to spend more on conspicuous goods, inconspicuous goods, and other expenditures than those in smaller cities. In fact, they spend on average 15% more on the first two categories and 20% more on expenditures in general. Part of this may be explained by cost of living—big cities like Los Angeles and New York are expensive places to live. In addition, wealth—both the profit generation of huge firms, banks, and film studios, and those who work in these high-paying industries—tends to be concentrated in big cities. In general these cities are dense, vibrant, and full of social events that drive the purchase of visible goods and offer the context where they are valued. When it comes to conspicuous consumption, smaller cities (those with populations of 125,000–329,000), by contrast, spend hardly more than those metros with fewer than 125,000 people (see table 2.7). With respect to inconspicuous spending, one explanation for the higher expenditure level might be the nature of jobs in bigger cities that lend themselves to the benefits of inconspicuous services. Major metros are home to a great number of professionals who work long hours and earn incomes that would lend themselves to inconspicuous consumption. The offerings available in bigger cities present another reason for increased spending there, including, for example, an abundance of labor-driven goods and services, whether nanny agencies or housekeeping firms, museums and opera

Table 2.7. Ratio of consumption by metropolitan area size (less than 125,000 = 100.0)

	Conspicuous	Inconspicuous	Other expenditures
More than 4 million	114	115	119
1.2–4 million	110	112	112
0.33–1.19 million	112	112	108
125–329.9 thousand	106	112	105
Less than 125,000	100	100	100

houses, and those repair shops for fixing high-end watches and jewelry. Big cities generate more profits and house some of the richest people in the world, from Russian oligarchs to Hollywood moguls to Wall Street hedge fund managers. This confluence of hyper-wealth and productivity in big cities translates into lots of spending power and as a result, the retail stores and service industries set up shop there and profit from such spending.

As we have seen, over the past decade and a half, income level increasingly separates how we spend and subsequently how we live and the fortunes of future generations. The wealthy of the twenty-first century are far savvier and more sensible than Veblen's leisure class—they are channeling money into education, and goods and services that save them time and provide a better quality of life. Yet, like Veblen's rich, today's top income groups take part in conspicuous consumption, too.

But conspicuous consumption is not the leitmotif of just the wealthy; it is omnipresent and, in fact, one might argue its democracy has made it so accessible that other income groups may choose to spend on status goods rather than on things that may shape their and their children's well-being in the long term. But we must also consider that those inconspicuous goods are far more expensive and getting more so each year. Those who are devoting more of their money to status goods and less to college fees may not even have the option of the latter. Say, for example, you have an extra $100. You can buy a handbag, a pair of shoes, or some electronic equipment. What that money won't do is make even a dent in a $50,000 tuition bill or an annual health insurance premium. One could argue that every dollar counts (this is the old adage put forth by many a father lecturing on the value of saving and compounding interest). But consider the psychology underpinning how and why we spend: The shoes or iPhone accessory provide instant gratification, as does being able to *actually* pay for college tuition for those who can. But being able to devote only a small amount of money toward something that costs so much (and thus still remains unattainable) doesn't really offer any benefits or satisfaction. So for some, the iPhone case offers more gratification than the small contribution to the tuition bill because the latter is simply too far out of reach to even consider.

Wealth is only part of our understanding of why we spend what we spend. Our consumption is influenced by our youth (or loss thereof), our relationship status, whether we have an MD or an associate's degree or neither, and whether we live in a big city or a small town. Multiple factors shape our desire for status, or our lack of interest in conspicuous consumption. Those who conspicuously consume are not always the same ones who inconspicuously consume (except the wealthy and the educated, who do both in droves). Regardless, what we spend and how we spend matters. Much of our consumption is linked to who we want to be and to our values—not all conspicuous consumption should be judged. Some forms of conspicuous consumption, like that with regard to race, may be an effort to thwart discrimination. For many of us, consumption is about fitting in.

Inconspicuous consumption, however, is the most consistent distinguishing spending practice of the elite, and is what truly separates them from everyone else. In the next chapter, I will look more closely at how inconspicuous consumption, which is often invisible and reveals status but often only to one's peer group, is perhaps the most pernicious divide between the elites and the rest. The practices of inconspicuous consumption, which can be both incredibly expensive but also nonpecuniary, offer a freedom and mobility that conspicuous consumption can't buy.

CHAPTER 3

Ballet Slippers and Yale Tuition: Inconspicuous Consumption and the New Elites

In the beginning, Essie Weingarten just liked nail polish colors. In 1981, Ms. Weingarten packed up her bags and displayed her initial 12 nail polish colors at a trade show in Las Vegas. In her collection she had, as she explained, "a true red, a blue red, a pink red and an orange red," along with the translucent pink and white tones that made her famous. Essie was the first in the business to push the sheer colors, of which Ballet Slippers has become the iconic shade along with Vanity Fairest (Essie #505), Baby's Breath (#5), Sugar Daddy (#473), and Mademoiselle (#384). As Essie explained, "I personally loved the look and nobody was doing it." In 1989, Queen Elizabeth's hairdresser sent a note to Essie requesting Ballet Slippers, Essie #162. As Essie recalls, "About two years after it came out, I received a letter from the Queen's hairdresser [with the request] complete with Royal seal. I thought, 'I've arrived.'"

In the decades since, Ballet Slippers and its sheer sisters have reigned supreme as the de rigueur nail polish colors for a particular group of women within Beverly Hills, New York's Upper East Side, and London's Kensington. Given the cult following by this aesthetically conscious elite group of women, and the Queen of England no less, surely there must be something special about Ballet Slippers—iridescent sparkles, unique mineral composition, or some attribute that would make its cult following so obvious. Yet, once applied, the color hardly screamed "notice me" or "I've just had a manicure." One coat leaves nails a slight blush, two coats creates an opaque white with hints of pink. Rather, this delicate color, almost childlike, merely signals subtly that a woman grooms herself.

My initial assumption about sheer nail polish among these high-society women was that its prevalence was a function of these women taking manicures for granted. Because well-groomed nails were such a quotidian part of their existence, it wasn't necessary to wear bold colors to announce the specialness of getting one's nails done. However, the phenomenon was quite the opposite: The women wore sheer colors precisely because their nails could *never* be taken for granted given the circles they ran in and the events they attended. They were a rarefied group who needed nails that assimilated within their social lives. The sheer color then became a symbol of an elite world where one's appearance *always* mattered.

Ballet Slippers is not worn by these women because it costs more— this nail polish is on the spectrum of affordable luxury goods, unlike the limited edition $20,000 Birkin bag or rare vintage wine. High-society women spend the same $7.99 for a bottle as the lady in small-town Pennsylvania pays for Essie's bright coral Geranium (#043). Yet both the Hermès bag and Ballet Slippers are status signifiers nonetheless.

Historically, professional manicures were very much relegated to high society and the affluent. "Getting a manicure before the 1980s was really special," Essie explained. "Before then, it was an outrage [to spend money on a manicure]." Then things changed. Starting in the 1980s, with the increased availability of low-wage service workers (located disproportionately in major cities), the price of manicures decreased such that average women were able to go to the salon. Now women can pop into a salon and have their nails done for $15.

Today, according to Euromonitor International, manicures are a $1 billion industry. Over a six-month period, 27 million adults had salon manicures and 32 million had pedicures. The trend continues to increase: From 2010 to 2011, manicure rates grew by 24%. Thus, a former habit of high society was easily translated by the masses. For Essie, nail polish became a democratic means to a former luxury and status good of the social elite—a taste of high society within reach. Today, Essie Weingarten's eponymous nail polish, Essie, is a household name to many an American woman and is sold in pharmacies and nail salons around the world.

With the decrease in manicure price, new colors have become more popular (blue, black, green, and flesh shades)—partially because manicures are so inexpensive that women can change their nail polish without it costing much. The manicure has become more disposable for everyone. Despite this trend, many women in high society and the professional world still wear sheer colors. It's hard to say which came first, the subtle colors as a functional or practical manicure or the fact that the subtle colors are a signal of a particular social position. Nevertheless, it is the way in which the manicure is translated—i.e., the color of choice—that makes all the difference. Unlike more material and ostentatious forms of conspicuous consumption, these nail polishes and the women who wear them illustrate a different barrier—the cost of information and knowing the implicit details that define a particular social stratum.

The choice of what color to paint one's nails is but one quotidian example of what the French sociologist Pierre Bourdieu would have called objectified cultural capital. In his landmark book, *Distinction*, Bourdieu argues that one's "taste" was less about the specific paintings on a wall or the car one drove and more about the cultural capital accrued through knowledge, social networks, and education that was indicated by those items.[1] Cultural capital (as opposed to economic capital or money) is the collection of distinctive aesthetics, skills, and knowledge (often attained through education and pedigree). Objectified cultural capital suggests that particular objects gain cultural or symbolic value that transcends, and is often greater than, any monetary value assigned. Thus social class is not produced through consumption (you can't "buy" your way automatically into the upper class) but rather it is attained through the adoption of values and aesthetics and the ability to decipher symbols and signs beyond materialism. These values, aesthetics, and taste form the "habitus" of everyday life—the ways in which we view the world and make normative judgments from our particular vantage point (as a rich, white person in Manhattan or poor African American in Mississippi, or a wealthy Latino in Miami, or member of the bourgeoisie in small-town America). The habitus is not simply the consumption patterns but the knowledge of what to consume. Thus, pale pink nail polish is the physical embodiment of the trappings of a particular social and economic class. The women know to paint their nails with Ballet Slippers as a commodified signifier of the cultural capital and habitus they glean from living an Upper East Side (NYC) life.

Most consumption choices are made at the intersection of the economic, cultural, and social values of particular classes and they are consciously and unconsciously appropriated to sort different groups from one another.[2] In an era where conspicuous consumption is accessible, social position is often truly defined by things we cannot see. Or, as Vance Packard remarked in *The Status Seekers*, "While Americans are ceremoniously egalitarian in their more conspicuous behavior patterns, they reflect, sometimes wittingly and often unwittingly, their class status by the nuances of their demeanor, speech, taste, drinking and dining patterns, and favored pasttimes."[3] Similarly, in the twenty-first century, social status emerges not simply from cars or watches but from inaccessible cues, information, and investments. For the aspirational class these signifiers are what I call "inconspicuous consumption"—that is, more subtle, less materialistic forms of conveying status particularly to others in-the-know. Sometimes these consumption choices aren't even intended to display status at all. Whether they are extraordinarily expensive versions of goods everyone buys, or investments in the life chances of their children, these new forms of inconspicuous consumption are goods and services purchased for the sake of making one's life easier, improving well-being (both intellectual and physical). Yet through both prosaic and profound inconspicuous consumption, these elites (whether the culturally rich aspirational class or just the rich) entrench their and their children's socioeconomic position.

The rise in inconspicuous consumption is a result of three important trends. First, so much of material consumption is accessible and overt that the aspirational class, both consciously and unconsciously, finds more obscure, codified symbols to reveal their social position.[4] Second, there is no "leisure class." The restructuring of the global economy prizes a meritocracy, who own the means of production through their minds, not land ownership. These labor market elites (many of whom are members of the aspirational class) believe in upward mobility and want the same for their children. Their dominant ethos—working hard and acquiring knowledge—is also the dominant cultural hegemony and spills over into all walks of life. Jonathan Gershuny observes that the relationship between work and leisure in contemporary society suggests that those who earn a lot of money work very hard to attain and maintain it, thus leisure time is the scarcest resource of all. He also observes that much of that leisure time is increasingly filled with consumer activities and to possess more leisure time paradoxically requires more work.[5] Today's labor market elites, particularly those in the aspirational class, devote money to freeing up that time and making the best of it through paying dearly for child care, housekeeping, gardeners, and luxury holidays. Finally, and most importantly, material consumption (particularly post-Recession) is less valuable than investing resources into the *consumption that counts*, like education, retirement, and health care, all of which price-out ordinary people but are critical conduits in the reproduction of aspirational class position and further separating the rich from the rest.

All of these latter consumption habits cost a lot of money but are not ostensibly about revealing one's status (even if they actually do). Inconspicuous consumption thus takes two, almost bifurcated, forms: *cost-of-information inconspicuous consumption*: inexpensive and nonpecuniary signifiers such as nail polish color and particular cultural knowledge, and *cost-prohibitive inconspicuous consumption*: incredibly expensive consumption such as child care, health care, and college tuition, which both significantly improve the quality of life for those who can afford it and simultaneously reinforce and retrench existing class lines. I will discuss each of these types of spending in turn. The key to most all inconspicuous consumption is that it is nonvisible except to those in the know, and is difficult to emulate without tacit information or a significant amount of money. Inconspicuous consumption is the source of the new class divide.

COST OF INFORMATION: NONPECUNIARY INCONSPICUOUS CONSUMPTION

This use of nonpecuniary means to demonstrate status is not entirely alien from Veblen's time. Veblen observed (and critiqued) the use of "manners" and "good breeding" as a demonstration of status. Acquiring manners and demonstrating them took time and was often possible only for those who led a life of leisure, exemplifying two important qualities of Veblen's upper class. Language has also always been a means to show social position—like manners, it takes time to acquire and practice particular word choices and turns of phrase. To quote the late social critic Paul Fussell, "Regardless of the money you've inherited ... the place you live, the way you look ... the time you eat dinner, the stuff you buy from mail-order catalogs … your social class is still most clearly visible when you say things."[6] Fussell goes on to discuss the "pseudo-elegant style" of the middle class: their discomfort in calling a toilet a toilet (rather, it is a restroom/lavatory/powder room), a drunk a drunk (he is someone "with alcohol problems"), or to comfortably use swear words or the word "death" (rather, it is "passing away" or "taken to Jesus"). Conversely, they are self-conscious using words that the upper classes use with reckless abandon: "divine," "outstanding," "super," "tedious," "tiresome." In their place, the middle class uses those umbrella words of banality: "nice" and "boring."

These observations get to class distinctions that transcend money and material goods: the "cost of information" and the cultural capital that one accrues through knowledge. Unlike conventional status goods, the new means by which members of the aspirational class define themselves are through goods that may cost just the same as they do for their middle-class counterparts but are only accessed through rarified information. As showy and material means of establishing status are more accessible, the aspirational class finds subtle symbols, cultural capital, and language to distinguish itself from other groups, and its members use knowledge as an important dividing line between them and the rest. Thus the aspirational class members shape and demonstrate their position through information they can attain only through their peers and position as purveyors of cultural capital. Just as Ballet Slippers does not cost more, there is a price to exist in the elite world where sheer nail polish is thought to be the standard, and the same holds true for other aspects of inconspicuous consumption. Nonmonetary, nonfunctional goods may cost the same in price, but the cost of information, rather than the actual cost of the good, is what creates the barrier.

This appropriation of value onto nonpecuniary behaviors is what the Columbia University sociologist Shamus Khan calls a "learned form of capital"; in other words, knowledge about ways of doing things becomes internalized, and acquiring it is an iterative process that in itself becomes valuable. In his study of Concord's elite school, St. Paul's, Khan argues that subtle forms of class assimilation, or "hidden curriculum," are in many ways more reinforcing of social position than more ostentatious and material symbols. The boys Khan interviewed discussed the hard work it took to gain entry into St. Paul's and asserted that they earned their success, but as Khan observed in his ethnographic work, most of them were seen to do very little work at all. In fact, the culture of success at St. Paul's was one of "ease" and effortlessness in their success. Walking to class without books was a marker of status, while those who actually carried huge backpacks of books and toiled away at the library doing homework were pariahs. "Hard work" was an important value to verbally espouse, emerging from a new generation of ostensibly meritocratic elites (who do in fact believe they have worked hard and deserve their position in the social pecking order). In reality, however, most of these students were as entitled as previous elites and their social behaviors were reflective of this. The belief in hard work becomes what Khan calls "a rhetorical cover" to mask what is actually privilege. "It is those students from advantaged backgrounds," Khan writes with NYU sociologist Colin Jerolmack, "who are most likely to succeed because throughout their lives, before even crossing the threshold of these spaces, they have developed the dispositions and cultural capital that give them an advantage over others. They feel at home within the institutions that reward them for exactly the type of behavior that is 'native' to them."[7]

To borrow an example from the sociologist Douglas Holt, the act of attending the opera is not the cultural capital, but rather the combination of the knowledge of when the performances are scheduled and where to buy the tickets, the appreciation of the music, the ability to reference the performance in discussion of other topics, and having people to share the experience with—and finally, the understanding that going to the opera is a valuable use of time.[8] Similarly, many of the observations made by *New York Times* columnist Paul Krugman could just as easily be made by simply thinking about massive inequality, unemployment, and the Great Recession's aftermath. Krugman's actual insights are less important than recognizing that reading Krugman is important. Reading the *New York Times* is a part of the aspirational class shared language, and citing Krugman (and knowing he is a Nobel Prize winner) at a dinner party is a significant part of fitting in with this group. The awareness of Krugman and the *New York Times*, not Krugman's thoughts in and of themselves (with all due respect), demonstrates cultural capital. But the value of the *New York Times* is place- and social situation–specific: Bringing up Krugman at a Manhattan dinner party would be met with approval or would be a nonevent that assimilates one into the group. In contrast, while Krugman's subjects (inequality, tax policy, presidential elections) may be of interest to those attending a Christmas party in small-town Pennsylvania, citing Krugman doesn't garner any social points. Herein lies the value of Ballet Slippers as greater than its $7.99 price tag.

Cultural capital is shaped by far more than money and objects. Many Bourdieu critics believed that his theories of cultural capital and habitus didn't apply in the United States because Americans are not known for their taste in high art and aesthetics. But Holt makes the point that Bourdieu's observations are not relegated to highbrow behaviors. Rather, his understanding of how shared aesthetics and values are formed by particular social groups can be broadly applied. Gilded Age elites made huge efforts to establish their distinct position, while those of today's aspirational class tend to be "cultural omnivores" in their consumption patterns, reflecting their knowledge, worldliness, and open-mindedness as a result of education and immersion into diverse environments (whether travel abroad or the international student body of their alma mater).[9] Vance Packard observed this of upper classes more than 50 years ago in his dissection of class behavior: "The average person of the lower group feels anxious in the presence of strange foods, and considers them fraught with danger. A Midwestern society matron reports her astonishment to find that her maid will not touch many of the very costly foods she serves the guests, such as venison, wild duck, pompano, caviar. Even when these are all prepared, steaming and ready to eat, the maid will cook herself some salt pork, turnip greens and potatoes. These are the foods she knows."[10]

The members of today's aspirational class fully embrace their cultural omnivore status through many different forms of cultural capital and totemic objects. They pride themselves on going to hole-in-the-wall ethnic restaurants instead of Applebee's, buying local farmers' eggs, and wearing TOMS shoes because these signifiers of cultural capital reveal social and environmental consciousness, surely acquired in the pages of the *New Yorker* and at the elite universities they attended. Even if they have full-time careers, the attainment of such knowledge implies that they either have the conspicuous leisure time to read or stroll famers' markets, or that they value the acquisition of this type of information as a worthy use of their time. In his study of class in America, Holt described this type of cultural capital as "authenticity and connoisseurship," which was prized among the upper classes (regardless of price point), whereas the lower classes valued things if they were expensive. The lower classes share "collective signals of [material] luxury" compared to the premium that the upper class places on individuality and shared knowledge of contemporary nonfiction writers and Cannes film festival award-winning documentaries. Similarly, in a study of contemporary upper-middle-class music tastes, the sociologists Richard Peterson and Robert Kern found that their music preferences were not relegated to opera and classical music, but rather ranged from everything from hip-hop to pop to folk along with the expected highbrow inclinations. As many of the upper middle class attained their status through higher education and professional position (the former of which tends to be associated with greater tolerance), Peterson and Kern speculate that perhaps these new elites are in fact more open than previous generations. More cynically, one might interpret the new elites' diverse "nobrow" consumer choices as a symbolic boundary that stakes their rarified social position. In other words, that they know to have diverse and idiosyncratic consumer choices may suggest a cultural sophistication that only comes with the education and knowledge that propels them into their social position.

This evolution from overt wealth (or the pretense of wealth) to discreet signals of class is present in aspirational class food too. Indeed, exotic or authentic food has become a legitimated signal of cultural capital for the aspirational class—and one that is shared across the economic gradients. While only the top income groups may be able to write checks for their kids to go to Stanford, the consumption of particular types of food becomes a unifying form of objectified cultural capital for all members of the aspirational class. Today's aspirational class circulates around cafés and restaurants that offer several different presentations of kale on the same menu, almond lattes, and gourmet comfort food. Stews rather than soufflés, chicken pot pie, artisanal mac and cheese, and beer (so long as it is craft) have become de rigueur signals of aspirational class culinary life and can be found in a variety of settings, from meals made by a banker's wife to those of a hipster screenwriter's Sunday brunch with friends. Sure, this food is more expensive than McDonald's, but most of it is still at a price point that members of the aspirational class can afford, and due to their cultural capital, they believe this type of food is worth the cost. While this type of cultural capital appears more democratic, as the sociologists Johnston and Baumann observe, foodie culture reaffirms Bourdieu's basic thesis that everyday cultural forms create and maintain social status.[11] Kale salad may not seem as overtly snobby as the opera but it's still a means of preserving class lines, albeit more subtly.

The accrual of particular types of knowledge and the sharing of cultural capital mean that the new elites use this information to buy particular things and act in particular ways and to further solidify their position. Or, as Khan writes, "Culture is a resource used by elites to recognize one another and distribute opportunities on the basis of the display of appropriate attributes."[12] Nail polish color is more subtle and less expensive than yachts and handbags, but the choice to wear one color over another involves acquiring knowledge as to what is aesthetically appropriate and appreciated by one's peer group. When to write a thank you note, how to hold one's fork, how many books to walk to class with (i.e., none at all)—are also learned behaviors that appear costless but are actually embedded in the experience of being in a particular socioeconomic group. "What appears as a natural, simple quality," Khan remarks, "is actually learned through repeated experiences in elite institutions."[13]

While the 1920s Gilded Age elites and today's "nouveau riche" (think of the stereotyped Russian oligarchs or Hollywood celebrities) may make great efforts to distinguish themselves in overt ways from everyone else, members of the aspirational class use discretion to separate themselves. Consider that even the wealthiest aspirational class kitchens often decorate with copper pots, rustic Stickley dining tables, and Aga-like stoves that resemble those used in the kitchen of Downton Abbey, rather than the upstairs formal baroque style of English aristocrats. Casualness in all facets of life has become a part of aspirational class habitus. In this respect, the aesthetics of the aspirational class are in line with those of bobos. As David Brooks writes in his book *Bobos in Paradise*, "Educated elites are expected to spend huge amounts of money on things that used to be cheap ... We prefer to buy the same items as the proletariat—it's just that we buy rarefied versions of these items that members of the working class would consider preposterous. So we will buy chicken legs, just like everyone else, but they'll likely be free-range ... we'll buy potatoes, but we won't buy an Idaho spud. We'll select one of those miniature potatoes of distinction that grow only in certain soils of northern France." For bobos, the downplaying of status resulted from discomfort with their newly acquired wealth. For the aspirational class, the choice of particular fabrics, wood, or foodstuffs has to do with acquiring knowledge of what is superior, more environmentally friendly, and more humane. We find these subtle signs of class in everything from what the aspirational class eats (gourmet, organic, and humane comfort foods), where they buy groceries (farmers' markets and Whole Foods), what they wear (organic cotton and made in the USA with no labels), and what they talk about (articles in the *Wall Street Journal* or the most talked-about podcast, which at present is *Serial*). All of these subtle cues suggest knowledge and a value system acquired through extensive acquisition of knowledge—and an aspiration to achieve a higher cultural and social way of being and a nonchalant worldliness about books, news events, and so forth. As many aspirational class members are ostensibly part of the "meritocratic elite" or at least educated with such an intention, these cues suggest membership but also reveal the cost of information to acquire it (college educations, reading highbrow publications, being up-to-date on food production practices).

Just as ease and insouciance are part of being on top of the pecking order at St. Paul's, staged informality has become a common aesthetic among the aspirational class. The former British prime minister David Cameron (a well-bred Eton and Oxford boy and distant relative of the queen) received a media bashing after his government minister, Francis Maude, shared his affection for hosting "kitchen suppers" with fellow elite cronies (including Cameron), a sort of upper-class version of slumming it. Our upper classes no longer have multicourse dinners every night with strange and obscure silver kitchen utensils, but the downgrading of "dinner" to a casual "supper" further distances the cultural elites from everyone else who keeps the meal special. The origin of the term "kitchen supper" again hails from the days of British lords and ladies and their servants who ate their dinner in the kitchen away from the aristocrats they served. Today, the term has been coopted by the elites themselves to imply that one has a dining room (and thus the kitchen supper is a separate type of meal); in addition, the decision to

forgo the dining room implies the choice to be more casual and intimate. Charles Moore, the *Telegraph* writer and Margaret Thatcher biog-
rapher, remarks of the kitchen supper eaters, "[They are] disclosing an
assumption—we have a nice dining room but we'll be all relaxed with
our pals and won't use it."[14] Or as Katrin Bennhold wrote of "supper-
gate" in the *New York Times*, "[When] Francis Maude, the British Cabi-
net Office minister, spoke of 'kitchen suppers,' the media reminded him
that most voters had 'dinner' (middle class) or 'tea' (working class) and
not necessarily the option of eating in a dining room";[15] thus suggesting
the implication that the kitchen was one of at least two options. Or as
Rachel Cooke wittily wrote in the *Guardian*,

> Who, apart from Francis Maude and his friends, uses it? And what, ex-
> actly, does it mean? In fact, it takes a while to unpick it, for within these
> two words lurk such a dizzying array of assumptions. The knowledge that
> one's kitchen is big enough to contain a table. The suggestion that, else-
> where in the house, there might be another room where, on a more im-
> portant occasion, one might also eat. The deft swerve around the words
> "dinner party" (these, being aspirational middle class, are presumably
> non-U[16] in Maude-ian circles) and "meal" (also non-U, though I've no
> idea why; I'm only aware of this at all because a horrible old Etonian I
> once met ticked me off when it fell sluttishly from my lips).[17]

Similarly, saying one went to a "small school in Cambridge" when everyone knows you mean Harvard suggests the downplaying of something
that is actually prized and rare, just like the option to have dinner in the
dining room or the kitchen. A household's rule of taking one's shoes off
when entering suggests too much regard and preciousness for the house
(nouveau), while the aspirational class wouldn't dare imply their house
was worthy of such care (even if it actually is).

The relationship between status and nonpecuniary inconspicuous
consumption can perhaps be best observed in the behaviors of those on
the lower economic gradient of the aspirational class: hipsters—those
young, 20-something-year-old urban denizens working in film or
screenwriting or publishing—who barely make enough money to pay
the rent, let alone attend parties with the queen of England or the head
of Citibank. Yet for this drolly ironic subculture, information about
what is cool or in the know is all they have and thus they too engage in

nonpecuniary means of inconspicuous consumption that allow them to define their social position by reading and referencing obscure blogs and Twitter feeds, carrying NPR canvas bags, and riding fixed-gear bicycles. They drink hemp milk, not dairy; drive old Mercedes revamped to run on veggie oil instead of second-hand Honda Accords; buy fast food at food trucks rather than McDonald's; even though these goods are more or less comparable in price. (Incidentally, McDonald's now serves kale salads, surely a response to the new emphasis on healthy eating championed by both health professionals and the aspirational class.) Yet the veggie oil car (despite smelling like a plate of French fries when it trundles by) and the almond butter (which really does taste almost the same as peanut butter) convey cultural capital for members of the aspirational class. These practices and goods are not more expensive but are established and coopted through an insider's game of information on local subculture, hole-in-the-wall dive bars, and the whereabouts of particular food trucks.

The new mannerisms and consumption practices of the aspirational class are not ostentatious even if they often imply wealth or knowledge. Unlike a Prada logo, these habits are not recognized as conveying status in a ubiquitous way. In the twenty-first century, there is a reversal of sorts of historical depictions of the elite classes and cultural capital. Thank you notes and good manners are still prized, as they were in Veblen's time, but superfluous notes or overly precious manners appear to be trying too hard.[18] Some members of today's aspirational class distinguish themselves through an active downplay of labels and ostentation and an upgrading of their cultural capital and signifiers—behaviors and information that are simultaneously inaccessible and costless. Hipsters may not be labor market elites (although many are), but they draw their elitism through rarified information too. They know who to read, who to follow on Twitter and Instagram, and particular types of insider language and obscure (almost fetishized) objects of consumption, whether almond lattes, green juice, or the $12 Casio calculator watch.

All of these practices reveal what Max Weber called "styles of life."[19] Thus, money and status, while related, are not the same thing. Rather, people of a similar income bracket do not necessarily behave and consume in the same way; behavior is determined more by how one got there, where she came from, and where she lives. This observation captures what Bourdieu meant when he believed it was impossible to be upwardly mobile simply through material goods. Bourdieu would observe that status then becomes a product of who we socialize with and the information and cues we pick up as a result.[20] Taste and style of life are passed on from generation to generation and learned at a young age or through membership in a particular group. If one is not brought up within an elite habitus, one remains an outsider. This explains why we see the true upper class of Britain poor as paupers but status rich, and why Tony Soprano, with his big New Jersey suburban house, would never be invited to attend a Met gala or to serve on the board of the New York Public Library. In a crushing scene in Dominick Dunne's best-selling novel *Too Much Money*, the imprisoned billionaire Elias Renthal tells his estranged aspiring high-society wife, "You still haven't gotten those people straight, Ruby. You still want to be one of them.... I know about the baron in Paris, who went back to his dyke wife rather than marry you.... she has lineage, like a title ... and all that stuff. You don't."

The essence of taste and habitus implies layers of status and acquired knowledge which may be a function of money but is not entirely explained by money alone. Thus, nonpecuniary inconspicuous consumption revolves around tacit knowledge, cultural capital and habitus, and what Michele Lamont calls "symbolic boundaries."[21] Lamont, a sociology professor at Harvard University, believes that Bourdieu's conception of cultural capital is too rigid and ignores other measures of status, particularly morality, which Lamont believes is highly important (but different) across the upper middle classes. Morality is a class issue that transcends conventional economic and even cultural lines. It is not enough to be rich or well-off or to know that reading the *New York Review of Books* or the *Paris Review* matters, but even one's values on marriage (mistress or not?), success (power or fame?), and what to spend one's money on as a general principle, are markers of where one fits in, and these matters become the redlines that classes don't cross. For example, in France, the male professionals Lamont interviewed for her study were much more comfortable talking about extramarital affairs than their American counterparts (even if statistics would suggest the latter participated just as much). While definitions of success were specific to each country, the upper-middle-class values of France (power and fame) and the United States (the implication of money) were consistently shared with their countrymen. Unlike accruing capital, which suggests that simply after having a certain amount one is a part of a particular group, symbolic boundaries imply lines drawn; thus they essentially allow us to exclude and include some people and not others. As the late social critic A. A. Gill sums it up, "After a bit, the money stops working."[22]

COST-PROHIBITIVE INCONSPICUOUS CONSUMPTION

Of course it's not so simple. Many of the things that are not about money are of course absolutely about money. Economic choices uphold social mores and consumption choices. The inverse is, of course, true too: Social mores and consumption choices are a result of economic options. You could be very poor and read the *New Yorker*, but there's a lot more to a subscription than simply the magazine itself. The *New Yorker* suggests socioeconomic and cultural position, but there are a whole host of other things that uphold it. Reading these publications implies an educated life, and a value system placed upon culture and knowledge (and the luxury to have such a value system). Most of the readers trolling through the pages of the *New Yorker* and the *New York Times* are likely to have $40,000-plus college educations (and graduate degrees too) from elite institutions and spend time with similarly educated people with whom they trade opinions and information. The *New York Times* costs $2.50 for the daily paper, $5 for the Sunday edition (the daily habit adds up), but comprehension of all those SAT words and cultural allusions (Camus, Foucault, Freud) implies a whole host of expensively attained knowledge. Cultural capital (and symbolic boundaries) costs money even if not all money can purchase cultural capital. Cultural capital is not about material goods and yet is still largely drawn from material wealth, even if the choices almost seem natural and habituated (more on this practice as status signifier in chapter 4). Understanding the value of these nonmaterial signifiers relies largely on spending time with others who also place significance on the newspaper and the well-groomed nails (and organic vegetables, direct trade coffee, and so forth). Without the shared experience, the sheer nail color and the strawberries are not so important. Much of aspirational class shared experience is based on information that costs money, even if it is materially invisible, just like the kids at St. Paul's who know to walk without books and make their work appear effortless. As Khan remarks, "The apparent easiness of these characteristics implies that if someone does not know how to embody [them] ... it is somehow their fault as they do not naturally have what it takes."[23]

But these nonpecuniary signals of status are underpinned by a type of consumption that truly excludes everyone but the rich. Whether college tuition, child care, or luxury holidays, these investments are cost-prohibitive for most Americans, and also genuinely affect the day-to-day and generational outcomes of those who are able to afford them compared to those who cannot. In short, this is consumption that is not about status as much as quality of life. Returning to Jonathan Gershuny's observations on leisure and work: Most rich people today work many hours to make their money, and as a result lose the very time that could be used for leisure.[24] Leisure is expensive. As a result, many of their consumption practices are directed toward recouping time and preserving their socioeconomic position for their and their children's futures. It is no surprise that this costs a lot of money. This type of pecuniary inconspicuous consumption can be divided into three key categories: *labor-intensive* (utility-driven over status), *experience-driven* (non-utilitarian but also not status-seeking), and *consumption that counts* (investments in the quality of life and well-being of oneself and one's children). These three types of inconspicuous consumption are symbiotic: As society in general has less time, one significant expense is the outsourcing of the drudgery that takes up time that could otherwise be used for fun. Hiring a nanny and paying for direct flights creates more time for weekend getaways—all of which can be very costly. Paying for college tuition, good preschools, and retirement is not only incredibly expensive but secures the upward mobility of the wealthy members of the aspirational class and their offspring, while excluding everyone else who cannot afford these goods. In the following section, I will look at these trends more broadly and how the rich (many of whom are members of the aspirational class) spend compared to the rest of America.

For starters, the rich have always spent more than everyone else on inconspicuous consumption, and less on conspicuous consumption than they do on education, child care, tuition, SAT courses, political contributions, and other nonvisible spending, but this trend has significantly increased in the Recession aftermath.[25] While the top income groups tended to spend essentially the same on conspicuous and inconspicuous consumption pre-2007, after the crisis their consumption habits changed significantly, with huge drops in conspicuous consumption after the crisis, followed by a slight uptick but never returning to previous levels from 2008 onward. As the economist Robert Frank observes, with the outcry over inequality in full swing, public hedonism and overt luxury spending have become flashpoints in the debate (which is not to say they aren't spending money), and thus those in top income groups find new channels for their money that are known only to those in their circles (whether it's a live-in housekeeper or, for the very rich, NetJets to Art Basel Miami).[26] Conversely, the middle class, those in the 40th to 60th percentile income bracket making on average $47,000 a year, are returning to their pre-Recession conspicuous consumption behavior while reducing their spending on inconspicuous consumption in the post-Recession period. Historically, they have always spent significantly more on conspicuous expenditures than inconspicuous consumption, and at the height of the financial crisis barely reduced their spending on clothes, watches, cars, and other Veblen goods (see fig. 3.1).

In fact, in absolute dollars, only the top three income brackets are spending more today on inconspicuous consumption than they did in 1996—the middle class and lower income groups are spending less during the same time period. Overall, the upper income brackets are spending 5–10% more on these goods than they did in 1996. For the average American household, inconspicuous consumption accounts for about 10% of all expenditures. For the top 1%, 5%, and 10% income groups' expenditure share devoted to inconspicuous consumption is 22.9%, 19.7%, and 17.4% respectively, up to 80% more than the national average. Contrast these shares to the middle and lower income groups where inconspicuous consumption accounts for just 9–9.5% of total expenditures. As a household moves up the income chain, its members tend to spend more on inconspicuous consumption.

The wealthy now spend almost 5.5 times more than the national average on inconspicuous goods (versus 2.5 times more than the nation on conspicuous consumption) and almost 12% more than they did in 1996. The middle class, by contrast, spends 40% less on inconspicuous consumption as compared to the US average, and 20% less as compared to 1996.

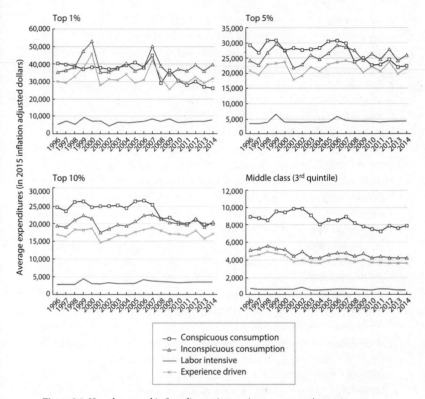

Figure 3.1. How they spend it. Spending on inconspicuous vs. conspicuous consumption by income group. Data source: Consumer Expenditure Survey, Bureau of Labor Statistics.

LABOR-INTENSIVE AND EXPERIENCE-DRIVEN INCONSPICUOUS CONSUMPTION

It's no surprise that the upper income groups devote significantly more money to these consumption habits, which free up time and make life run smoother. It's also no surprise that most people cannot afford these types of spending. Much of it requires labor, which doesn't get much cheaper over time. No matter what technological advances the world develops, some tasks still require the hard work of real people. Economist William Baumol observed that a Beethoven string quartet would always require four musicians putting forth the same degree of effort regardless of increased productivity or technological innovations that might make other industries more efficient (the manufacturing sector, for instance). And, even as the musicians' productivity remains the same, their real wages will increase due to inflation and economic growth, or what Baumol called the "cost disease." This is true, too, for many service industries like daycare and lawn care. Controlling for fads and fashions in childrearing (as I will discuss in chapter 4), taking care of children has been a fairly straightforward task for centuries, yet the cost of a babysitter or nanny's labor has increased significantly. More practically, child care is an industry that just won't be automated. (No one is going to let a robot take care of their kids.) And while there is such a thing as a roaming automated vacuum cleaner, the detailed aspects of housekeeping require a person scrubbing tiles and polishing coffee tables. The same holds true for music instructors, veterinarians, and dog walkers. Even with technological innovations, people are still crucial in many areas of life management and upkeep.

These macro changes in society and economics show up in consumption patterns. Looking at the actual numbers, the top 1% spends 10–20 times more than the middle class on child care. The top 5% and 10% also spend significantly more on child care: in excess of 6–8 times more in absolute dollars than the middle class. While it is logical to expect that the more money people have, the more they spend on making their lives easier, these upper income groups also spend a greater *share* of their total expenditures on child care, suggesting they are prioritizing child care over other consumption choices. They are spending two to five times more of their share of expenditures on child care than the middle class does. Similarly, domestic services, which include gardening, security, and housekeeping, are more prized by the upper income groups both as demonstrated by absolute dollars spent and share of total expenditures: the top 1% spends about 20 times more on domestic services than the middle classes, and double even that of the top 10%. As with child care, the wealthy clearly also choose to make these services a priority over other expenditures: The top 1% spends four to five times more of its total household expenditures on domestic services than the middle class. In general, the top 5% and 10% spend similar shares of total expenditures on domestic services as the top 1% (although the top 1% still

Table 3.1. Expenditures on child care by year and income group (in 2015 dollars)

	1996	1998	2000	2002	2004	2006	2008	2010	2012	2014
All households	140	135	118	104	95	114	108	103	106	110
Top 1%	885	995	1,025	606	596	893	984	1,507	963	2,110
Top 5%	389	380	400	409	354	517	519	564	452	676
Top 10%	383	325	302	342	286	384	378	387	401	429
60–89th percentile	166	160	128	104	99	114	110	100	79	101
40–59th percentile	72	94	68	53	60	56	47	39	60	41
0–39th percentile	47	43	60	35	31	36	29	30	42	31

spend the most on child care) (see tables 3.1–3.4.). Do they have bigger houses than the less well-off and thus might need extra help? Possibly. But the top income groups also have the option to have someone else mop their floors, mow their lawn, and water their plants, while the data suggest that lower income groups do these chores themselves.

The findings on labor-intensive inconspicuous consumption align with the extensive work of Suzanne Bianchi and her colleagues. Bianchi finds that despite the fact that there are more women in the workforce today than in the middle of the twentieth century, and despite the fact that parents in general work more than ever, today parents are spending more time with their kids than in the "family-oriented" 1960s. Using time diary data over several decades starting in the 1960s, Bianchi and colleagues find that cultural norms around parenting are changing. Parents are more involved with their kids voluntarily, and there is an "ideal of shared parenting" that lessens the traditional load on the mother.

Table 3.2. Share of expenditures on child care by year and income group (%)

	1996	1998	2000	2002	2004	2006	2008	2010	2012	2014
All households	0.25	0.23	0.20	0.17	0.16	0.18	0.18	0.18	0.18	0.19
Top 1%	0.52	0.58	0.55	0.35	0.34	0.49	0.57	0.88	0.54	1.22
Top 5%	0.30	0.28	0.31	0.31	0.27	0.35	0.37	0.42	0.33	0.51
Top 10%	0.34	0.28	0.26	0.29	0.25	0.30	0.32	0.34	0.34	0.37
60–89th percentile	0.26	0.24	0.19	0.15	0.15	0.17	0.16	0.16	0.12	0.16
40–59th percentile	0.17	0.22	0.16	0.12	0.14	0.12	0.10	0.09	0.14	0.09
0–39th percentile	0.15	0.13	0.18	0.11	0.09	0.11	0.09	0.09	0.13	0.10

Table 3.3. Expenditures on domestic services by year and income group (in 2015 dollars)

	1996	1998	2000	2002	2004	2006	2008	2010	2012	2014
All households	237	252	286	264	292	330	325	305	342	343
Top 1%	2,372	2,380	3,432	2,121	2,552	2,720	2,628	2,368	2,627	3,020
Top 5%	1,286	1,436	1,432	1,338	1,412	1,761	1,637	1,579	1,681	1,651
Top 10%	853	1,002	991	947	1,022	1,244	1,195	1,126	1,176	1,190
60–89th percentile	191	181	237	211	264	266	297	266	286	306
40–59th percentile	103	109	143	147	130	159	131	141	187	159
0–39th percentile	129	125	150	121	129	138	127	118	162	158

Bianchi finds that parents give up more of their leisure time to be with their children. The management of parents' time toward finding more of it to spend with their kids suggests the role of inconspicuous consumption in making this possible.[27] Bianchi also reports that even though women are working more in the twenty-first century, they are actually spending the same amount of time, if not more, with their kids as the stay-at-home moms of the mid-twentieth century.[28] Part of this change is a result of larger reconfigurations of how society uses time and what is valued. Take the case of housework: While cleanliness standards have not necessarily gone down, housework is less valued as a reasonable use of a working mother's time. Bianchi finds that households now rely on domestic service (e.g., housekeepers and gardeners) and men pitching in so that mothers can spend time with their families.[29]

Table 3.4. Share of expenditures on domestic services by year and income group (%)

	1996	1998	2000	2002	2004	2006	2008	2010	2012	2014
All households	0.42	0.43	0.49	0.44	0.50	0.54	0.54	0.53	0.59	0.59
Top 1%	1.39	1.38	1.85	1.24	1.44	1.48	1.52	1.38	1.48	1.74
Top 5%	0.99	1.06	1.09	1.01	1.06	1.19	1.18	1.19	1.23	1.25
Top 10%	0.76	0.86	0.87	0.82	0.89	0.98	1.00	0.99	1.01	1.02
60–89th percentile	0.29	0.28	0.36	0.31	0.39	0.39	0.44	0.41	0.44	0.47
40–59th percentile	0.24	0.25	0.33	0.32	0.30	0.35	0.29	0.33	0.43	0.36
0–39th percentile	0.41	0.37	0.44	0.36	0.39	0.41	0.38	0.37	0.50	0.49

Experience-driven goods, such as travel, wine, lodging out of town—the fun parts of life—are also a significant area of top income spending. The rich spend more than the middle and lower income groups by substantial margins. In fact, when it comes to experience-driven goods, the top 1% and 5% are dramatically different from everyone else. In 2014, the top 1% spent, on average, $32,000 on having fun, while the middle class spent $3,600. Experience-driven goods and services account for 16–18% of household expenditures for the top 1% and 5% but just 8.2% for the middle class. The top 1–5% spend 50–70% more on experience-driven goods as a share of total expenditures than the average household, while the middle class spends 20–25% less. Finally, the top 1%, 5%, and 10% are spending significantly more on this type of consumption than they did in 1996 (both in absolute dollars and as a share of total expenditures), while everyone else is spending 15–25% less.

One might argue that, aside from the rare few virtuosos, learning the violin by age three equally falls into a category of non-utility. Some things—going to the opera, learning the saxophone (or trying to), and taking exotic holidays—while not performing a utility per se, are also not done for conspicuous status either. Most people who play saxophone aren't doing it in public, and while the opera can indeed be a social scene for some, others attend for the sheer enjoyment of the music and drama (as is the case for exotic travel and attending museums, for others). This type of experience-driven consumption, not utilitarian and not status-driven, is most prevalent among the upper income groups. Overall they spend five times more on these goods than the middle class. In the case of musical instruments, the wealthy, from the top 10% to the top 1%, all spend significantly more than the middle class (see table 3.5). Similarly, the top income groups spend significantly more on recreation and nonbusiness travel (see table 3.6). While the top 1% spends more in absolute dollars, the top 1%, 5%, and 10% each spend more or less the same share of their total expenditures (around 0.1%), while the middle class spends significantly less both in dollar terms and share of expenditures. This suggests that recreation, like instruments and other inconspicuous goods, is not, and perhaps cannot be, a priority. Post-Recession, the top income groups are spending more on musical instruments and other inconspicuous consumption while the middle

Table 3.5. Spending on musical instruments by income and year (in 2015 dollars)

	1996	1998	2000	2002	2004	2006	2008	2010	2012	2014
All households	113	103	134	99	84	65	77	47	41	37
Top 1%	476	134	385	364	310	141	156	83	340	493
Top 5%	233	157	215	205	180	124	317	87	135	153
Top 10%	207	172	204	189	157	113	226	107	116	101
60–89th percentile	125	118	191	126	99	80	76	56	41	38
40–59th percentile	89	96	94	71	61	52	52	32	27	26
0–39th percentile	74	54	54	43	49	30	27	19	18	17

class has returned to its pre-Recession conspicuous consumption levels but not its pre-Recession inconspicuous spending levels.

Recent data on luxury holidays illustrate the general trend of the wealthy spending more on experiences and, in the process, pulling further and further away from everyone else. According to Virtuoso, a network of thousands of travel agents, over the past seven years, travelers who spend at least $100,000 annually on trips have increased the rate of their spending two to three times as compared to the "regular traveler" (or those who spend "just" $10,000 annually on trips). National Geographic Expeditions, a company that designs round the world trips to far-flung destinations like the Galapagos and Antarctica, recently offered a 24-day trip (including stops at the aforementioned locations) for $77,000. The trip sold out.[30] These "bespoke experiences" are more than just expensive and fun. Traveling like this has the second-order effect of

Table 3.6. Spending on recreation by income and year (in 2015 dollars)

	1996	1998	2000	2002	2004	2006	2008	2010	2012	2014
All households	45	45	42	41	41	39	30	28	26	23
Top 1%	295	103	163	160	130	182	206	102	102	116
Top 5%	148	121	127	117	131	115	127	77	95	60
Top 10%	120	114	100	95	104	91	95	75	73	56
60–89th percentile	54	53	48	52	49	53	33	31	29	28
40–59th percentile	23	26	23	24	22	21	17	20	15	12
0–39th percentile	18	16	25	16	14	11	8	8	8	8

generating cultural capital and symbolic boundaries and numerous non-pecuniary signifiers of being well-rounded, knowledgeable, and probably interesting at dinner parties.

CONSUMPTION THAT COUNTS

There's no question that there exists both a symbolic and an economic boundary between the girl who takes private violin lessons and the girl who does not, as is the case for those who have the luxury to take vacations or can afford nannies. All of these consumption practices create class lines that are more stratifying than conventional goods, because they enable some people to accrue experiences, knowledge, and skills, or what Khan calls a "learned form of capital." In isolation, whether one knows how to play violin or not isn't what gets a kid into Harvard (as much as those Tiger Moms wish it to be the case). Rather, the violin is significant in conjunction with all the other experiences and circumstances that matter: whether her parents have the money to send her to an elite preschool and secondary institution, whether they can afford test prep and extracurricular activities that make her an "interesting" applicant, and who in the family's social networks knows someone at Harvard admissions. Better yet, who else in that little violin-playing girl's family already graduated from Harvard? This mosaic of attributes is increasingly a necessity for top universities and reveals where inconspicuous consumption is most pronounced and has the greatest implications for inequality and future generations.

I mentioned earlier that the Great Recession fundamentally changed particular consumption habits: The richer households now spend significantly less on conspicuous consumption and more on inconspicuous consumption, while the middle class only slightly reduced its conspicuous consumption through the crisis (returning to pre-Recession conspicuous spending levels) while decreasing its inconspicuous consumption spending post-Recession. As this chapter and the previous one document, the wealthy and the middle class are now exhibiting almost opposite spending patterns. Nowhere is this more evident than in the *consumption that counts*. In education, health care, pensions, and personal insurance, the top income groups (particularly the top 1%) are spending much more than the middle class both in absolute dollars and in share of total expenditures (see figures 3.3–3.5). These are not small numbers: The top 1–5% spend on average 5% of their total expenditures on education, while the middle class barely spends 1% on education (see figure 3.2). Since the Great Recession, there has been a gradual overall uptick in top income group education spending and a decline in the middle class's education consumption. In 2014, the top 1% spent 3.5 times more in absolute dollars and share of expenditures on education than they did in 1996. In 2014, they spent 860% more than the national average, while the middle class spent 50% less and the lower income households spent 70% less than the national average on education. Despite skyrocketing college tuition, as a share of expenditures, the poor and middle-class income groups are spending exactly the same as they did in 1996 on education, and less than a quarter of what the top income groups devote as a share of total expenditures. Education is perhaps the biggest tangible example of the divide between the haves and have-nots in America. While the rich are redirecting greater portions of their income to education, the lower income groups are unable to keep up even as a share of expenditures (let alone in absolute dollars). The results suggest that the middle class and lower income groups are not deprioritizing education, but they simply cannot afford the rising tuition fees across all levels of education from preschool to high school to college. According to the Labor Department, college tuition has increased 80% in just ten years (2003–2013), while the cost of other types of consumer goods, like housing and food, has grown at just 23% and 30% respectively, and the overall consumer price index has increased 27% in the same time period (see figure 3.3).[31] In major cities, even preschool fees climb into the tens of thousands (yes, that's tuition for three-year-olds), which was the cost of a good state university education just 15 years ago.

You can argue that there is a conspicuous component to education—most parents brag about where their kid goes to college. But the bragging is still secondary to what education actually provides: knowledge, a degree, social networking opportunities that are essential to get ahead and improve one's life chances. Unlike in Veblen's time, when education was thought to serve no real function, today a college education quite literally defines and predicts one's future income, occupation, and class. Education is essential and perhaps the consumption habit with the greatest utility over the long term.[32]

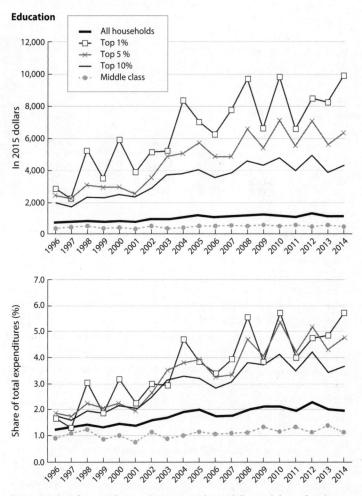

Figure 3.2. Spending on education by income and year, dollars and share of total spending. Data source: Consumer Expenditure Survey, Bureau of Labor Statistics.

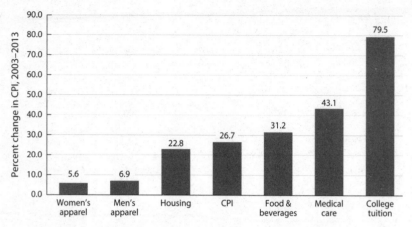

Figure 3.3. The rate of college tuition compared to other consumer goods.
Source: D. Kurtzleben (2013). "Just how fast has college tuition grown?" *U.S. News and World Report.*

With regard to health care, the top 1% spends far and away more than everyone else, but all of the upper income groups are spending dramatically more on health care in the post-Recessionary period (see figure 3.4). While the middle class spends the most on health care as a proportion of their total expenditures, the top earners are experiencing the most rapid increase in share devoted to health care. This investment in health paves the way for better day-to-day maintenance of health (and chronic health problems) and better lives as they grow older. Preventative health care is a crucial component of overall well-being, and the ability to invest ongoing in one's health is indicative of overall quality of life. In addition, the best health insurance often garners the best health care. The rise of "concierge medicine" requires a patient to pay an annual fee or retainer for Fee for Care or Fee for Extra Care (FFC or FFEC), which means that a doctor limits her number of patients to provide additional time and greater care for those who are willing to pay a premium.[33]

Perhaps most alarming, the top 1% are spending significantly more in terms of both absolute dollars and share of total expenditures on personal insurance and pensions: about 20% of the top 1%'s expenditures are in this category, compared to 8% for the middle class. In 2014, this

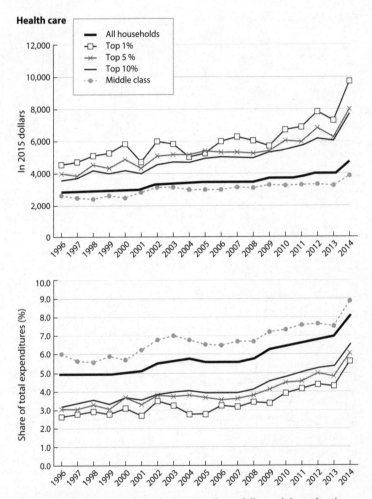

Figure 3.4. Spending on health care by income and year, dollars and share of total spending. Data source: Consumer Expenditure Survey, Bureau of Labor Statistics.

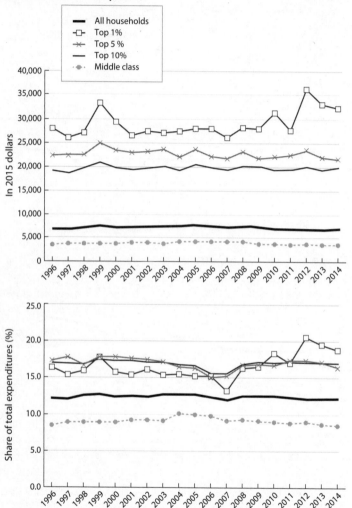

Figure 3.5. Spending on retirement by income and year, dollars and share of total spending. Data source: Consumer Expenditure Survey, Bureau of Labor Statistics.

distinction amounted to an average of $32,500 a year for each top 1% household and less than $4,000 for the average middle-class household (the top 5% and 10% households were spending $20,000–$22,000 in 2014) (see figure 3.5). Again, these investments allow the top income groups to maintain a better quality of life into retirement in a way that the middle-class and low-income groups cannot afford to. Thus, top income groups are not just living good lives in the present but making sure this standard is maintained into the future and for family members should anything happen to them. Far more expensive than more obvious signs of status like a watch or bag or car, these investments genuinely shape life chances and intergenerational mobility.

If you have more money you can afford the more expensive elements of life—education, health, and retirement savings. Ironically, despite the fact that all of these items are essential for a good life and create lifelong returns, they are also the investments that are most out of reach, particularly for the middle class and the poor. A financed SUV, perhaps signaling some upwardly mobile position, is fairly affordable to a middle-class household, and is significantly less expensive than a top university's tuition fees, or putting away the requisite 15% a year for retirement. Good health insurance costs thousands of dollars a year, and that does not include anything that might be considered a specialty health cost, like allergy testing or dermatology. The increase in disparity is not a result of the middle class spending less on these categories as much as it is a result of the rich spending significantly more (see figures 3.3–3.5). In fact, Hyojung Lee and my colleague Gary Painter have documented what they believe is a rising inequality in spending on "key human investment categories" after the Great Recession. A look at general consumption patterns would suggest that the gains brought forth by the Industrial Revolution and mass production have given everyone a chance at the good life. But no matter how many Coach handbags and minivans a middle-class family consumes, it's not the same as having the available funds to send one's child to Princeton. Even more alarming, Lee and Painter find that the vast differences in education spending between the wealthy and the middle- and lower-income groups does not start with college but rather at a much earlier age (elementary and secondary school tuitions), which sets in motion the divergence across socioeconomic classes more than a decade in advance, making it nearly impossible to catch up.[34] We may find a leveling of the playing field in conspicuous consumption, but cost-prohibitive inconspicuous consumption has become the new division between the rich and the rest.

In thinking about these types of inconspicuous goods, I am reminded of a chilling passage of C. Wright Mills's *The Power Elite*. Mills, a mid-twentieth-century Columbia University sociologist, was concerned that the elites of America were finding ways to make upward mobility virtually impossible for everyone else. In arenas of life that impacted life chances for oneself and society as a whole—politics, government, public figures, prestigious occupations, and degrees—the elites kept everyone else out. The problem with this pattern was that they then became the people who made decisions for all of society. The elites essentially created an "accumulation of advantages" and were only invested in other elites and their interests, leaving aside the concerns of everyone else. Mills did not believe this situation was actively nefarious, but it was sinister nonetheless because the disregard for others' concerns created an even greater divide between this "power elite" and everyone else. "The upper social classes have come to include a variety of members concerned with power in its several contexts, and these concerns are shared among the members of the clubs, the cousin-hoods, the firms, the law offices ... They spread into various commanding circles of the institutions of power," Mills writes. "Accordingly, in the inner circles of the upper classes, the most impersonal problems of the largest and most important institutions are fused with the sentiments and worries of small, closed, intimate groups ... Without conscious effort, they absorb the aspiration to be—if not the conviction that they are—The Ones Who Decide."[35] Mills's observation could never be truer than it is today.

In the twenty-first century, elites are further reaffirming their position by spending more on those goods and experiences that radically inform and shape their quality of life and future success and intergenerational mobility. This pattern of spending is apparent in the choices of wealthy members of the aspirational class, and more broadly, the top income groups. With their nonmaterial choices on what to spend on, these new elites are deviating even more from the consumer patterns of the middle class, never mind the lower income groups and the truly poor. These deviations create the norms, symbolic boundaries, and cultural capital that exclude everyone else, and make very obvious the differences between these two disconnected societies. Further, and more disconcerting, the things the wealthy aspirational class actually spend money on—education, health care, child care (not silver spoons, fancy cars, or fine china)—are the very things that build social capital and create class boundaries across generations that are almost impossible to overcome with material goods. Because paying for elite universities may seem more laudable than spending on silver spoons, and the aspirational class work hard to earn the money to pay the tuition, they may believe that their position is richly deserved. The fortunate children at the receiving end of those tuitions and violin lessons will also believe that their social position is more deserved than the birthright elites of previous eras. They have spent their entire life learning musical instruments and second languages, and taking test prep courses, such that they believe they have earned their position. Perhaps in some instances this observation is fair. But as Khan has pointed out in his work on this new meritocratic elite, of which many of the aspirational class are members, "Meritocracy is a social arrangement like any other: it is a loose set of rules that can be adapted in order to obscure advantages, all the while justifying them on the basis of shared values."[36] So yes, students at Princeton likely work hard, but many are in an elite position, financially and culturally, from the beginning, to even be accepted to such a prestigious university in the first place. Along the way, most students have acquired the sorts of knowledge and cultural capital that make it easy to assimilate into the Princeton student body. Research by Stacy Dale and Alan Krueger suggest that it is not elite education in and of itself that produces upward mobility. (In fact, Dale and Krueger conclude that it is likely "unobserved characteristics" that explain the success of those who attend elite universities, rather than the universities themselves.)[37,38] The blending of values, information, and class is becoming more stratified than ever and almost impossible to untangle. As the next two chapters will show, aspirational class consumption patterns are often imbued with a sense of morality and deservedness. The essential privilege that gives rise to such practices and behaviors in the first place is all but ignored.

CHAPTER 4

Motherhood as Conspicuous Leisure in the Twenty-first Century

In my playground set, the urban moms in their tight jeans and oversize sunglasses size each other up using a whole range of signifiers ... But breast-feeding is the real ticket into the club ... So I was left feeling trapped, like many women before me, in the middle-class mother's prison of vague discontent: surly but too privileged for pity, breast-feeding with one hand while answering the cell phone with the other, and barking at my older kids to get their own organic, 100 percent juice—the modern, multitasking mother's version of Friedan's "problem that has no name."

—Hanna Rosen, "The Case against Breastfeeding,"
Atlantic Monthly (April 2009)

For us Anglophone mothers, the length of time that we breastfeed—like the size of a Wall Street bonus—is a measure of performance ... We all know that our breastfeeding number is a concrete way to compete with one another.

—Patricia Druckerman, *Bringing Up Bébé*, Penguin Press (2012)

In 2012, the American Academy of Pediatrics (AAP) reaffirmed its long-standing recommendation that all children be exclusively breast-fed through 6 months old and continually breast-fed through 12 months.[1] Countless studies have reported the substantial benefits of breast-feeding a child rather than using infant formula (stronger immune systems, fewer gastrointestinal problems, less frequent earaches, and even higher IQs). A more recent UK-based study links breast-feeding to increased upward social mobility and decreased downward social mobility, suggesting that the combination of particular nutrients in breast milk along with the skin-to-skin mother-child bonding improves neurological development and emotional stress levels, thus enabling a child to thrive and subsequently move up the social ladder.[2]

Many critics note that some women are physiologically unable to breast-feed or have trouble with their milk supply; consequently, such a recommendation generates enormous amounts of pressure on women. However, according to a lactation consultant whom I interviewed, fewer than 1% of women fall within the aforementioned category, whereby they have trouble with their milk supply such that they are unable to breast-feed at all. As an added benefit, breast milk is free, breast-feeding is associated with lower postpartum hip-to-waist ratio (read: more post-pregnancy weight loss), and is a lot less messy than putting together a bottle of infant formula. At first glance, it seems simple (i.e., just breast-feed your child), but when you dig deeper, it's much more complicated.

For starters, according to the Centers for Disease Control, just 16.4% of children are exclusively breast-fed through 6 months, 27% are breast-fed (in conjunction with other food) through 12 months, and just three-quarters initiated (which could mean they were breast-fed just one time, for one day, or one week)—a far cry from the goals of pediatricians and Health and Human Services.[3] Regional studies suggest wild discrepancies across states too: A study of a small town in northwestern Pennsylvania reported that just 13% of children are breast-fed at all at 6 months.[4] In Oregon and California, 40% of mothers are still breast-feeding their babies at 12 months of age, as compared to 10% for Mississippi and 11% for Alabama.[5] In these former more bohemian states, women may feel a greater pressure but also a greater cultural acceptance to breast-feed.

But the single leading indicator of breast-feeding is education level —17% of college graduates exclusively breast-feed through the first six months, compared to just 9.3% of those without a college degree. In fact, 95% of women with a college degree or higher initiate breast-feeding versus 83% of women with just a high school degree or GED (these numbers are almost exactly the same for the father's level of education).[6,7] Being wealthy helps. In a CDC study of breast-feeding rates from 1999 to 2006, 74% of high-income mothers initiated breast-feeding versus 57% of low-income mothers. Of those women coming from households earning 400% or more above the poverty line, almost 96% breast-feed versus fewer than 83% of those at or below the poverty line.[8]

On the surface these numbers don't make sense. Breast-feeding is free, it's better for the baby, and it's better for the mother, yet it's prac- ticed mainly by women who could afford the best formula out there and, as college-educated women, many have full-time, high-pressure jobs (particularly the over-30 set, who often have children at a later age, after completing their education and establishing themselves in a ca- reer). In fact, as a result of all of the overwhelming evidence that breast- feeding is good for both mother and child, the AAP stated explicitly that "choosing to breastfeed should be considered an investment in the short- and long-term health of the infant, rather than a lifestyle choice."

Nevertheless, lifestyle—and socioeconomics—seem to be important factors in whether or not women choose to breast-feed. While the os- tensible economics of breast-feeding do not explain the statistics, social mores and what one's work group deems acceptable explain these breast-feeding rates. Breast-feeding in the twenty-first century, like many other aspects of motherhood, has become an issue of class and its accoutrements.

Mothering, writ large, has become a new channel for engaging in what Veblen termed conspicuous leisure. Breast-feeding and birthing practices are the most obvious examples of this, as playing sports or studying Greek were in Veblen's time. Unlike a Louis Vuitton bag or a luxury car, these signifiers are not explicitly expensive but they do re- quire significant investments of time, an even more precious commodity in modern society. Like in Veblen's era, much of contemporary conspic- uous leisure is suggestive of money. While many aspects of motherhood seem costless—birthing choices, co-sleeping, carrying your baby, breast- feeding—women can only engage in these activities if they have the lux- ury of time and leisure and membership into cultural and social groups that encourage this form of motherhood. Certain maternal choices demonstrate the possession of both time and cultural capital that is truly impossible for many women to attain.

In 1957, the French semiologist and linguist Roland Barthes wrote a small but powerful book entitled *Mythologies*. Barthes argued that through the dominant values upheld by society we create "myths" around particular practices and consumer goods, which become "signifiers" of particular messages or dominant belief systems.[9],[10] In his chapter "Wine and Milk," Barthes discusses the symbolism of red wine and framing of red wine as an egalitarian and healthful substance. Red wine's color suggests vitality, a substance thought of as "the juice from the sun and earth." Like the English royal family drinking tea or milk from Dutch cows, red wine is the "signifier" of French culture and a "collective morality" and "décor for all facets of French life."[11] In fact, red wine is so synonymous with the French that when President René Coty was photographed with a beer on his coffee table rather than a bottle of wine, the nation was shocked. But this depiction of red wine ignores and glosses over other negative aspects of the drink. For example, that people get drunk from wine is not a goal but rather a consequence. (By extension, bad things that happen when one is drunk are more superficial or theatrical rather than truly evil.)[12] Or, as Barthes observes, red wine is as much a part of French capitalism as culture: The land used to grow grapes is taken by settlers in Algeria "who impose on the Muslims on the very land of which they have been dispossessed, a crop for which they have no use, while they actually lack bread."[13] Similarly, in his chapter "Steak-Frites," Barthes discusses the prestige of this national dish and the semi-rawness and visibility of blood in *saignant* (rare) steak which symbolizes strength and nature—the act of eating a bloody steak almost suggests these qualities "pouring into man's very blood."[14] In contemporary times, we know that steak is equally a signifier of industrialized food systems and a host of heart problems brought on by saturated fat. But the myth of red wine like that of steak-frites is a function of how society chooses to interpret it. As Barthes remarks, "Myth is neither a lie nor a confession: it is an inflexion."[15] Similarly, the choices around motherhood become embedded in a value system determined by elite members of society. Breast-feeding thus becomes a Barthesian mythology: the twenty-first century signifier of what motherhood ought to be.[16] Similar to Barthes's red wine, this semiology obscures and distorts the nuances of how difficult it is to breast-feed, why some mothers actually have the choice to do so and why others do not. Indeed, it is an inflexion of motherhood as upheld by the ideologies of the dominant aspirational class.

Ask Corky Harvey, the founder of the LA–based breast-feeding and baby boutique The Pump Station. With outposts in Santa Monica, Hollywood, and throughout the city, Harvey's little boutiques garner an almost cult-like following. Her stores offer everything from high-end newborn onesies to CPR classes to breast-feeding classes and consultations, replete with breast pump rentals and sales (thus the name of the store). A new mom can find anything she needs for her baby. Before the average upper-middle-class Angelino mother gets pregnant, she likely doesn't know what The Pump Station is; thereafter it almost becomes a rite of passage to attend classes and get one's Medela breast pump "serviced." Yet, as Harvey herself explained, "We would never survive in rural Mississippi or NE Pennsylvania," where the notion of a breast-feeding boutique would be hilariously weird.

What is weird in Mississippi is the status quo in California. Many of the discrepancies in breast-feeding rates can be explained by the fact that women of different social and economic groups are simply treated differently and presented with different choices. Breast-feeding may be free, but to a certain extent, formula is free too. The biggest purchaser of formula in the nation is the US government, which channels much of it through Women Infants and Children (WIC), the federal assistance program for low-income pregnant women and mothers. As Harvey put it, "Why wouldn't you take it for free if you're poor? Medicine plays a role [by not advocating heavily enough with mothers]. For instance, in cultures like low income African Americans in Atlanta Georgia nobody breast-feeds and if you do you're a fool … As my son, who is a physician in Atlanta, explained to me, 'Mom, it isn't even discussed here.'" The research suggests that mothers who are eligible for WIC (and use it) are less likely to breast-feed than mothers who are not.[17] There have, however, been improvements with the new WIC package that was introduced in 2009, resulting in some studies showing WIC mothers significantly increasing their exclusive breast-feeding rates.[18] Another pediatrician, who worked at a community clinic, explained to me that, in the past, in some populations, the women were given a shot of Depo (a birth control medicine) almost immediately after birth. Depo has the effect of significantly reducing milk supply when given right after birth versus being administered 4–6 weeks later. As the physician explained, "I used to have to tell them [the women visiting her clinic], 'Do not let them give you that shot.'" She went on, "Luckily now, the obstetricians who take care of our clinic patients have been educated and have stopped routinely giving Depo to the women right after delivery. If you have a family who shows up [at the clinic] and they are feeding their children formula at three days or two weeks of life, you need to ask them why, since most of these mothers are doing it because of breast-feeding challenges and not because they wanted to give their child formula."

Despite the health imperative, breast-feeding at 6 and 12 months remains a rarefied practice. It is mainly prevalent in particular cultural and class groups—women with higher education levels who learn about the benefits of breast-feeding and women of higher income groups who can afford the insurance to deliver in baby-friendly hospitals with round-the-clock nurses and lactation consultants providing breast-feeding classes, expensive and efficient breast pumps, and help throughout the mother's entire stay. One of the other significant predictors of breast-feeding success is duration of maternity leave: Those mothers who receive fewer than 12 weeks of maternity leave have up to four times higher odds of failing to establish breast-feeding.[19] In the United States, good maternity leave is a rare thing for all women, but those who receive it are primarily women in high-level professional jobs. The irony is that women with ostensibly higher pressure jobs (e.g., managers, lawyers, CEOs) are those who have better maternity leave and thus are better able to breast-feed successfully. Of course, their education level and access to knowledge around the benefits of breast-feeding are closely linked to their choice (and also their attainment of these professional high-powered positions). In recent years, as many as 10% of highly educated women (i.e., master's degree or greater) are "opting out" of work to stay home with their children. These women also tend to be affluent and have a working spouse,[20] all factors that indicate higher breast-feeding rates.

Consider the alternate and far more realistic universe that most moms face. "How can you pump if you're a cab driver, or you're working in an industrial setting, where there is no support, no break and even though it's the law but no one cares?" Harvey asked. "You'll get fired. So formula is easier." Or, as the sociologist Cynthia Colen summed it up, "In the United States, where only 12 percent of female workers and 5 percent of female low-wage workers have access to paid leave, most women are required to forgo income in order to breast-feed. This may be a less-than-ideal situation for middle-class women but an impossible situation for poor women who already are having trouble making ends meet. No wonder, one of the most critical determinants of who starts and who continues breast-feeding is socioeconomic status."[21] This precise distinction is why Sheryl Sandberg can pull off being a top executive at Facebook while breast-feeding two kids, while the average hourly worker cannot.[22]

In other parts of the world (just as in the United States), good maternity leave is associated with higher rates of continued breast-feeding (see figure 4.1). As the journalist Hannah Rosen calculates, "Let's say a baby feeds seven times a day and then a couple more times at night. That's nine times for about a half hour each, which adds up to more than half of a working day, every day, for at least six months. This is why, when people say that breast-feeding is 'free,' I want to hit them with a two-by-four. It's only free if a woman's time is worth nothing."

To the rest of the world, the battles on the *New York Times* opinion pages about the moral imperative of breast-feeding may seem like aspirational class navel gazing—it reflects a debate completely detached from most mothers' lives, and indeed it is. The Mommy Wars—to breast-feed or not, the stay-at-home versus the working mother face-off, C-sections, and home births—are debates for a particularly privileged set of women.

To actually talk about the nuances and choices of motherhood (rather than simply being a mother and taking care of one's children) implies the luxury to do so. "We focus on motherhood as the province of privileged women with no greater struggles than whether or not it is possible to have it all," writes Mikki Kendall in *Salon*. "Meanwhile, mothers who do not fit into this narrative feel excluded. Motherhood is supposed to be a choice, but what kind of choices are mothers making? Concerns over access to food, healthcare, education, even safety somehow don't make the main stage of these discussions. At its base, motherhood encompasses all of that, and mothers who don't have many choices (or, in some cases, any choices) need support that they are not getting."[23] Nancy Chin is a professor in the University of Rochester's Department of Public Health Sciences and author of a number of key studies on low-

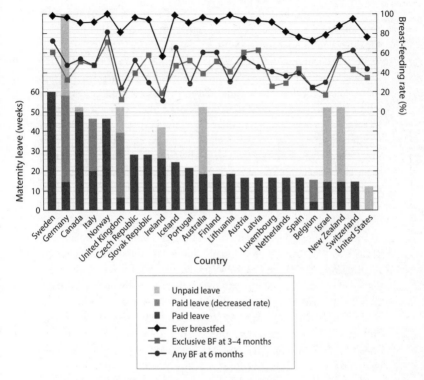

Figure 4.1. Maternity leave and breast-feeding (BF) rates.
Source: *State of the World's Mothers*, Save the Children, May 2012.

income women's breast-feeding experiences. As she put it, poor women spend most of their days dealing with risk ratios. "Every day you are exposed to risk—so if you have a 100% chance of running out of food by the end of the month, a 75% chance of being evicted, a 50% chance of the baby's daddy not being around," Chin explained, "then a 10% chance of an ear infection because of formula feeding doesn't seem so bad. [Further], low-income women don't necessarily feel safe enough to breast-feed in public if they live in unsafe neighborhoods."

Society is incessantly judging the mothering practices and consequences of lower socioeconomic groups—and that certainly has an impact on the mothers' decisions. As Chin illustrates, "If you're a poor woman, you feel you are constantly under surveillance. [For example], the other confounder is that mothers who stop breast-feeding often say, 'I didn't have enough milk; it was insufficient.'" Chin continues, "The medical view is that's a rare condition, so [if you don't have enough milk then] you're not doing this right." Given that breast-feeding requires a whole host of resources and time that poor mothers may not have, low-income mothers are limited in their ability to breast-feed, even if it is not physiologically based. Breast-feeding might be the ideal choice, but these women often do not have the chance to do so. As Chin explains, "Can you imagine if you're a low-income mom, and you're worrying about feeding your baby and they [the doctors] say 'It's your fault.' [If you're that mother] you're going to say, 'Let's just give that child a bottle.'"[24]

Yet if you subscribe to the thesis put forth by Joan Wolf, a professor at Texas A&M and author of the 2010 book *Is Breast Best?: Taking on the Breastfeeding Experts and the New High Stakes of Motherhood*, all of this debate may really be just aspirational class self-preoccupation. Wolf argues that we have not even statistically proven that breast-feeding is actually better than formula.[25] As Wolf remarked in a 2013 interview, "When it comes to other outcomes, such as intelligence or obesity or diabetes, etc., it is simply not possible to separate any benefits that have been attributed to breastfeeding from the general health behavior of women who choose, for various reasons, to breastfeed." In the same interview, Wolf continues, "Mothers who breastfeed promote health in all sorts of ways that could have a positive impact on obesity, IQ, colds, etc."[26] A 2014 study of breast-feeding focused on "discordant siblings" —those where one child was breast-fed and the other not. The sample, some 1,773 sibling pairs, enabled a wide-scale analysis to tease out the extent to which breast-feeding (rather than other hidden variables) might explain the health, achievement, and other metrics of success over formula-fed babies. Turns out, at least according to this study, breast-feeding confounds a more basic explanation: socioeconomic class. Those siblings born to wealthier (and healthier) mothers thrived regardless of being formula or breast-fed. And in fact, it is a circular causation: Breast-fed babies tend to be born into families with higher incomes, more educated parents, and safer neighborhoods.[27] Or as Hanna Rosen candidly admits in *The Atlantic*, "One day, while nursing my baby in my pediatrician's office, I noticed a 2001 issue of the *Journal of the American Medical Association* open to an article about breast-feeding: 'Conclusions: There are inconsistent associations among breast-feeding, its duration, and the risk of being overweight in young children.' Inconsistent? There I was, sitting half-naked in public for the tenth time that day, the hundredth time that month, the millionth time in my life—and the associations were *inconsistent*?"[28]

I can relate. I live in a bohemian bourgeois Los Angeles neighborhood filled with farmers' markets and cafés obsessed with the art of coffee making. Other than the artists who live here, the neighborhood is filled with families who are drawn to the playground and public space and, especially, the really good public school district. Our tastes may be slightly different from our counterparts in the suburbs, rural America, or the East Coast, but just like parents across America, childrearing and the values that surround it are the most important aspects of our lives.

One fine morning when my oldest son was just more than a year old, I was strolling down our street and ran into a woman I'd seen around. We started chatting across from a housing construction site with a large and active cement truck (a perennial attraction for little boys). Her son was a few years older than mine, and at some point she commented on my use of an Ergo baby carrier with my already enormous child. I said that my back was killing me and I was trying to figure out how to get him out of it, to which she responded by recommending one she had purchased for her bigger child which allowed her to "breast-feed him in the grocery store." I tried not to skip a beat but I was certain that kid of hers was over three years old, so between the baby carrier and the public breast-feeding of a child swiftly entering pre-K, this woman immediately became a source of fascination. As we continued talking she went on about the ongoing "nighttime feedings" (something most moms are happy become less frequent after 5 months old) and the co-sleeping (she in his bed, not he in mom and dad's bed) and the fact that only children were special, and that having multiple children was "different… not necessarily worse" (although her inflections clearly indicated that it was, indeed, actually worse).

I consider myself a baby-led mom. I never even remotely "sleep trained" (and for that I spent years on the brink of exhaustion). I would have made the La Leche League proud with my dedication to breast-feeding way past the recommended year. Yet even I was unable to make sense of this mom's approach. Here's the thing: True to aspirational class mothering, as I said good-bye and walked away, I couldn't decide whether to judge her for being a crazy person who was setting up her son for years of psychotherapy or feel bad and insecure for not being as much of an alpha mom as she. At that time, my husband and I were trying for a second child and suddenly I thought, "Maybe I'm being a bad mom by having another child. Here I thought having more kids was fun and fulfilling, but maybe I'm doing something that is clearly both different … and worse." To be a mother, whether in Santa Monica or St. Louis, is to feel judged on an almost daily basis. But, unlike Chin's mothers who are worried about simply being able to breast-feed (or feed) their children at all, upper-middle-class mothers genuinely stress themselves out over breast-feeding tenure and organic peaches. Such anxieties seem absurd. Unless you're in the thick of it.

It goes on. As one young mother in San Francisco remarked, "Here, many pregnant women join a prenatal yoga class, take childbirth classes, and join Golden Gate Mothers Group. GGMG is a mothers group that has an active online forum and hosts events, playgroups, and meetups … Depending on preference and need, a pregnant woman in San Francisco might have a mix of acupuncture sessions, chiropractor appointments, working with birth doulas, and even taking hypnobirthing classes. Getting through pregnancy can seem to involve a whole team of people, not just your partner and OB."

Given this level of micromanaging of pregnancy and early childhood, it's not surprising that my friend who got breast implants (ok, a boob job) and cracks open the bottles of formula at our local playground elicits stares of shock (simple disdain would be easier to handle). Moms sit around comparing first sentences (not first steps, mind you) and boast about how much wild salmon their toddlers can consume, and then there's the breast-feeding bragging rights and casualness to the whole practice—at the playground, coffee shop, nursery. I'm grateful. I certainly am one of those moms who liked being able to meet a friend outside of the house for a coffee and yet know I could feed my baby in peace. But public breast-feeding is a luxury of this little myopia of society. Or, as the mother from San Francisco reported, "After my baby was born my new mom friends from my prenatal yoga classes would send me text messages inviting me to join them at post-natal yoga classes (with baby) and 'discover your baby's RIE' classes. Other moms have told me about music, swim (starting at two months!), and language classes for parent and baby." These are not the things Nancy Chin's low-income moms are fretting about, even if they wish they could.

Breast-feeding as status signifier is something of a new construct. Historically, having a wet nurse symbolized wealth. Let's take the case of France, which still remains the United States' counterpoint in mothering today, with books such as *Bringing Up Bébé* demonstrating the virtues of the French modus operandi as compared to America (less indulged, better behaved children, skinnier moms, and virtually no breast-feeding at two to three months postpartum).[29]

The values upheld today were in place some 300 years ago as well. In eighteenth-century France, the rule among the upper classes was to send one's children off to wet nurses, whose occupation it was to breast-feed other women's children. The upper-class decline in use of wet nurses only occurred in the latter half of the nineteenth century, when the practice became commonplace among women working in factories during the Industrial Revolution (in 1869, more than 40% of all babies were commercially nursed). Remember, infant formula was yet to be invented and the use of animal milk caused infant mortality of up to 50%, thus any woman who was unable to be with her baby round the clock found herself in a predicament (for the wealthy it was mainly a matter of convenience and freedom from maternal duties). While one cannot say with certainty that the adoption by lower-class women deterred the wealthy from wet nurses, two important events coincided with the mainstream use of wet nurses and decline among the upper classes. First, the increasingly wide-scale use of wet nurses in France encouraged an official government regulation of the practice through the Bureau des Nourrices, which primarily made sure the wet nurses were paid for their service. In post-Revolutionary France, however, the bureau emerged significantly weaker and unable to imprison debtor parents (i.e., those parents who used wet nurses but did not pay for their services). In fact, those parents who couldn't pay were dismissed as charity cases, rather than penalized. This in combination with the country's general economic distress forced the bureau to close its doors in 1876.[30]

In its place, and due to the increasing demand for wet nurses by factory workers, a commercialized, private "business" arose, which was less regulated and subsequently mismanaged. While the nurses were almost certainly paid and at higher wages, they were also less carefully supervised: They were not subject to a strict medical evaluation and could take on children outside of work with the private firm. The lack of regulation and management caused a host of issues, from increased infant mortality to the spread of syphilis.[31] These health concerns caused great alarm and made wet nurses a much less desirable option to those who had alternatives.

Second, and hardly unrelated, the upper-class consciousness began to change. From doctors' reproach to the outcry of Rousseau in the mid-1700s, maternal nursing was considered the more morally sound approach. Among both the middle and upper classes, a "revolt of conscience" emerged with regard to hiring wet nurses to do the duty of a mother. Even though it had been practiced for many years among these very same economic elite, the use of wet nurses by mothers, unless they had rare physical limitations, was now thought of as essentially criminal.[32] Thus, as the historian George Sussman remarks, "It would appear that in Napoleon III's capital—and perhaps all over his empire—a paradoxical position had been reached: The demand for wet nurses had never been greater because the cities and the female working population in the cities had never been larger, while at the same time the idea of maternal nursing, and perhaps the revulsion against commercial nursing, were spreading downward from the upper levels of society."[33] Breast-feeding one's own child began to be viewed as a sign of high society. But things changed again—the invention of formula, the adoption of breast-feeding by other parts of society, and changing dynamics in the workforce. Thus, the status signals of motherhood changed as well.

In the early twentieth century, for fashionable women in England and America, infant formula became the more accepted means of feeding one's baby. Wet nurses (not as popular in these countries as in France) were working-class and rural women and thus the distinction between whether one fed her child maternal milk or formula (or had a wet nurse do it instead) became a distinct class issue—poor women nursed, wealthier women did not. In addition, wealthier women were convinced of the "scientific" and modern superiority of manmade formulas over nature (even though it was clear through the medical studies of the time and the great Margaret Mead herself, that infants were more likely to survive and thrive on human milk). There was another implicit deterrent to breast-feeding: Fashionable society women who did not want to be burdened by the social limitations of nursing could point to modern medicine and even popular literature, which characterized upper-class women as physically weak and "unable" to nurse.[34] Yet, as in most cultural arenas, the habits of the rich were emulated by the lower classes too, and soon formula was ubiquitous and breast-feeding declined rapidly. By the middle of the twentieth century, many middle-class American families chose the bottle over maternal milk, and from 1946 to 1972, universal rates of breast-feeding fell to 22–25%. Additionally, middle- and upper-class motherhood became a different experience, or what the historian Janet Golden calls the changing "cultural meaning of motherhood": rather than basic nurturing and survival, more affluent women were thought to be responsible for character-building.[35] A dramatic increase in overall breast-feeding rates in the 1970s was followed by a decline in the 1980s. That dip in the 1980s is explained by the same factors that influence low levels of breast-feeding today: poverty, lack of education, lack of employment, race, and WIC. Public awareness, medical intervention, and access to more advanced breast pumps have all increased the rate of breast-feeding overall, and particularly with socioeconomically disadvantaged groups. Gains in those disadvantaged categories account for much of the increases in breast-feeding from the mid-1980s to the present day (although these rates are still significantly lower than those of higher income and highly educated Caucasian women, who have been breast-feeding at a static rate since the 1970s).[36]

Contrast this trend with the French. Upper-middle-class French women, unlike their American counterparts, do not see breast-feeding as *de rigueur*. Today in France, barely half of women are still breast-feeding when they leave the hospital a few days after giving birth, and breast-feeding after a few months is thought to be a genuine oddity, let alone breast-feeding in public or keeping up with the AAP's 12-month recommendation.[37] For French women, the badge of postpartum status is losing weight quickly and looking sexy again, contrary to the American mold of tent dresses and justifying one's mom clothes as a result of being preoccupied with breast-feeding and attachment parenting.

In the United States, the now dominant practice of breast-feeding among upper-middle-class, educated non-Hispanic whites is rooted in something else too: the overall return to nature as superior to modern science, and the luxury to engage in the time-consuming practices that go with this ethos. Since the 1960s, the natural childbirth movement and the increase in home births have been adopted by well-educated, Caucasian women.[38] Part of this evolution in how we give birth to and raise children is clearly rooted in the cultural revolution of the 1960s; it has now become the norm for conventional, affluent, educated white women to spend hours reading baby books, attending birthing classes, writing detailed birth plans, and in general getting very prepared for the business of having a baby. One of the ongoing conversations among them is the distinction between the natural birth versus one involving an epidural (the C-section is, theoretically, at least, an emergency-only option for these mothers). Women of this set not infrequently believe that the extreme pain of an unmedicated labor and delivery is part of the full experience of giving birth, while others worry that epidurals are harmful to the baby (although no medical evidence supports this concern). In fact, drug-free births are almost a rite of passage and the home birth is the holy grail, as giving birth goes. Yet these cultural and social beliefs are powerful and shape how women make decisions, so much so that they can put their own health in jeopardy. Emergency C-sections after 30 hours of home birth labor are not unheard of. In some medical opinions, while epidurals can slow labor, the pain and stress of natural birth can be bad for the baby.

Newborns room with their mothers in the days following delivery, "baby-friendly" hospitals offer constant lactation support and immediate "skin-to-skin" contact. In fact, the pressure to be a baby-friendly hospital is so great that hospitals aiming for this distinction refuse to provide even a drop of infant formula in the early days, even before a woman's milk comes in and a baby might be starving. According to one obstetrician I spoke to, even one drop of formula means a child has not been "exclusively breast-fed" for the first six months, and thus the hospital's statistics and subsequent ranking are compromised. And mothers are onboard with this no-formula mantra. As another physician I spoke to described, "A baby will be born with low blood sugar and we will need to give it sugar water. The mother will freak out and say that her baby is to be exclusively breast-fed, completely ignoring the medical imperative to give the baby sugar for her well-being."

All of these new norms place a greater emphasis on nature rather than scientific medicine, a far cry from the gestalt of the mid–twentieth century. The luxury of time enables a mother to attain the information about these practices and to engage in them. Of course, as noted earlier, frequent breast-feeding, home births, and parenting classes involve time, acquisition of knowledge, and often money (or the luxury to trade money for time). In the example of breast-feeding, learning to nurse effectively, particularly with no supplemental formula, can involve practice, a number of classes during pregnancy, and, for some, encouragement from lactation specialists. Natural births, too, involve extensive classes on breathing and muscle relaxation rather than simply arriving at the hospital and relying on the doctor. A vaginal delivery takes a significant amount of time (e.g., waiting for a woman to go into labor, to dilate, and to deliver the baby). And those wishing for natural births by refusing medicine that induces or speeds up labor invest even more time in their child's birth. While the national rate of C-sections is more than 30%, non-Hispanic whites and Asians, and particularly educated non-Hispanic whites, are the least likely to have one, leading researchers to conclude that C-sections, outside of emergencies, are most associated with poor-quality medical care.[39] Twenty-five years ago, the *New England Journal of Medicine* reported the exact opposite finding: The majority of C-sections were occurring among wealthy, white women, suggesting that high socioeconomic status rather than medical indication drove this delivery outcome.[40]

Today, the highest order of childbirth among wealthy American women is the home birth, again suggesting the changing tides of status and values in the whole childbirth and motherhood experience. More than 2% of well-educated, non-Hispanic white women (that's 1 in 49) choose a planned home birth, and that number has continued to rise over the last ten years and shows no signs of slowing down. When a profile of midwife Ina May Gaskin and the home birth movement made the feature article of the *New York Times* magazine, it became clear that while the home birth movement may not statistically dominate delivery among the rich and educated (yet), as a cultural interest and genuine alternative, it's become a desirable way of doing things. At the very least, home births are worth talking about among those who have the luxury to do so.[41] Home birth is indeed a privilege for those who can afford to pay out of pocket (insurance doesn't cover it).[42]

A look at different places and different social groups makes it clear that even when we think we are making clinical or medical decisions, our social and cultural environment matters. In the early twenty-first century, while affluent women in the United States are considering natural or home birth, South American women pride themselves on C-sections as a way to avoid vaginal stretching, schedule their deliveries, and have control over their lives. Some 80–90% of private hospital deliveries in Brazil are Cesarean, some up to 99%. The World Health Organization believes that a rate exceeding 15% of women having Cesarean deliveries is too high. Or, as NPR put it succinctly, "C-Sections Deliver Cachet for Wealthy Brazilian Women ... The emphasis on status begins at birth—and cesarean deliveries are the Louis Vuitton of the maternity world."[43] In China, the Cesarean rate is 50%. (The number one reason why? "Everybody else is having surgery.")[44]

Practices of aspirational class conspicuous leisure extend beyond birth and breast-feeding. Parenting styles also have become symbols of socioeconomic position. Consider attachment parenting: Advocated by Dr. Sears, it requires the mother to be around her child nonstop, to continue to breast-feed on-demand extensively after one year, to co-sleep until five years old (or whenever the child is ready to leave his parents' bed), and to "wear" one's baby most of the day. This approach is parenting in the extreme, and admittedly has its anthropological merits: Sears found that children in less developed countries who were comforted by their mothers round the clock tended not to cry so much, and were much more secure in the long term. The geographer Jared Diamond came to a similar conclusion observing the childrearing habits of more primitive societies where co-sleeping, extended and on-demand breast-feeding, and mother-to-child skin contact are omnipresent well into the toddler years. Children were much better off (and less likely to be socio-paths). The time compression of Western society and its working mothers, Diamond argues, has created the social constructions of scheduled sleeping and feeding we associate with modern childrearing.[4]

While not economic per se, the social practices of upper-middle-class motherhood are in and of themselves elitist and exclusionary, and they rely on cultural and symbolic capital and extensive unencumbered time that is not a part of most families' prosaic interactions and daily life. Nevertheless, by virtue of engaging in these parenting behaviors, upper-middle-class parents acquire the material means that ultimately reveal their conspicuous parenting and therefore their and their children's social position. Day-to-day objects like the Baby au Lait designer nursing covers, Ergo and Baby Bjorn baby carriers, and cloth or compostable diapers operate as efficient signals of this particular type of motherhood. The nursing cover itself is not expensive or even overly conspicuous; rather it is a material sign of an often expensive and time-intensive mode of parenting. Thus, the increasingly in-vogue practices of attachment parenting, home births, and breast-feeding signal an elite position vis-à-vis most American mothers who face time and money constraints that prohibit them from these behaviors. I don't mean to suggest that women engage in these practices for the sake of status, but I am reminded of my own experiences in dissecting these phenomena.

I became a mother in my early thirties, and prior to the birth of my first son I had babysat for fewer than ten hours in my life. When I found out I was pregnant, I had little more than a vague notion that there were benefits to breast-feeding, and yet, without much prompting, I took breast-feeding classes, learned infant CPR, did my research to find a great obstetrician and pediatrician, and read dozens of books and articles on childrearing. As I write about motherhood, I realize I am the very woman I write about.

As I write, I continue to ask myself the extent to which my choices are conscious, and if conscious, what are my motivations? They are not status-driven in any intentional way (there are much easier, less time-consuming ways to attain social position), they are not a response to medical evidence (I am a mere layperson on such matters). Rather, I am propelled by something that transcends empirics: my friends and all those mothers at Mommy&Me playgroups and the playground—essentially the milieu in which I exist every day. But truthfully, I do not absorb these practices in such a conscious manner. In my habitus, this is just how we do things; it is in the air. It feels unconscious and intuitive, like one's personal sense of morality or the desire to eat when hungry. Yet national statistics show me there is nothing unconscious about my decisions. My choices are influenced all the time by where I live, financial means, and the resources offered close by and those mothers also engaging in these practices thus affirming my choices: Living in California, getting paid maternity leave, being able to afford a breast pump, knowing that lactation consultants exist (let alone talking to one), taking classes on mothering which espouse these practices, having email access to my obstetrician and pediatrician who answer all and any of my questions at all times of day and night. This style of motherhood, like other styles of life, to use Max Weber's term,[46] may not be material or ostensibly conscious, but its implications and influencers are just as dramatic and wide as the more physical consumer objects that divide across race and class lines. To quote the sociologist Annette Lareau from her book *Unequal Childhoods*, "Individuals carry out their lives within a social structure."

The question then emerges, why have some mothers (and parents more generally) adopted practices that are difficult, time-consuming, and sometimes even painful instead of using that very same time for leisure? In Veblen's time one would not have made such an effort during leisure time. Veblen defined conspicuous leisure as the *unproductive* use of time, time that was not used for any greater utility. In short, leisure was actually leisure: People watched sports, went to university to study the "Classics" like Greek and Roman simply for the sake of learning (rather than practical application), went on extensively long holidays, and lived a life of idleness.[47] But it's not just mothers who channel money and time into things that are far from leisurely. As a 2008 analysis shows, for all parents, as income and education increase, leisure time and housework decrease, yet simultaneously, time with children increases. The Brookings Institute scholars Garey Ramney and Valerie Ramney find this trend has been going on since the mid-1990s. High socioeconomic women spend two to three times more time with preschool children than those of lower socio-economic groups.[48]

Why, Ramney and Ramney ask, would parents whose own time is increasingly economically valuable, give more of it away for "free" (i.e., to spend time with their kids)? These scholars believe that the answer lies in "cohort crowding"—it's so much harder to get into an elite college these days that elite parents need to focus more time on priming their children. Or as these economists put it, "We argue that increased competition for college admissions may be an important source of these trends. The number of college-bound students has surged in recent years, coincident with the rise in time spent on childcare. The resulting 'cohort crowding' has led parents to compete more aggressively for college slots by spending increasing amounts of time on college preparation."[49] As a study in the journal *Demography* reports, wealthy, educated parents are not just spending more time with their children, they are also spending significantly more money on them. While historically that money was devoted to the teen years, after the 1990s, most of the financial resources of wealthy families have been devoted to under-six-year-old children and those in their mid-twenties.[50] In short, schlepping one's child to those pre-K Saturday morning violin lessons really may pave the way for Princeton.

These parenting practices fit into the frame of what Annette Lareau calls "concerted cultivation." Whether pursuing breast-feeding to increase baby's IQ, or art classes at the age of three, or lacrosse in high school, aspirational class parents see their children as developmental projects and initiate structured and cultivated modes of parenting to maximize their children's future success. As Lareau notes in her book, these choices in parenting both suggest present social class and impact future social, educational, and work outcomes. Along with the structured activities from birth to high school, children of upper-middle-class families are encouraged to question authority, engage in constant negotiation with their parents and, through their various engagements, become socially adept. Contrast this type of parenting with "accomplishment of natural growth," which Lareau argues is the dominant style of parenting among poor and working-class parents. This type of parenting emphasizes respect for authority, more parental directives (i.e., "go wash your hands" rather than an extensive discussion on the origins of germ theory), and far less structured activity (e.g., fewer music classes, play dates, and gymnastics). These aspirational class children are reared to feel empowered, and tend to have larger vocabularies and greater social aptitude (but are criticized for being entitled), while the working-class kids, often more independent, learn the skills of following orders that are thought to be important in their future work in more rote jobs (but also limiting for upward mobility).

For upper-middle-class children to engage in highly cultivated leisure activities, they require geographical, cultural, and financial access.

Aspirational class parents (even the overworked ones) use their precious free time to cultivate this structure: They sign their kids up for extracurricular science classes, AYSO soccer, art classes, SAT prep, and they engage in extensive conversations around any array of topics their children wish to speak about. This type of parenting exhibits intense peer effects, where parents in this social echelon are trading notes and suggestions, and competing on the playground, on parenting listservs, and at school events, and in a way that low-income parents have not the time, information, or capital to participate in. As Lareau surmises, "Children grow up within a broad, highly stratified social system."

THE PRODUCTIVE LEISURE
OF THE ASPIRATIONAL CLASS

Whether parenting or exercising, paradoxically for the twenty-first century aspirational class, conspicuous leisure is actually quite productive. This contradiction is due to the fact that today's "leisure class" is not actually leisurely. Conspicuous leisure still exists but it has changed in two profound ways. First, today's aspirational class, many of whom have built themselves up through hard work, infuse even their leisure time with productivity and value. Second, key conspicuous leisure activities in Veblen's time—going to college, playing sports—are now essential tickets to upward mobility.

Excepting the rare trust fund families and a few children of oligarchs, most people make their own money, and those who make the most money also work the most. The economist Robert Frank argues that these labor market elites actually experience "leisure inequality" (certainly by their own doing). The most educated and most affluent have, in absolute terms, much less free time than the less well-off. They are so accustomed to being overproductive in their work lives that it carries over into their leisure time, including their intense and active focus on childrearing. Such devotion to children is born out of love but also stems from a parental belief that this effort increases their offspring's well-being and future success. This last point is where childrearing is not just suggestive of social position through conspicuous leisure, but actually reproduces class and socioeconomic position. Spending extra time reading to one's children, playing with them on the floor, and providing the time, patience, and financial resources for sports and test-prep classes may be time-consuming in the present, but it also grooms these children for a bright and successful future.

Whether mothering or shuttling a child to hockey lessons, there is a constant pressure to be productive in work and in life, and this observation extends beyond parenting. The economist Staffan Linder uses the term "harried leisure class" to explain the cycle of working more to spend more, a cycle he calls the "paradoxes of affluence."[51] Because of the way in which the current capitalist economy works, to build up assets one must sacrifice time and time of course is not storable. Thus, in the cycle to attain money to consume more, we end up with less time to simply enjoy the pleasures of life. These socioeconomic conditions come from a long-standing observation of modern, industrial, and post-industrial society. Many members of the aspirational class achieved success there through hard work, and that ethos, the "Protestant work ethic" in the popular vernacular, spills over into all facets of their lives. One can trace the austerity and all-work-no-fun to Puritanism, but really the Industrial Revolution explains the rise of a new class of workers who attained capital and social mobility through hard work rather than nobility and bloodlines. Productivity is highly valued and is rewarded through economic success and in turn social position and status. Unless you are Bill Gates (who dropped out of Harvard, anyway), it is challenging to achieve upward mobility, let alone become truly wealthy, without a college degree. The university, Veblen's veritable institution of conspicuous leisure, is the sine qua non for any member of capitalist society. Those very "idle" courses—classics, the humanities, poetry—are a dying breed as students seek out business, finance, and economics degrees.[52] These latter course choices are an even further turn from Veblen's notion of leisure—learning is not simply about being well-bred or well-read; it's about translating knowledge into productivity. Sports and learning the violin—again conspicuous leisure activities during Veblen's time—are now productive and proactive measures to make one seem desirable for university. These activities become the means for achieving acceptance into college. Playing football or running track, learning three instruments or four languages gives one a fighting chance at the Ivy League. Sports are now a means to be awarded a scholarship and show diversity and well-roundedness in an applicant. In the United Kingdom, the "gap year," that is, the noncompulsory year between graduating from high school and starting university, allows students to travel the world, embark on fascinating internships, and work in the developing world. All of these activities are laudable, but they are also a part of the grooming process for university and making oneself more interesting to admissions committees.

These transformations have prompted new means for twenty-first-century elites to suggest social position through conspicuous leisure. Today, conspicuous leisure, so removed from its origins as a bastion of idleness and nonproductivity, allows the aspirational class to make moral judgments about their behavior (and others). As the next section will show, they find the material means to show it.

LULULEMON'S GROOVE PANT AND PRODUCTIVE CONSPICUOUS LEISURE

In the 1950s, Lotte Berk, a former ballet dancer living in London, needed to figure out a way to pay the bills. With the help of an osteopath (who was helping her recover from ballet injuries) she created an exercise routine similar in method and results to Pilates and yoga, but, it turns out, was even better. Breathtakingly difficult and strenuous, Berk's approach focused on core stability and very specific toning exercises, with humorous and suggestive names including "the Prostitute" and "the French Lavatory," perhaps due to the repetition of pelvic thrusts throughout the workout. Berk, described in one profile as "a bubbly German Jew who narrowly dodged the Nazis," opened her Manchester Street Studio in the carpeted, drafty, dark basement below her friend Vidal Sassoon's salon in West End London.[53] Between the two of them, this location developed a devoted clientele among the Swinging London's glamorous set. Sassoon styled the ladies' hair and Berk shaped the figures of a celebrity clientele that included Joan Collins and Barbra Streisand. As the *New York Observer* put it, this approach to exercise was "the original, the mothership—the grand dame of making your ass smaller and higher and not quite so flat. It was there before step aerobics and spinning and

Pilates and Tae Bo and a New York Sports Club or yoga center on every corner."[54]

In the 1960s, a young Midwestern woman named Lydia Bach showed up at the Manchester Street Studio and was entranced by the transformative effects of the exercises and the following that Berk had cultivated. Making a deal with Berk (not a particularly lucrative one for Berk), Bach took the exercise routine across the pond. In 1970, Bach opened up the Lotte Berk Method studio on 67th Street in the heart of New York City's Upper East Side and later opened another studio in an old potato barn in the Hamptons, on Bridgehampton's Butter Lane, so clients could still attend classes during summer holidays. Upper-crust WASPs, celebrities, and New York socialites attended the classes in droves—the very social x-rays chronicled by Tom Wolfe (who was also a client of Bach's). As Bach herself reported, "I had all three generations of the Kennedys … in one class." For many years, the studios were "a well-kept and expensive secret of New York's upper crust," as the *New York Observer* put it, and Bach refused to franchise or make deals with others to open up more studios in New York or other cities (Bach briefly opened a studio in Los Angeles). At $30 a class in the 1970s (that's $183.87 in 2015 dollars), only the rich could afford it anyway. But its success and cult following made it hard to dissuade others from copying. These exercises really worked. Because the exercises isolated specific muscles through discrete movements, one's body really looked different—toned and tightened in ways that an ordinary run, game of tennis, or visit to the gym could not accomplish. Within a few decades, offshoots began showing up around New York City and ultimately major metros around the country. Burr Leonard and her then-husband Carl Diehl met Berk and studied at the Lotte Berk Method studio before opening their first The Bar Method studio in Greenwich, Connecticut in 1992. In 1999, they opened three more studios in Darien, Westport, and New Canaan Connecticut. From a socioeconomic and demographic perspective, all of these Connecticut locations were essentially the suburban equivalents of New York City's Upper East Side. A few years later, two of Bach's star students left the Lotte Berk Method studio and started Core Fusion, which was housed in New York City's fancy "exhale" spas. Not only did DeVito and Halfpapp catalyze an exodus of most of Bach's instructors, but given the glamorous backdrop (and spa benefits) of Core Fusion's new home, many clients also left. Bach's approach was no-frills and her studio, increasingly decrepit, was housed in an old brownstone, which one client called "a dump" and remarked, "I think of my grandmother's toilet."[55]

Since these early offshoots, a number of different barre studios have opened across the country—Pop Physique (Los Angeles, New York, and San Francisco), The Bar Method (after Connecticut it opened in dozens of places around the country), and perhaps most famously, Physique 57 (New York City, the Hamptons—in the old Lotte Berk studio, and Beverly Hills). Each emphasizes different measures of yoga, Pilates, and ballet using varying weights and a ballet barre.

Irrespective of where one attends, barre classes are the consummate example of twenty-first-century conspicuous leisure. Sure, there are differences in clients, peer group for one's conspicuous leisure, and style of dress, but the effect is the same: These classes signal financial stability and free time for leisure activities. This conspicuous leisure operates on a number of levels. From a strictly economic perspective, each class is expensive by any global standards (ranging from approximately $10–$40 a class) and to achieve the desired effect one must attend classes two to four times a week. Even if each class doesn't cost $183.87, it still adds up pretty quickly.

But there are more social and cultural signals that emerge from attending barre classes. As conspicuous leisure is suggestive of luxury of time, the hour-long classes themselves reveal one has the capacity to attend and perfect one's body. Those who attend the Monday 11 am class (or its equivalent in the middle of a workday) are revealing conspicuous leisure to everyone else who has also shown up. In and of itself, this behavior suggests flexibility or affluence or both in one's career, or for some, the luxury of not working at all. As Pop Physique's Deric Williams remarked, "A single mom in Kentucky can't do that … We used to have childcare [in the studio] but we stopped because most people had babysitters and nannies."

Second, people who go to these classes tend to wear particular clothes to class, and to run errands. As Jennifer Williams, the former ballet dancer and co-founder of Pop Physique, remarked of her time as an instructor at The Bar Method, initially she wore nondescript workout clothing, but in the early 2000s, as she taught barre class in San Francisco, Williams noticed, "Every woman in the class had those pants with the little symbol. I realized 'I have to have those pants.'" Those pants, Lululemon's Groove Pant, is the signature piece of the company's collection and materialized as the badge of the new urban conspicuous leisure. The pants are indeed very flattering (black, bellbottom style, and made of a thick spandex blend that sucks everything in). Still, the Groove Pant requires one to actually work out to look good in them and to have the financial means to purchase a pair (they sell for $100 per pair, and one presumably needs more than one pair if exercising several times a week). So in one fell swoop, the wearer of these exercise pants fully transmits the wearer's conspicuous leisure. Each of these exercise studios also offers its own line of clothing with t-shirts, tight spandex, and the standard grip socks "necessary" for barre work (often the bottom of the sock is designed with a grip made out of the studio's logo or name and prevents slipping on the barre or hardwood studio floor). In more recent years, many offshoots of Lululemon's Groove Pant have appeared, including capri yoga pants with mesh cutouts, wild geometric printed leggings, and Stella McCartney for Adidas gear sold at Barney's. Even those who do not religiously attend exercise class can evoke the patina of conspicuous leisure through the adoption of casual sportswear like Athletica or Lululemon as a part of their regular wardrobe. Designer workout clothing has become part of the aspirational class mythology.

Finally, and most importantly, if one has the time and money to attend cardio barre classes several times a week, it does start to show. As the *New York Observer* less than delicately put it, women who attend these classes do look physically different from their non–barre workout class attendees. So merely by picking up coffee, stopping at the grocery store, or going out to dinner, those who attend classes at Pop Physique, Physique 57, The Bar Method, or any permutation of cardio barre class, reveal their conspicuous leisure by simply living their lives. And if one is ever concerned that the world is unaware of the hard work of such conspicuous leisure, there is always the "healthy selfie," which is a photo taken post-workout that can be instantly posted to Facebook or Instagram, or one's blog.

This trend is visible through other types of conspicuous leisure, where many aspirational class members find the material means to make them conspicuous via the clothes, the bottles of water carried to and fro, and the murky green pressed juices slugged down after a workout, along with simply being a member or regular at elite exercise studios. In her book *Fit for Consumption*, the sociologist Jennifer Maguire looks at how using free time for fitness fits into the larger gestalt, viewing leisure time as an occasion for productivity and personal development. The opportunity to appropriate one's time for exercise is a sign of social position and luxury and, as Maguire argues, studios and gyms were quick to reinvent themselves and their fitness regimes accordingly. As Maguire observes, "The future of exercise was being reformulated. Clubs sold fitness as a leisure lifestyle activity ... Health club memberships and physical appearance were interrelated status markers in an overall lifestyle package." Places like Equinox and Core Fusion, initially places to exercise, also began to offer luxury services and amenities; thus, frequenting one of these facilities in and of itself suggests social position. As n+1 co-founder Mark Greif writes, "Modern exercise makes you acknowledge the machine operating inside yourself. Nothing can make you believe we harbor nostalgia for factory work but a modern gym."[56] So, leisure is productive always and the goods and services accompanying them—certainly conspicuous consumption of a sort—are an efficient means of showing the world that you use your leisure time to stay in shape and perfect your abs. The *Economist* recently reported that while many industries were damaged by the Recession, exercise (in the form of gyms, clubs, classes) has remained robust and has grown. The industry's health, in a manner of speaking, is owing to the increase in elites working out. For example, those in the top quintile exercise more than six times more minutes per week than those in the bottom quintile. As the magazine observed, "sweating on purpose is becoming an elite phenomenon.... Where once 'prosperous' was a synonym for overweight, being fit (and thin with it) is a marker of status."[57] Or as the sociologist Harvey Molotch remarked, "Leisure once meant utter whiteness and lack of muscle tone. Now you need some affluence to *have* muscle tone. The working-class men used to be the only people with biceps, working at fast food gives you no biceps."

These examples are no different than that of the social mores of privileged modern motherhood. "The fact that breast-feeding requires endurance, inconvenience and in some cases physical suffering, only increases its status," writes the journalist Patricia Druckerman.[58] Women who are spending the year on maternity leave aren't getting daily manicures. Instead, they spend their time breast-feeding, bonding with their child, trying to get a head start on verbal skills. All of these practices are productive but suggest the glut of otherwise luxurious time that most moms don't get.

Aspirational class productivity in leisure spills over into all facets of life. Some members are never able to just relax. Even watching television —*Mad Men*, *Breaking Bad*, *Game of Thrones*, or HBO's latest epic—is about being a part of the cultural zeitgeist. How else can an individual seem informed (and intellectually productive) at a dinner party if he's not spending free time doing things that make him seem smart and culturally aware? And if a member of the aspirational class doesn't actually have the time to watch TV or read books, forms of media from Twitter to the Daily Beast allow overly productive people to pretend to be watching or following the latest cultural happenings, television programs, or book publications so that they can appear to spend more time reading the newspaper and the *New Yorker* than anyone actually does. "What we all feel now is the constant pressure to know enough, at all times, lest we be revealed as culturally illiterate. So that we can survive an elevator pitch, a business meeting, a visit to the office kitchenette, a cocktail party, so that we can post, tweet, chat, comment, text as if we have seen, read, watched, listened." Karl Taro Greenfield writes in the *New York Times*, "What matters to us, awash in petabytes of data, is not necessarily having actually consumed this content firsthand but simply knowing that it exists—and having a position on it, being able to engage in the chatter *about* it. We come perilously close to performing a pastiche of knowledgeability.... It's not lying, exactly, when we nod knowingly at a cocktail party or over drinks when a colleague mentions a movie or book that we have not actually seen or read, nor even read a review of. There is a very good chance that our conversational partner may herself be simply repeating the mordant observations of someone in her timeline or feed."[59]

When members of the aspirational class are being so productive with their limited leisure time, they lose sight of what a luxury it is to spend time this way. They are very busy demonstrating and signifying the unique ways in which their time is used doing things that are fundamentally different from everyone else. "Just as they want a return on their investment and philanthropy," writes economist Robert Frank, "rich people now want a return on their leisure time." So part of that time is also used to judge those who aren't doing these things with their time: infant formula rather than mother's milk? Poisonous! The culturally illiterate who spend time watching lowbrow sitcoms? For shame! In other words, part of modern conspicuous leisure is a cultural and moral superiority directed toward those who don't participate in these behaviors and an assumption that this lack of participation is always a choice.

The truth is much more complicated. These behaviors that seem so natural, that many members of the aspirational class think everyone should engage in, are deeply embedded into the social norms of the educated elite and their social groups. Breast-feeding and natural births are "intuitive" or "instinctual," or so the mind-set goes. But they are a luxury, make no mistake, even if they are tiring and feel like work. Intuitive as such practices feel, they are not an obvious or easy option for the middle and lower classes. On this point, it's worth referring to one of the greatest thinkers of the twentieth century. Daniel Bell wrote *The Cultural Contradictions of Capitalism* in 1976 and it remains one of the most potent commentaries on modern society. Bell argues that society has taken the economic advantages offered by capitalism and its work ethic to create new sensibilities and massive freedom in our social behavior and cultural styles. Those who would once have been relegated to a lifestyle reflecting the austerity and frugality of this Protestant work value system (think William Whyte's *The Organization Man*) are now embracing new forms of cultural behavior such as the avant garde (does it even exist anymore?) and bohemianism. Our economic productivity offers us the chance to be culturally liberal, or "cultural omnivores," as sociologists refer to this particular bastion of new elite society. We remain very productive, and this quality defines the aspirational class and how its members got there. But the outward status markers of such productive success lie in accompanying lifestyle and consumption choices.[60] Bell's great contribution in this respect is that society has culturally shifted so that anti-bourgeois lifestyles (even bohemian) have become a signifier of higher economic status. Or as David Brooks remarks, bobos make every effort to turn consumer choices into sacred and moral decisions (water purifiers, private meditation classes, lactation consultants, and slate Zen bathrooms). These choices that seem to be instinctual or a return to a more natural way of living are actually a product of how capital allows us freedom to be this way. "Mindfulness" may seem like a virtuous return to the pre-digital age and suggest anti-capitalist sensibilities, but it takes time and money to learn and practice meditation. Copper cookware, much more environmentally sound than its Teflon counterpart (and of course closer to nature using a natural element), costs $1,500 a set, while the latter goes for $50. Or, to quote historian Frank Trentmann again, "Morality is woven deep into the fabric of our material lives."[61]

The extent to which status decisions are a reflection of wanting to show off to the world or the basic human desire to be accepted is hard to disentangle. While we do not feel much sympathy for the woman buying the Hermès Birkin handbag in an effort to feel accepted (see also *The Primates of Park Avenue*), the woman who makes a choice to breastfeed, to have a home birth, to quit work to spend more time with her child, to exercise more for health reasons, seems a bit more authentic, deeper, or at least aiming for a greater good—but the ability to make these seemingly wildly different choices emerges from the same socioeconomic class and accrual of cultural capital.

Thus simultaneously, there is a clear backlash to America's new type of conspicuous leisure—it creates even more social stratification and inequality than any form of designer handbag. At least in the case of the handbag, it's clear that those with money get the luxury version. With conspicuous leisure, we assume that if someone isn't doing something it's a moral choice. We ignore the socioeconomic limitations (or the freedom, for the affluent members of the aspirational class) of how people make decisions. Why is that person overweight or another less culturally aware? Perhaps because they work for an hourly wage, and thus don't have the resources to buy expensive fresh vegetables or the "productive leisure time" to attend evening Pilates classes or read the *New Yorker*. In the case of motherhood, aspirational class society makes women feel badly if they end up using infant formula or have a C-section. Mothers disapprove of pacifier use, while simultaneously using their very own finger to soothe their babies.

For aspirational class parents, sweetened drinks and Doritos are the toddler equivalent of smoking. As a recent study by sociologist Caitlin

Daniel reports, it's not that low-income parents aren't aware of the benefits of children eating vegetables and "healthy food," it's that they can't afford the waste if the children refuse to eat it or throw it on the floor. For most young children, outside of fatty, tasty items like chicken nuggets and French fries, it takes 8 to 12 tries of broccoli, salmon, or other more virtuous foods before a child will properly eat it. So every time a poor mother spends her minimal income on Brussels sprouts that end up on the floor, she is not just wasting money she doesn't have but is also giving up the opportunity to buy something her child will actually consume. As Daniel remarked, "Poor parents not only have to calculate how much their food costs, they must also consider what happens if no one eats it." Daniel also studied well-to-do parents. Upon asking one such mother how she felt about the waste of food and money associated with her toddler's food rejection the mother remarked, "Honestly, it never crossed my mind."[62] And yet such an aspirational class mother will gasp at the sight of a fellow mom purchasing her young child a McDonald's happy meal for lunch, secure in her own decision to make her toddler a bento box of perfectly grilled chicken and a rainbow array of vegetables. This aspirational class mother has the very best intentions to provide healthy food for her own child, but she forgets that the former mother almost never has that choice.

Consider the maelstrom of aspirational class parenting: the elite, private preschool. Tuition runs $10,000–$40,000 a year and wait-lists start before a child is even born. Forty-five-year-old dads race out of work to pick up their kids by 5 pm (only to work into the wee hours after bedtime). Some dads work in the broadly drawn "creative class," and thus their flexible hours allow them to join their children for lunch. Stay-at-home moms, some with Ivy League graduate degrees, are shopping for organic vegetables and organizing play dates and music lessons while their children are at school. These are parents who, steeped in Lareau's concerted cultivation, spend most of their free time thinking about how to make their children's lives better. Yet, by default, in many of their decisions they are subconsciously judging those who make different ones, oblivious to the fact that each decision ultimately rests on the economic and social freedom a mother does or does not possess, and that this freedom is derived almost entirely from her position in a capitalist society.

Not all conspicuous leisure is about status, nor are all breast-feeders alpha moms looking down upon the rest. In fact, many members of the aspirational class who engage in exercise, attentive parenting, and acquisition of cultural knowledge are doing it with good intentions. But the point remains that the mythologies that surround twenty-first-century conspicuous leisure are those of a dominant social class who has the luxury of time and knowledge to partake. As the next chapter will demonstrate, this luxury of affluence and information can inspire very important social movements and pushback not just against conspicuous consumption, but also against the very means of production that transformed capital, consumption, and status in the first place.

CHAPTER 5

Conspicuous Production

For most consumers that Earthbound Farm organic baby arugula from
Whole Foods isn't an opportunity to dismantle the infrastructures of the
modern world; it's simply salad. Dressed with a little Tuscan extra-virgin
olive oil, a splash of sherry vinegar, some shavings of Parmigiano
Reggiano, and fleur de sel from the Camargue, it makes a very nice
appetizer. To insist that we are consuming not just salad but a vision of
society isn't wrong, but it's biting off more than most people are able and
willing to chew.

—Steven Shapin, "Paradise Sold," *New Yorker*, May 15, 2006

Beyond the renovated industrial lofts of downtown Los Angeles, through
the rapidly gentrifying Echo Park and the already hipsterized Silver
Lake is Glassell Park. While much of East LA is going the way of Silver
Lake and Los Feliz, Glassell Park is rarely mentioned in the gentrification discussion. This is partially due to the lingering gang activity, and
persistent reputation for crime (whether accurate or not). The area also
lacks parks, cafés, bookstores, and the other sort of amenities that the
young, urban creative types seek out. Physically, it lacks the interesting
architecture of downtown, the natural beauty of the West Side's ocean-
front, and the hills and bohemian art scene of the East Side. Unlike most
of Los Angeles, there's empty space, seemingly plenty of it. The industrial corridor along San Fernando road remains pretty active. Big trucks
park outside the warehouses and factories, and blast down the road toward the Interstate 5. There is the glamorous noir of the Hollywood
Hills that feels just out of a Raymond Chandler novel, and then there's
Glassell Park, where the noir feels like something more akin to *Escape
from LA* with Kurt Russell raging around a fiery urban wasteland.

But these demerits allow Glassell Park to play home to what could easily be the next big wave in American industrial activity. For in Glassell Park, there are big, old warehouses being used for exactly what they were designed for—not nightclubs, artist studios, or big gallery space (although there is certainly some of that too)—but for making stuff. These warehouses are not out in the middle of Minnesota, but rather in the heart of one of America's major metropolitan areas. And what's going on here is both a new concept for America and a return to previous, almost pre–Industrial Revolution production of small-batch, artisanal products made, packaged, and sold in the same country of origin, with a clear story and road map from conception to production to consumption. Here in Glassell Park, I got to see this phenomenon really happening, and how it could fundamentally change America. While in Veblen's time status was a function of the product itself, in the twenty-first century status emerges from how the product is made and its point of origin. Rather than conspicuous consumption, today many goods attain their status from their conspicuous production.

This particular story starts with the coffee shop Intelligentsia. Intelligentsia, born out of Chicago in the late 1990s, is one of the first post-Starbucks success stories. Unlike Starbucks, which has 13,000 stores nationwide, Intelligentsia only has nine—a few in Chicago, one in San Francisco, two in Los Angeles, and a newly opened branch in Manhattan, near the High Line in Chelsea. The important thing to keep in mind when talking to anyone who works for Intelligentsia is that it is nothing like Starbucks, barring the fact that both companies have convinced consumers to spend five dollars on a cup of coffee. However, where Starbucks adds a dollop of caramel and a cup or two of milk to make the consumer's money worth it and essentially creates a liquid dessert, Intelligentsia has managed to get consumers to spend the same amount for a plain cup of coffee, dairy and syrup not included. In fact, the line around the block at the Silver Lake shop is mainly for their slow-brewed obscure coffees from faraway parts of the world, not cappuccinos and certainly not the decadent 510-calorie Pumpkin Spice Latte, which, if requested, would get you laughed right out of the store onto Sunset Boulevard. Where Starbucks made its fortune in bringing luxury to the masses, Intelligentsia makes its (smaller) fortune proclaiming its rarity.

Intelligentsia belongs to an emerging group of companies focusing on "specialty coffee." For most people, Starbucks would be the obvious example of such a consumer good. However, Starbucks may be a step up from Maxwell House and Nescafé, but it mainly operates in a space that produces coffee-esque drinks, where coffee is not necessarily the whole point. To put things in perspective, Starbucks is one of the biggest purchasers of dairy products in the United States. Specialty coffee companies are a different breed altogether. Intelligentsia's claim to fame is that it focuses on the coffee beans, how they are roasted, how the coffee is brewed, and perhaps most importantly, where the coffee comes from in the first place.

I arrived one Wednesday morning to Intelligentsia's Glassell Park Roasting Works warehouse, where I was greeted by Mark Zambito, the manager of the Silver Lake coffee house. Mark and I had met a few weeks back to talk about Intelligentsia as a consumer good, and in listening to his discussion of "craftsmanship," "select harvesting," "green buyers," and in-house "educators" to train the baristas (almost daily) how to brew particular coffee beans, it became apparent that something else was going on. Most of us have been brewing some version of coffee since we were teenagers, but specialty coffee is more akin to wine than tea or Coca-Cola, and the process of acquiring beans and roasting them (never mind actually making a cup of coffee) took such an amazing amount of time and resources that I was surprised that a cup of Intelligentsia coffee didn't cost more.

Zambito is the picture of Silver Lake, or Williamsburg, or any other hipster enclave. Thin, small, wearing a tie and vest, Zambito is soft-spoken, but when he does talk it is clear that he is incredibly knowledgeable about all things coffee, and is equally passionate (or even more so). Zambito doesn't spend much time talking about how good Intelligentsia's coffee tastes; in fact he focuses mainly on the process of making good coffee, starting with how the company acquires the beans. As he explains, coffee cherries (that's what they are before they are picked and roasted into coffee beans) do not ripen evenly in a bundle. So in order to get the ripe cherries, they have to be handpicked, then put in water to see which cherries sink and which ones float; then the ripe floating ones are skimmed off for production. If you're Starbucks, with 13,000 stores, the sheer cost of labor for all that handpicked coffee would be prohibitive, but for Intelligentsia, it's possible.

Of course in order to handpick the right coffee cherries at a large scale that serves several major American metropolitan areas, Intelligentsia still needs some larger structure of operation and a good, trustworthy relationship with coffee farmers, most of whom live and grow coffee in East Africa and Central America. Intelligentsia gets farmers to fastidiously pick perfectly ripe cherries by simply paying them more. Starbucks, famous for its "fair trade" (which has been criticized as a bit of a misnomer), doesn't hold a candle to the practice of "direct trade," whereby Intelligentsia works with the farmers themselves, removing the middleman.[1] According to those I spoke with at Intelligentsia, this practice gives farmers 25% more money than fair trade, and also allows Intelligentsia not only to supervise harvesting, but also to enforce fair labor practices and environmental sustainability, both essential aspects of the company's policies. Intelligentsia sends staff to far-flung parts of the world to develop relationships with farmers, establish trust, and then oversee the farms and harvesting processes. This part of the company is wholly separate from the coffee roasting, brewing, and selling business.

This area of the business is run by Geoff Watts, one of the owners of Intelligentsia and a green coffee buyer for the company. He was charged with acquiring the unroasted, immature green-colored coffee beans, essentially the beginning stage of the entire process. Watts is the opposite of Zambito—he looks nothing like the Silver Lake denizens he employs and who patronize Intelligentsia. The day I met him, he was wearing a flannel checkered shirt without a hint of irony. He has nice, thick, floppy hair and looks like he'd be more comfortable in Humboldt County than in the heart of LA. Watts's business acumen and articulation are so impressive that I asked him where he got his MBA; he replied he had a bachelor's degree in philosophy and mainly picked up the knowledge on the job. Watts used to oversee all of the coffee buying, but as Intelligentsia grew, more buyers were necessary and now he only manages 20%. But that 20% requires detailed dedication and extensive research. "We see coffee farmers as our partners and we need a team. We can invest in roasters and baristas but how the coffee is grown is 60–80% of the coffee, so we need them to do a good job. We went down there [to

Central America] and saw how destitute they [farmers] are and that they were making bad coffee but not because they can't make better coffee but because they didn't have the resources."

Watts continued, emphasizing his point with his hand, "You need to plant the right coffee, harvest selectively. We pay them to pick only the ripe fruits, put them in hermetically sealed bags to protect them. If they can do this, we'll pay a really great price. We also pay based on the real cost of production, not the futures market [like other coffee buyers]. We invest in a lot of these farmers so they have finances, resources, and knowledge. We bring them to our stores, bring them all together to meet the other farmers, we bring in scientists on the frontiers of coffee quality research so they can learn [and] learn from each other. A farmer from Kenya will show El Salvadorian farmers their techniques and vice versa."

With roasting machines in Los Angeles and Chicago, the company is able to roast all of its own beans, primarily selling in its own stores but also to other small specialty coffee shops and more recently in Whole Foods and other upscale grocery stores. This is another interesting aspect of their production process. Intelligentsia has managed to acquire some of the last of the Gothot Ideal rapid roasting machines, highly sought after roasters from the 1940s and 1950s that are no longer made. Stumptown specialty coffee, with eight locations nationally, also uses 1950s-era Probat roasters (the company that bought out Gothot), and this is a selling point for them too. Standing next to one of these machines as the coffee beans were being churned over slowly and methodically, I asked the roaster why these machines were better than something more technologically advanced. The flames for roasting, he explained, were at the top rather than the bottom of the roasting tin, which allows for a more gentle and precise roast. While I still can't figure out why Probat doesn't just make more of these machines, without question the rarity and return to a previous era is part of the appeal (along with the distinct taste of the coffee beans). All parts of the production process are transparent. When you buy a pound of coffee from Intelligentsia you will see the farm, country of origin, roast—every aspect is outlined on the bag.

After all the due diligence, it would be hard to say that Intelligentsia is ripping anyone off with their $5 coffees. This company really cares and spends a shocking amount of time getting things right. Their dedication, from the very first green coffee cherry to the small cup of coffee sold at Chelsea's High Line Hotel, housed in an old seminary, is remarkable. Intelligentsia workers, whether baristas or the founders of the company, are both knowledgeable of and involved in every precise aspect of the production process, and this process is tied inextricably to the company's identity and unique selling points and actual product. All of this is what makes the coffee taste good both physically and metaphysically. Intelligentsia would have attracted employees like Watts and Zambito, but it couldn't successfully sustain a business, with lines out the door, in the heart of Los Angeles and Manhattan, if it didn't have consumers who cared about the exact same things. Consumers' desire for these less ostentatious forms of consumption is crucial to conspicuous production's success.

I found this out the morning I arrived at the Intelligentsia Roasting Works just in time for what specialty coffee brewers, buyers, and baristas call a "cupping," which is the process of tasting particular roasts and coffee beans and determining the precise ratio of water to grounds and the brewing method and timing to produce the best flavor. The taste tests commence after the coffee grounds have been extracted for 15 minutes—whereby hot water is poured over the coffee grounds and then the grounds rise to the top of the water. After the fifteen minutes are up, the tasters "break the crust" and scoop the grounds off the top. Then, over the course of 45 minutes, two cups of each coffee are tasted (to ensure quality control) for a total of three "passes." Akin to a religious ritual, the cupping is an almost silent production, bar the slurping and spitting noises, as the tasters move around the table evaluating the coffees brewed at different temperatures. For each pass, each taster scribbles down various notes, marking the coffee's acidity, sweetness, and emerging compounds—whether chocolate, toffee, or berries—creating an aggregate score out of 100. The first pass focuses on sweetness and acidity, the second on flavor and aftertaste, and the third makes small adjustments to early assessments. Watts explained, "For example, you thought you tasted blackberry but it's actually raspberry." Only after each coffee is scored by each taster and the comments and scores discussed are the farm, bean, country of origin, and roast revealed.

At this particular cupping, the four tasters were considering 13 different coffees and, despite a seemingly subjective process of evaluation ("reminds me of caramel apple," remarked one taster. "I got that black-berry when it was kind of hot," "I tried to say it's 'dark chocolate' but actually it tastes like mold," said one of the young women), they generally arrived at the same conclusions, scoring a Kenyan bean roasted in Portland with the highest mark of that day's cupping (90/100).

The process of evaluating specialty coffee is not unlike that of tasting this year's Bordeaux wine, and the coffee tasters may not be as skilled as sommeliers but they operate within the same space. Assessing specialty coffee involves a process of tasting at different stages and different temperatures and quantifying a seemingly subjective and taste-driven product. And the coffee cherries, how and when they were picked, and seasonal fluctuations determine the ultimate score, just like grapes for wine. Therein lies the key distinction between Intelligentsia and Starbucks, and it transcends taste. Rather, what makes Intelligentsia fundamentally different from Starbucks is that its founders, producers, and customers all really care about where the stuff comes from. Starbucks may stamp "fair trade" on its pounds of coffee, but Intelligentsia buyers actually become friends with their coffee farmers and fly them to Los Angeles to meet the rest of the staff (and some of their customers).

THE RISE OF CONSPICUOUS PRODUCTION

This latter point is the key to understanding not only Intelligentsia but also the rise of a social and economic consciousness and awareness emerging across the Western world and its cultural, post-scarcity goods. The rise in specialty coffee is really the story of conspicuous production and it can be seen at grocery stores, clothing boutiques, farmers' markets, and restaurants across the world. Conspicuous production goods are a key type of aspirational class consumption. For the aspirational class, we are what we eat, drink, and consume more generally, and this is why for some goods the opaque process of production has been replaced by transparency for every step. This transparency doesn't simply add value—it *is* the value—of many cultural goods. We will eat the smaller, sadder apples from the farmers' market because we met the farmer and we know he didn't put any nasty chemicals on his fruit. We will spend three times more on a linen shirt because we know it was picked up from a small shop somewhere on the Amalfi coast, and we met the store owner who personally made the voyage and met the tailor (and his children). We will slather on organic coconut oil instead of Retin-A, and eat in restaurants that charge $20 for mac and cheese because they list the originating dairy farm in chalk on a rustic sign in the front. Or, as Mark Greif observes in his book *Essays Against Everything*, "When you eat the supermarket tomato that tastes terrible, it is 'terrible'; when you bite into the heirloom tomato that happens to be tasteless and watery, you adjust it to taste 'real.'"[2] The production, rather than the consumption, becomes the key conspicuous status signal embraced by this new formation of the economic *and* cultural system, which is why we see the unemployed hipsters at the same coffee shop as the successful Hollywood screenwriter. Finally, after centuries of diametrical opposition, these two groups have banded together as the aspirational class, and they want and value the same things.[3] The emergence of conspicuous production in the twenty-first century revolves around three key forces: the backlash against globalization, the rise of information and the premium on transparent information, and the luxury to care about these things as a result of a post-scarcity, postmodern society and its values. We see this transformation in where we buy groceries, the restaurants we frequent, what we wear, and even our toothpaste. Capitalism, historically dividing the capitalist from the proletariat, has been turned on its head.

MORE THAN JUST ARUGULA: FOOD AS CONSPICUOUS PRODUCTION

We may thank Starbucks for introducing the idea of the $5 cup of fair trade Kenyan coffee, but Whole Foods is the mainstream, mass-produced leitmotif of the conspicuous production movement. Founded in 1980, Whole Foods emerged from the bohemian tradition of Trader Joe's and the crunchy Berkeley Bowl and somewhere along the way started selling arugula and chard for five bucks a pop. Over the course of the last several decades, Whole Foods' founder, John Mackey, has transformed his natural food store, originating from his Austin apartment, into a $9 billion-plus enterprise with more than 300 locations.

People who shop at Whole Foods are not oblivious to its contradictions of capitalism. Affectionately called Whole Paycheck, the grocery store beams purity, goodwill, and a return to nature—but all at a shocking price tag that is unaffordable for most of society. Whole Foods shoppers know that they can get organic tomatoes for half the cost at Trader Joe's, or even the local chain, but the grocery store creates an entire shopping experience that for many is worth the price. Even people who probably don't earn the income to afford luxury food (those same unemployed playwrights and artists buying $5 cups of coffee) end up in the store's deli buying sweet summer kale salad for $11.99 a pound. Since the regional stores have quite a bit of autonomy, local distinctiveness emerges. In New York City's Columbus Circle location, jazz plays softly, while others, like the Orlando, Florida outpost, offer chair massages. Glendale, California's Whole Foods doesn't offer massages but indie music plays in the background, with a pressed juice and coffee bar at the entrance. Even though shopping at Whole Foods is not marginally but significantly more expensive than Trader Joe's (which offers similar kinds of food) or Albertson's or Giant (which has more common brand-name food), many still trek to Whole Foods every week, telling themselves that the food is better there than at other, more convenient grocery store locations.

But consumers may be telling themselves something because they want to believe it. I'm not a foodie, so these minor nuances in taste are lost on me, but I end up shopping here too. Honestly, I, like many a fellow grocery shopper, go to Whole Foods mainly because of the Whole Foods experience. The stores tend to be relatively big, not very crowded (or offer very efficient check-out lines even in the heart of Manhattan), there's reasonably good music, and coffee, juice bars, and various amenities offered while shopping. Then there's humane chicken, strawberries without pesticides, and weirdly colored vegetables that make a consumer feel virtuous and counterbalance the bars of chocolate and coffeecake that may also be piled in their cart. All of these items have stories of the places where they are created and the people who create them built into their branding. "Zen muffins" from a small neighborhood in Los Angeles, whole milk with a little picture of the farm where the cows roam freely and happily, Mary's free-range Heritage farm turkeys from California's San Joaquin Valley, and yes, Intelligentsia coffee.

This storytelling is so effective that even the chocolate and the coffee cake seem less bad, maybe even good for you, compared to similar forms found at other grocery stores—even though surely they are not.

Whole Foods makes you believe you are a better global citizen and healthier person by shopping there even if the calorie content, nutrition facts, and price tag will quantitatively and insistently tell you otherwise. A wide-scale Stanford University research project studying the importance of organic foods compared to conventional fruit and vegetables revealed that the former were no better for us in a meaningful way. Or more plainly put, as my sons' pediatrician wearily remarked when I was discussing Plum's Organic Peach baby puree with him, "Did you eat organic when you grew up? I didn't. We're fine, aren't we?"

But Whole Foods' success isn't about organic products or better tasting food. Whole Foods' secret lies in how it effectively creates an identity and story to which people wish to subscribe. The key to understanding Whole Foods and the whole conspicuous production movement itself is recognizing that it is about the process and its implications rather than the product itself: Buying Whole Foods groceries signals consumer awareness, an animal rights ethos, environmental consciousness and, more broadly and perhaps most significantly, being an informed and conscientious member of society, just like Intelligentsia does on a much smaller scale. One does not attain any such attributes at a local Safeway or Giant, which, fair to say, is a neutral shopping experience for most. To understand the powerful consumer identity of Whole Foods, simply consider that it's one of the only chain grocery stores to offer one.

When asked how Whole Foods selects locations, Mackey himself explained, "Well, there's no more important decision that you're going to make than where you locate a store. If we're going to invest, depending on the size of the store, anywhere from $8 million to $20-plus million in capital for a new store, and sign a lease of usually 20 years or longer, we're making a long-term commitment and putting up a lot of capital." Mackey continues,

> So we spend a lot of time and energy sorting through that. We do site analysis. We analyze our competition in an area. We look at the demographics of who's living there. We look at education levels, income. There's a whole bunch of variables, but I think by far the most important

variable is the number of college graduates within a 16-minute drive time
… I can tell you that about 80 percent of our customers have college degrees. I can speculate that our customers, on average, are better educated
and better informed. And a college degree, while not a perfect proxy for
that, is the best we have in terms of demographic data that we can get. If
people are going to change their diets and become more health conscious,
they need to be generally better informed.[4]

Mackey is right. Education level correlates with higher levels of knowledge and higher income levels, much of which is linked to greater concern for animal welfare, fair trade, and environmentalism. We're more
likely to find animal rights activists among the metropolitan elite than
in gun-slinging NRA territory in rural Pennsylvania, which is why we
see Whole Foods mainly in urban areas and their close hinterlands. But
more importantly, Whole Foods propagates the group identification attributes to which members of the aspirational class espouse and aspire.
Just walking into the grocery store suggests one's values are on track or
certainly will be guided correctly during the shopping experience. Even
if one shops at the store weekly, there is always a social, political, and
spiritual place just out of reach, and Whole Foods' pressed juices might
get you there. I feel like a jerk when I turn up at the checkout without my
reusable bag, and am catapulted into better person status when I buy
the step 4 humanely treated beef for $15.99 a pound. Whole Foods al-
lows us to consume our way to a particular type of persona, and the
Whole Foods reusable bags, 365-product line, and organic local red
chard are the conspicuous goods that uphold this identity. So actually,
that Earthbound Farms baby arugula is more than just salad.[5]

Whole Foods offers the conspicuous production story to millions of
people in a fancy, highly commodified package. Yet, the same concept
emerges less formally from farmers' markets, curated clothing boutiques,
and farm-to-table restaurants popping up in small, affluent towns and
major metros around the Western world. Coined "localism" by travel
sections in newspapers and special features on Umbrian cheese, these
entrepreneurial ventures convince consumers that in addition to buying
something for themselves, they are doing a public service to small-town
business owners. In the general vernacular, localism describes the production of goods, particularly in arts and crafts and cuisine, which

develop from the resources and skills of a local region and are sold within that market. It makes consumers feel as though they've returned to the trade and agrarian society of the pre–Industrial Age. It used to be enough that buying shoes from Italy or perfume from France provided authenticity.[6] Today, consumers demand more: where the product is made, how it is made, and that the production process is fair, non-exploitative, and environmentally conscious are all important factors. These data points justify both the products and our choice, as consumers, to buy them.

Farmers' markets perhaps most closely embody the merging of localism and conspicuous production and successfully exist in the heart of distinctly non-agrarian cities across the United States. Any weekend afternoon in Los Angeles, New York City, San Francisco, or Notting Hill offers half a dozen such gatherings of farm-fresh produce heralding from pastures and fields located in the city's hinterlands. Farmers' markets allow farmers to sell directly to consumers, essentially turning Karl Marx's alienated labor on its head. Or as Elizabeth Bowman, who runs the Altadena Farmers Market just outside of Los Angeles, explained, "Farmers' markets are about reinstating that trust between the producer and consumer of a good [and making it] a direct relationship ... [But] in terms of time and what you get back, the tents, the insurance, the gas mileage, it is actually much harder to find people to commit to show up to the market. [Given the above variables], you're pricing under market value for issues of food justice." Indeed, from an economies-of-scale or -scope perspective, the farmers' market makes no sense—there aren't significant advantages for the farmer or the consumers, who would otherwise be Whole Foods customers perhaps avoiding long lines and the parking lot. People don't go to farmers' markets for deals—most of the fruit and vegetables are the same price as in upscale grocery stores—nor do they go to get diversity of produce. After all, the farmers only sell what's in season, rather than the cornucopia of flown-in exotic, out-of-season fruit found at the average supermarket in the dead of winter.

Yet, despite the unprofitable and constricting elements of the business, farmers' markets are growing in great strides: According to the USDA, in the past five years the number of farmers' markets in the United States has nearly doubled from 4,685 to more than 8,000 markets nationally. Since 1994 (the earliest documented figures on farmers' markets), the number has increased almost 500%.[7] Simultaneously, Whole Foods (certainly very profitable but operating under the same ethos) has grown 350% over the past 15 years, operating 365 stores, primarily in the United States. All of these heirloom tomatoes and pesticide-free blackberries are underpinned by another surprising trend: For the first time since World War II, the number of agricultural farms is growing in America.[8] In the UK, farmers' market revenues grew 32% from 2002 to 2011.[9]

These statistics are part and parcel of a number of other unforeseen trends occurring within food production. Farmers' magazines are gaining a greater following (and new ones are being published even today), farm-to-table restaurants are becoming commonplace, and community urban farms are the norm from Brooklyn to the Mission to Santa Monica. The ethos reinforcing these changes is perhaps most famously championed by Alice Waters, the godmother of the slow food movement and founder of Chez Panisse, one of the most challenging restaurants in the world at which to get a reservation. Opened in 1971, Chez Panisse serves all organic, local, and biodiverse-sensitive cuisine. Chez Panisse remains expensive and exclusive (not necessarily by Waters's design, but surely a result of the ongoing demand for slow food in Berkeley, California where the restaurant is located). Slow Food is a movement focused on sustaining local ecosystems, and as such the cuisine is regional and derives from seasonal ingredients local to the production and consumption. In recent years other restaurants and local establishments are taking Waters's cue and putting the produce from farmers' markets in front of many more of their diners as well. Forage, a Los Angeles farm-to-table restaurant, works directly with urban home growers (that is, people who are not farmers on a large scale but harvest small crops of vegetables and fruit, often grown in their backyard). Forage's website features pictures of the farmers and the particular produce they provide to the restaurant—figs from Pasadena brought by Malika, Santa Monica apricots from the Lewis's backyard, and so forth. Forage also features the home growers' own blogs, in which they provide explanations for growing produce and general modus vivendi. (Forage's chef, Jason Kim, used to be the sous chef for the award-winning Lucques and is a protégé of Waters herself.) As Eugene Ahn, Forage's head of PR, explained, "Jason was immersed in the values [of Waters] ... Here in this world of restaurants, it's so critical that if you want to be authentic, being able to share that with other people, falls into this category of making available your process to others." But Kim wanted to do something Waters couldn't do. While Forage operates largely under the same principles as Chez Panisse, the restaurant is much more egalitarian. "[Jason had] rarified but accessible values towards food. He wanted to take the $50 dining experience and make it a $15 experience—something you can experience daily."

Indeed, that is exactly the experience of Forage, a small restaurant barely noticeable against the bustle and endless automobile traffic of Sunset Boulevard. Yet inside it's packed with bohemian locals, ironic hipsters, screenwriters, and affluent, educated stay-at-home moms having lunch with their kids. Around the world, newspapers from Hong Kong to London are writing up its practices and cuisine. The food really does taste good, and as with Intelligentsia, I'm puzzled as to how they pull it off and why they charge so little for all that effort. The same could be said for Bare Burger, a chain with outposts in Los Angeles and New York, which offers all organic, pasture-raised meats, or Shake Shack, a national fast food chain that produces hormone- and antibiotic-free hot dogs and burgers and cage-free chicken. Both of these chain restaurants manage to offer their environmentally conscious food at affordable price points. Commitment to values rather than profit drives conspicuous producers. They could make more by charging more or lowering standards, but these actions would challenge their basic ethos of how things should be made and sold.

In ways big and small, the organic, slow, and farmers' food movement is part and parcel of twenty-first-century conspicuous production. What makes it so pervasive and prolific is its ability to bring together people from opposite ends of capitalism's spectrum. Or, as one observer put it with regard to the magazine *Modern Farmer*, "That means the magazine has attracted readers who include an Amish farmer and vegetable supplier to Whole Foods, Brooklyn rooftop farmers harvesting kale and broccoli and myriad young farmers going back to the land."[10]

The environmental awareness and social consciousness that Whole Foods and farmers' markets propagate is what inspires many of its dedicated consumers. What the sociologist Josee Johnston calls the "citizen-consumer hybrid" of ethical consumption is the way in which we use our consumer choices as a form of social practice. By shopping at Whole Foods, consumers "vote with their dollar" and signal their belief in animal rights, sustainable agriculture, and fair trade, essentially politicizing their grocery store experience—why else would anyone spend so much money on the same bread, beef, and vegetables that could be bought elsewhere for significantly less? Alison Alkon's study of farmers' markets reveals that both the farmers and the consumers are actively willing to sacrifice for what they believe is a more morally sound, sustainable food system. Consumers realize that they are paying a premium to shop at farmers' markets but see that as the "cost" of supporting local and ethical food practices, while farmers consciously sacrifice more lucrative financial opportunities to be a part of a greater social good.[11]

But Johnston would argue this is naive and self-interested nonetheless, particularly on the part of the consumers. As she points out, the environmental awareness and social consciousness that give Whole Foods items (and farmers' markets) a cost premium are actually about meeting personal desires around identity rather than necessarily enabling collective action to solve larger social problems. Johnston posits that it's easy to be ethical and a "good citizen" at Whole Foods, where consumers are offered an array of consumer choices within a milieu of jazz music, cappuccinos, and ease (not exactly the same experience as being a Peace Corp volunteer).[12] From Johnston's perspective, shopping at Whole Foods makes consumers feel good about themselves, but it does not actually make the world a better place. Similarly, the idyllic depiction of the farmers' market and local food movement in general is what scholars have called the "white farm imaginary," which is the over-valorizing of the white farmers and vendors that hides the under-represented minorities who are the actual laborers toiling away. Patrons of farmers' markets self-identify as ethical supporters of local family farmers, and this practice itself becomes a status marker. The "community imaginary" of the farmers' market (showing up with one's basket to visit vendors from nearby farms) allows these customers to feel good about themselves without meaningfully engaging minority groups or poorer classes who remain excluded from these mainly white, privileged experiences. For these critics, Whole Foods and farmers' markets act as enclaves for white, affluent people to feel empowered in their omnivorous cultural tastes and to find others just like them without actually helping the world.[13] In his critique of Michael Pollan's *Omnivore's Dilemma*, n+1 writer Mark Greif observes that this "luxury food trade" essentially satisfies the elites' desires while also making them seem deeper and thereby justified for good health and the environment. Greif takes particular umbrage against Pollan's distaste for the mainstream success of organic food. Implicit in Greif's critique is that Pollan no longer supports such organic farming precisely because the masses now have access to it, and thus Pollan seeks ever more elitist food practices. "His [Pollan] championing of it [grass farms and smaller producers] entrenches a form of localism that stays dependent on the patronage of a few buyers at the very top of the income distribution, where Pollan seems to sit."[14]

The critique of this type of conspicuous production is not without substance, but it also ignores the upsides to the new emphasis on humane and socially conscious food practices. By participating in food practices and culture that espouses sustainable values and environmental awareness, this smaller group of consumers may over time change larger social norms by supporting farmers who can, by virtue of increased demand for their goods, in turn produce food at lower price points for a wider market. For food policy experts like Paula Daniels, the elite's changing ideology and consumer practices around food at first may be a privileged position, but over time their hope is that as a result of more support for the industry, more people are able to access local, humane, and more sustainable types of agriculture, which would serve a greater good. Daniels, who is the founder of the LA Food Policy Council and founding chair for the Center for Good Food Purchasing, believes that social change often comes through the market, even if it starts with just a few. As Daniels explained to me, "Market forces have a great impact, environmental and local values build a midscale level of environmentally conscious food products. [By way of example], California is the largest agricultural economy by dollars and volume because California produces the greatest number of high value specialty crops. [The state is also the] highest in production of organic agriculture, something like 22% of all organic production in the US." Daniels continued, "What does that mean? That means we have more acreage in production that is pesticide-free, not using hormones and using practices that are much better for the environment. With market demand for organic, we start increasing that potential [for more sustainable agriculture practices]."

For Daniels, this approach creates a larger market and also greater capabilities for the farmers. In the case of Whole Foods, Daniels cites the grocery store's experience in Hawaii. As a native, Daniels recalled that when she lived there, the grocery stores were limited in their offerings and quality. But when Whole Foods opened stores in Hawaii it directly supported local farmers. As she explained, "Whole Foods made agreements with local producers of food ... and increased local food production. I have personally witnessed this. The local produce section in the Whole Foods Markets in Hawaii is even better than many of the Whole Foods stores I shop in LA. The impact they've made is that these otherwise subsistence farmers in lower income communities like Waimanalo are now beneficiaries of Whole Foods' consistent demand."

The end goal for sustainable food experts is that environmental, humane, transparent food production is the norm. As Daniels, who is a lawyer by trade, recalled,

> I remember when recycled paper was being introduced. It was expensive and not [readily] available. I was practicing law at the time and we used a lot more paper then, more than we do now. I was part of a state bar committee that reviewed rules for the state and a proposal came to require the use of recycled paper. My view then was we need to require people to do this then the market place will catch up. You know now that [this] is the case: you can go to Staples and buy 100% consumer waste paper that will work in your printer and it is cheaper [than standard paper]. I'm pretty convinced we can do this with food systems. That system is more complex ... [But if we] create more scale, more support for local economies and farmers, we can encourage more wide-scale regenerative production practices.[15]

FASHION AND THE NOT-MADE-IN-CHINA MOVEMENT

In 1919, in his treatise, *The Economic Consequences of the Peace*, John Maynard Keynes, commenting on the diversity of consumer choice at his disposal, remarked that "The inhabitant of London could order by telephone, sipping his morning tea in bed, the various products of the whole earth."[16] This observation was pre–World War II and pre-globalization as we know it. Yet in many ways fashion has returned to a pre–mass produced world where point of origin matters as it did with Indian tea and Persian silk. Fast women's fashion in the form of H&M and Forever 21, and the standardized goods made en masse and anonymously in China, Vietnam, and Mexico, have made Western consumers less interested in the big, global brands, particularly those that are produced in far-flung parts of the world with a slapped-on American label. This type of consumer good is increasingly criticized for being cheaply made, ersatz, and part of a general concern that we simply buy too much stuff.

The story of conspicuous production is really powered by consumers demanding something different and authentic. This new demand, while seemingly niche, plays into the development of local boutiques that sell only small-batch designers and raw denim whose weave comes with a unique story and place of origin. In these types of boutiques, those rare items on the rack that are in fact made in China are rebranded as "Designed in Scandinavia" (or France, or some such reputable point of origin), with a subtle second line to the label, "Made in the People's Republic of China"—as if this location is any different at all from China itself.

One such place that captures the return to place in product is Urban Rustic, in Carroll Gardens, Brooklyn.[17] With battered, unfinished wood floors and mason jars for glasses, this small boutique only sells food and drink sourced and made in New York, a business model that seems precarious in the long term, but thus far has been wildly successful. The shelves are lined with candy sticks from a bygone era, fresh simple flowers seemingly picked from the owners' backyard, and beer and pickles proudly brewed and brined (respectively) in New York. For all of these examples, the products and the stores in which they are sold possess a distinct story that imbues them with authenticity and value. It's no longer enough to buy an Italian suit or Parisian perfume. The entire production process (and materials used) are far more centralized and specified, right down to the neighborhood and artisan who made them. This type of store has popped up all over metropolitan America and its affluent hinterlands. The goods inside these boutiques are artisanal and strongly tied to their place of production. For example, the Broome

Street General Store, which has two locations in Silver Lake along with an online presence, offers Barbour waxed coats from England, St. James striped cotton t-shirts (the company that has dressed the French military since the 1800s), and Mast Brothers' chocolate from Brooklyn.

Another example, Bucks & Does in Los Angeles, operates a front office as a boutique with handpicked, expensive items from around the world and a back office filled with sewing machines, fabric, and a dozen seamstresses and designers who also produce clothing sold in the shop and distributed to other boutiques around the city. Just down the road from Forage, Bucks & Does (and Mohawk General Store, another boutique a few stores down) is fashion's equivalent of conspicuous production—a curated assemblage of clothing, shoes, and accessories taken from specific cities and regions known for producing these goods and materials. Struck by the list of designers I'd never heard of scribbled on a chalk sign outside the store, I decided to take a look. The moment I walked in, the young store clerk showed me some beautiful gray cashmere sweaters that were "just picked up in Ireland by the store's owners"—this description was the only selling point the young man gave me to convince me to buy the sweater.

Industry of All Nations (IOAN) is another enterprise that also captures this pre–Industrial Revolution type of production. Located in Culver City, a formal industrial corridor of Los Angeles, IOAN works with small and medium-sized manufacturers around the world to design and produce indigenous basic goods from around the world. Like Intelligentsia, their model is one of direct interaction with the producer, which means the founders fly around the world meeting indigo dyers in India, sneaker makers in Kenya, silk producers in China, and so forth.

Juan Diego Gerscovich is the founder of IOAN, which he started in 2010. Gerscovich is not a fashion designer or businessman by trade. Initially an architect hailing from Argentina, Gerscovich became involved in fashion as an outlet for his social causes. As he put it, "We don't want to negatively affect others with our work. The way we live is to be good and do good. The minute you do something that you are harming others, that's no good. There are a lot of good young people who think like us, so that's the future of the world."

As an architect, Gerscovich appreciates beautiful things and the history and origin of how they came to be, and fashion, at least in theory, captures these qualities. Yet fashion, he explained, had gone away from producing goods with integrity and an authentic point of origin. As he explained, "The past three or four years, even a Burberry coat is made in China and it's such a disappointment. Imagine being English and making raincoats for the past 200 years and then getting a raincoat made in China. We buy stuff in China, but the correct stuff—like recycling plastics, China is very advanced in this." IOAN's vision is to work with local producers to make goods with a real story and a specific quality of material and manufacturing that is unique to that place and product. In the beginning, Gerscovich spent hundreds of hours trolling websites of manufacturers around the world to find the best producers of basic materials and then making contact, arranging visits and so forth. One such quest involved finding a business that still produced natural dyes. As Gerscovich put it, "It's almost dead [as an industry], but there are a few little spots in India where they do it. These businesses started doing organic cotton t-shirts and dyes 25 years ago! They were in India, not Paris or New York. And until now, no one gave them the opportunity [to sell on a wide scale to the Western market] until us."

Gerscovich has traveled extensively to meet potential manufacturers to produce these basic goods that, practically speaking, would be much easier, more efficient, and cheaper to produce in China. Yet, Gerscovich wouldn't have a business with that approach. As he explained, no one just wants a white t-shirt anymore. "I don't want to just see the product. I want to see the information. Like a politician's face, we need to know more about what is behind the expression, the explanation with information."

One such example is a small cotton sneaker manufacturer in Kenya. Prior to working with IOAN, the business sold its shoes solely on the dusty roads in Mombasa. Gerscovich found the company online, went to Kenya to meet the owner, and decided the sneakers were exactly what he wanted to sell. Named the "Kenyatas," IOAN's catalogue describes them as made of 100% African material and sold outside of Africa for the first time in the 40 years of the company's existence. "Before us, they used to sell their sneakers in the street markets on dirt roads. They didn't even have sizing. And in like six months, the shoes have sizes, they are selling in Tokyo, Paris (at Merci) and around the world. They are still selling their shoes on the streets of Kenya; that is their main business still, of course." A few years ago, one batch of shoes sent to Gerscovich arrived in a bag covered with red dust and a smattering of fingerprints. He determined that they were the fingerprints of the employees and the dust of the Kenyan roads. "At first, we were like 'oh God,' and then we thought, wow this comes with the dirt from the roads on the employees' fingertips.... it's real."

Along with their Culver City outpost, IOAN operates a very successful online store where they do most of their business. The success of IOAN lies in their commitment to their philosophy of production more than the goods themselves—after all, these companies are still producing basic t-shirts and cotton sneakers that could be mistaken for Fruit of the Loom by the undiscerning eye. Patrons of IOAN are opposed to the economic and environmental consequences of conventional manufacturing. IOAN explains itself as "inspired by how things are done. We are not creating a new brand just to fill up shelves. In this modern time it is so easy and in everybody's hands to do most anything, so the most important thing should be how we do these things."[18] In the fall of 2013, J.Crew sent Gerscovich a fan email stating how much the company loved what IOAN did. In March 2014, IOAN produced its first line for J.Crew's kids' line Crew Cuts, and some basics for men, and as Gerscovich explained explicitly, "We are producing the same stuff for J.Crew but without dropping an inch in our standards." Today, on J.Crew's website, one can find IOAN's specially dyed madras t-shirts for kids, fleece sweatshirts made with organic cotton hailing from India, along with an interview with Gerscovich in which he explains the importance of sustainability in clothing manufacturing.

"ETSY'S INDUSTRIAL REVOLUTION"

As Whole Foods made organic a global, mass market phenomenon, Etsy enabled artisanal goods to go mainstream. Etsy, established in 2004, is a sort of Ebay for artisans selling handmade boots, candles, jewelry, belts, paper goods, and pretty much any other product so long as it conforms to the company's production standards. Founded in 2005 in Brooklyn (of course), Etsy is what is called a peer-to-peer e-commerce company where members can buy and sell crafts, craft materials, and artisanal goods in their "Marketplace" arranged under a wide array of choices such as weddings, birthdays, men, women, and jewelry. Vintage goods are also sold (but must be at least 20 years old). More prolific and industrious sellers can open their own "shop" which sells a variety of different handmade and vintage goods, of which Etsy gets 20 cents for every listing and 3.5% of the sale price (most goods are sold for $15 to $20). The average seller is a college-educated woman in her twenties or thirties. Initially, Etsy only allowed handmade goods, but more recently (and despite criticism by the diehards), the company allowed producers to work with some small artisanal manufacturers provided the relationship is direct and it is still people rather than companies selling things. This revision of rules is a matter of practicality: As a marketplace, Etsy has become more successful than its producers can handle, and to actually fulfill consumer orders more hands (or machines, as it turns out) are needed. The proof is in the numbers. In 2010, Etsy generated $180 million in sales, and by the next year that figure jumped to $314 million.[19] In 2012, Etsy generated $895 million in sales; by 2013 that number was $1 billion. In 2014, the company boasted $2 billion in sales. In April 2015, Etsy went public with an IPO of $16 a share but opened at $31 a share. Yet despite these clearly capitalistic moves, the company aims to keep its philosophy and raison d'être in place. Etsy is still about the "life stories of the sellers," as *The Economist* put it in a profile of the company. For Etsy, its triumph is in the hands of consumers not producers, the former of which care an awful lot about where things come from and who made them.[20] Today, other than its billion-dollar sales figures, Etsy boasts a membership of more than 50 million registered users who are happily making or buying handmade goods from all around the world and unique versions of mainstream consumer goods.

CONSPICUOUS PRODUCTION GOES MASS MARKET

These more specialized firms are not the only ones embarking on conspicuous production. More mainstream companies may not be traveling the world for uniquely dyed cloth, but they are seeing the importance of the "made in USA" label (rather than China or India or Bangladesh) as a symbol of good quality and authenticity. Consequently, they are looking

for ways to construct at least the sense of authenticity, which for consumers is a sign of quality and social consciousness. They observed
what happened when globalization hit the United States' manufacturing economy at full speed. From the collapse of the manufacturing
economy in the mid-1970s, to the easing of import duties by NAFTA in
1994, to China's membership in the WTO in 2001, the US apparel industry experienced shocking contraction over the past 20 years, as jobs
moved to Mexico, India, and China. From 1990 to 2012, textile and apparel contracted by 76.5% or lost 1.2 million jobs. In 1991, American-
made goods accounted for 56.2% of all clothing purchased in the United
States; by 2012, that number had dwindled to just 2.5%.[21] The AFL-CIO
attributed a loss of 700,000 jobs to NAFTA alone. Technology didn't
help either—advances in machines automated much of the work for
which people were once needed. As a result, cities around the country
witnessed a hollowing out of their factories and an entire urban job base
disappeared, creating a crisis in our inner cities and the rise of permanent "joblessness," which created decade after decade of intergenerational poverty.

The shock of global economic restructuring resulted in consequences
that transcended the practical. American consumers and companies
became aware of the social implications of widespread American unemployment and concurrently the exploitation of developing-country
workers. Irrespective of the plummeting price of goods, it became impossible to ignore the human cost. The proof is in the recent upsurge of
the US manufacturing industry and the change in consumer and company preferences as documented by recent research. Indeed, a recent
survey by Boston Consulting Group found that more than 70% of consumers would prefer not to buy "Made in China"[22] and, according to a
New York Times study, 60% would pay more for "Made in the USA."[23]
In another study, 30% of manufacturers considered moving some production back to the States, while about 15% already had done so. Overall, US apparel manufacturing has experienced a significant turnaround
after globalization, NAFTA, and outsourcing led to decades of inactiv-
ity.[24] Much of the manufacturing resurgence can be attributed to small
firms: More than 75% of US manufacturing firms employ 20 or fewer
workers.[25] And while these small firms only account for 9% of the sector, these artisanal manufacturing businesses account for much of the

job growth in the post-Recession period.[26] As textile factories open up across the country, the job listings are piling up.

The problem is that a return to Made in the USA costs real money. Nanette Lapore, the successful New York City–based designer, who sells high-end clothing, recently joined forces with J.C. Penney. However, to make any of the 150 clothing pieces with the "Made in USA" label, there would be a premium in the price and one that would likely put off Penney's customers. As Lepore simply put it, "That [less expensive] price point can't be done here [in the United States]."[27] The problem is that cheap goods simply can't be made in America. Consumers who are socially conscious and want Made in the USA (or made in France, Italy, or England, for that matter) are willing to pay more. But, as the business journalist Stephanie Clifford, who has been chronicling the new wave of American manufacturing, put it, for those looking for cheap prices, "even when consumers are confronted with the human costs of cheap production … they show little inclination to pay more for clothes."[28] When the average piece of clothing in the United States sells for $13.49, it's pretty hard to convince an average consumer to pay double for a label no one else will see. Therein lies the contradiction of conspicuous production. It does not exhibit ostensible status in the good through a brand name, consumers are motivated by their internal values and preferences, and these more subtle markers become points of judgment for them and their peer group. The lack of obvious status takes away some of the impetus behind why people consume in the first place.

Yet, change is under way in certain parts of America, and not simply along the boutique-lined streets of the Mission, Venice, and the Lower East Side. Wages in the US apparel industry are up 13.2% since 2007 (compared to just 1.4% for the private sector)[29] and US textile exports are up 37% since 2010.[30] Part of this change in production is a function of consumer preferences. Even if the average American is not wholly buying into conspicuous production and its accoutrements of farmers' markets, pressed juices, and handmade slippers, American consumers are increasingly aware and concerned about where things come from. News reports of the Bangladesh fire that killed more than one hundred garment workers,[31] the Bangladesh textile building collapse that killed more than one thousand workers,[32] and more generally the unsafe labor practices and child exploitation associated with sweatshop labor all make the cheap clothes from China and its brethren less appealing.[33] In short, consumers are taking notice of globalization's discontents and slowly pushing back. Globalization may have brought $5 t-shirts but increasingly, consumers are willing to pay more to ensure that workers are well cared for. According to Perception Research Services, 80% of consumers notice, and 75% will be more likely to buy a product because of the "Made in the USA" label.[34] Keeping jobs in America is a part of the motivation for some, but those in the industry say that consumers are mainly concerned about quality and safety, and recent reports from abroad call both of these into question with outsourced goods. "We don't have the mass market mentality in the US anymore," observes Jeffrey Cornwall, a professor of entrepreneurship at Belmont University.[35]

HOW DID WE GET HERE? GLOBALIZATION, INFORMATION, AND POSTMODERN VALUES

The origins of conspicuous production can be found in mainstream society's increased awareness of environmental and social problems and, most importantly, the channels to do something about them. It all started with pandas. In the mid-1990s, the World Wildlife Fund launched a conservation campaign that gave even conventional, middle America pause. I remember being in high school in a small town in Pennsylvania, and suddenly I cared about rain forests in South America. I got the t-shirt, the bumper stickers, and could recite the statistics (today deforestation occurs at a rate of 20 football fields per minute).[36] Aesthetically, WWF puts out a good campaign. Developed in 1961, the WWF is universally recognized by its stark panda graphic, inspired by the arrival of the panda bear Chi-Chi to the London Zoo the same year.

But WWF has accomplished more than the proliferation of panda bear bumper stickers. From their 1960s efforts to preserve the life of the Galapagos Islands to their ongoing international rain forest campaign (particularly in the Amazon), WWF has made environmentalism and preservation a real and pertinent issue across the world. The organization's work has resulted in conservation treaties, a moratorium on commercial whaling, and documented proof of biodiversity loss. WWF has intervened in the logging in the Congo, pioneered efforts to curb carbon emissions, and made rain forest destruction a household topic.[37]

Even if WWF's mission is compelling and its work important, the organization's efficacy relies on people, donors, and other organizations willing to respond to and support their causes. In short, lots of different actors and institutions must work together to accomplish big goals around conservation and environmentalism. Environmentalism, after all, has been around for centuries, but change in our behavior is a much more recent occurrence. In 1845, Frederick Engels remarked upon the decrepit and degraded environment of England's industrial cities.[38] Henry David Thoreau wrote *Walden* in 1854. The 1960s and '70s brought major environmental awareness and subsequent action in the United States: Rachel Carson's *Silent Spring* (1962), the Clean Air Act (1963), the Water Quality Act (1965), Dr. Seuss's *The Lorax* (1971), and the Clean Water Act (1972).[39] These monumental moments in environmentalism may have shifted the dial on a macro level, but today many of us practice a quotidian environmentalism, which partially explains the rise of conspicuous production.

For starters, when did many Americans start using cloth bags at the grocery store? And start lining up multicolored bins for recycling? I used to think it was a city thing until I observed my mother, who lives in rural America, organizing all of her bottles and cans and *driving them* to the recycling center. She also uses cloth bags and gets mad with herself at the checkout line when she realizes she's forgotten them. When did caring about the environment become a way of life, a part of mainstream Western consciousness? I started wearing my WWF t-shirt in the mid-1990s and was organizing river cleanups with the Ocean Conservancy by the time I was 20 years old. Why did I, along with all of my friends and thousands of other middle-class folks around the world, start caring so much about the environment? Understanding mainstream environmentalism helps us understand why people conspicuously consume in the first place.

The phenomenon that explains much of these changes is "postmodern values," a term that was coined by the University of Michigan political scientist Ronald Inglehart. In his 2000 *Washington Quarterly* essay on the topic, Inglehart argues that we are able to care about environmentalism, feminism, and a host of other value-laden causes because we have the post-scarcity luxury to do so. In other words, we are no longer worrying about being fed and keeping the lights on and so now, as goes Maslow's hierarchy of needs, we can self-actualize. In a survey of thousands of people around the world, Inglehart finds that for the pre–World War II generations, material goods still matter significantly, but for the postwar kids who grow up in relative prosperity, what matters most are nonmaterial matters, such as self-expression and a sense of belonging. And this isn't a slight difference between the two groups. Inglehart finds that the older age groups cared about material goods more than self-expression and postmaterial values by a ratio of 14 to 1. After long periods of rising economic and physical security, Inglehart believes that values and priorities change, which is why the younger generations care more about environmentalism and less about materialism —and this trend continues throughout their lives. Inglehart believes that this shift from "modern to postmodern values" is taking place "throughout advanced industrial society." "If one grows up with a feeling that survival can be taken for granted, instead of feeling survival is uncertain," writes Inglehart, "it influences almost every aspect of one's world view."[40]

The transformation Inglehart observes revolves around two key hypotheses: the *scarcity hypothesis* and the *socialization hypothesis*. The scarcity hypothesis suggests that the socioeconomic context in which a person grows up reflects his values in the long term. Those who grew up with fewer resources put a premium on that which is in short supply. For the pre-War generations, there was still uncertainty about food, water, shelter, and many basic material needs being met. For the post-War generations (right up to present-day teenagers), who have lived largely prosperous lives and whose basic needs are met, there is instead an absence of meaning and purpose. The socialization hypothesis simply means that this transformation of values takes time. Thus, while the pre-War generation may have come into abundance, the values of frugality and the necessity for reserves remain in place. It takes time, in other words, for society to become accustomed to post-scarcity and then have a value system that reflects it. In fact, most of us have a value system that reflects the socioeconomic conditions of our childhood.[41]

As most of the consumers of Whole Foods, farmers' markets, and "Made in the USA" grew up at a time of great prosperity and peace, we are able to develop the postmodern values that prize fair labor and environmentalism. Paradoxically, those of us who have never experienced any of the atrocities of labor exploitation, compromised food sources, or the tragic effects of war are the very people who care so deeply about wiping out these problems and advocate social and economic change. Many of the things that preserve the environment, and emphasize labor rights and fair trade, actually slow down production and economic processes, and in the case of environmentalism, stymie them altogether. Postmodernity and conspicuous production are essentially at odds with globalization and the economic growth it has brought.

We would not even be aware of globalization's negative impact on the environment and on the labor movement if not for the Information Age, which makes data and details in all aspects of human society almost transparent. With a quick keystroke, we can search a topic on the Internet and return troves of information about corporate prices, government actions, and materials and chemicals used in our clothing. The Information Age has not only created transparency; it has made transparency a key value of our society. Whether Michael Pollan's *The Omnivore's Dilemma*, a polemic against industrialized food production and fast food, or the revolting documentation of McDonald's food production in Eric Schlosser's *Fast Food Nation*, or the presence of formaldehyde in Victoria's Secret lingerie,[42] consumers expose and are exposed to insider details about how products are made, and it turns out these things aren't made very well.

Thus, consumers now prize production information nearly as much as the product itself, and trust between consumers and the producers is essential. As Kevin Carney, owner of the small, conspicuous production boutique Mohawk explained, "You see a lot more people really wanting to know the story around each piece—nontoxic, no run-off into the environment." Or, as Eugene Ahn of the restaurant Forage succinctly sums up, "People want to know where the food comes from. There was a whole time when we did not know where things came from and now we know the consequences of not knowing: We have vastly compromised food sheds, natural resources, food not adding nutrition, instead adding toxins to our body. If we knew more about what we consume, we could make better choices. Knowing the process increases the value."

Elizabeth Bowman of the Altadena Farmers Market explained it by way of anecdote:

> We had a whole dialogue with our egg vendor. He has like 50 chickens and 50 ducks and he needed another outlet to sell. And he priced it all out and he called me and said, 'I need to charge a dollar an egg to make money and I'm making 10 cents profit per egg even to sell it at that price.' That doesn't even count for his time, his gas money, just feeding the chickens. Hours and hours of conversation about the one dollar egg and you know what, people bought those eggs! Because that was his story, and that's why they bought it.

"VOLUNTARY SIMPLICITY"

Much of this type of spending fits into what has been called alternative consumption—nontraditional, less materialistic ways to spend that are a reaction against mainstream modern capitalism. Money that is spent is done so in low-key ways and consumer goods aim to be modest and inconspicuous. Followers of this modus vivendi fit into what has been called "voluntary simplicity," which as the name suggests is the *voluntary* practice of limiting expenditures and signals of material consumption. This type of consumer draws inspiration from a long line of nonmaterial philosophies including those of the Quakers, Buddha, and Henry David Thoreau.[43] Those who participate in the voluntary simplicity movement tend to sacrifice money in exchange for leisure time or to seek out nonmaterialistic and environmentally conscious forms of consumerism.[44] Followers of this movement engage in three types of behavior: "downshifting," the practice of lower income consumption; "strong simplification," the application of a high-end lifestyle to pursue more meaningful activities (much of which falls within inconspicuous consumption), and "simple living," which is the rejection of urban conspicuous consumption.[45]

The ethos behind the voluntary simplicity movement links strongly to concern around the environment, socioeconomic equity, and a general distaste for mass market modern consumer behavior. While the main principle of voluntary simplicity is to downgrade one's consumerism, members of the movement do find signals to reveal their lifestyle choice, such as style of dress (understated, no labels), attendance at yoga classes, or purchasing food at farmers' markets. But like postmodern values in general, the voluntary simplicity movement is a function and luxury of prosperity, literally anathema to the experience of being poor and being forced to limit consumption.

While there are middle-class "downshifters," who have chosen less money and part-time work to regain leisure, many voluntary simplicity members are able to make this life decision because they can live off of accumulated wealth.[46] In short, one must be wealthy enough to afford to live simply. Further, the signals of being less consumerist are also expensive—those farmers' market eggs priced at a dollar each may be very much in keeping with the voluntary simplicity ethos and are hardly a flashy status item, but they are four to five times more expensive than the version that most people buy at a grocery store. The content of conspicuous production (Chemex coffee brewers, hand-knitted sweaters, the slow food movement) has shifted from the 1980s zeal for convenient products (Mr. Coffee, McDonald's) to an appreciation for the production process itself, but it comes with a price.[47]

ARTS AND CRAFTS AND THE POST–INDUSTRIAL REVOLUTION

Conspicuous production has historical roots in the Arts and Crafts movement of the latter half of the nineteenth century—a distinctly different setting than its contemporary urbanity. Arts and Crafts, emerging from rural England and pioneered by William Morris, was a reaction against both technology (recall the Luddites) and mass production and the erosion of artisanal workmanship as a result of the Industrial Revolution. While wildly successful aesthetically—think the Morris chair, Stickley wood furniture, delicate flower motifs—Arts and Crafts was ultimately not very successful economically. There was no way to slow down the Industrial Revolution, and fighting it made one a loser from the outset.[48]

The central tenet of the Arts and Crafts movement was anti-capitalism and anti-industry, and this underlying sentiment explained its ultimate failure as an economic force. Arts and Crafts referenced an artisanal pre-capitalist point in history that was more idealized representation than reality.[49] As the archeology professor Elizabeth Wayland Barber put it, "The truth is that almost none of the objects that we think of as hand-made truly are. And that has been the case for thousands of years," referencing a fragment of Egyptian linen from 2500 BC as one such rare, fully handmade item.[50]

While the Arts and Crafts movement was a purposeful reaction against capitalism, it was already being practiced (without a label) across rural England from Lancashire to Yorkshire as a way of being. For those in the English countryside, the rise in crafts, artwork, and local goods (and the use of barns and local resources to produce these items) was simply a mode of self-preservation for farms that were no longer sustainable solely through agrarian use. Though not politically motivated conspicuous production, localism has for some time been a practical reality and survival technique for rural communities who diversified and repurposed their agricultural land and infrastructure[51] into something more profitable.

Today the rise of conspicuous production is driven by similar anti-industrial sentiment but also by a number of social, economic, and cultural trends that are twentieth- and twenty-first-century phenomena. Environmentalism and postmodern values are the dominant forces that have changed how we consume. Conspicuous production, like voluntary simplicity, is a reaction against conventional mainstream capitalism. Paradoxically, while globalization takes identity away from the production process of goods, the Information Age prioritizes transparency. And, like the Arts and Crafts movement, today's conspicuous production is a simulacrum of a previous, more wholesome time. The rustic chalkboards in Whole Foods listing Swiss chard and new batches of artisanal cheese (what does "artisanal cheese" even mean?) evoke an earlier agrarian era, even if one is living in the heart of Chicago or San Francisco, with taxis blasting by and cell phones buzzing around as one picks up a locally cultured buffalo mozzarella. Part of conspicuous production is the romanticizing of an era removed from modern industry and mass production, and as the chalk-scrawled listings of fresh produce indicate, anti-technology too.

REVISITING KARL MARX

Unlike previous movements, however, conspicuous production is not anti-capitalistic. Rather, conspicuous production fully embraces capitalism, but reinterprets it. Herein lies the fundamental uniqueness of this movement. Unlike Morris and his followers, who were ultimately trying to do away with capitalism rather than work with it, the conspicuous producers are working within the system, not against it. Those who conspicuously produce are still operating within a market economy, but with different motivations and rules. Money is exchanged for goods, rarity is prized, and yet some of the other hallmarks of capitalism, namely exploitation, Marx's alienated labor, and the neoclassical theory of profit maximization, have been shunned to create a whole new economic ethos working with a capitalistic framework. As the Industry of All Nations' website defines itself, "I.O.A.N. is pure capitalism. We don't seek people in need; we seek productive people. There is nothing noble about suffering, there is nothing courageous about poverty; but industriousness, working for a better life, it is the bravest thing in the world. That's what we seek; the industry of the people, the Industry of All Nations." Without question it's clear that conspicuous producers are pioneering transparency and making their production process as straightforward as possible. Much of this effort is due to a social and economic consciousness against globalization and the resulting exploitation of people and the environment. But built into this process is also a refutation of what Karl Marx called "alienated labor."

In his book *The Economic and Philosophic Manuscripts of 1844*, Karl Marx, so horrified by the conditions of the Industrial Revolution, outlined four basic types of alienation that emerged from capitalism: Alienation from the worker to the product he produces, the worker to the production process, alienation of the worker and his identity as a human being (or what Marx called "species-being"), and the worker to humanity and the others with whom he worked.[52] In Marx's eyes, workers have no control over the design of the goods they are told to produce (via the capitalists), they engage in repetitive processes rather than any craftsmanship, they don't know the people who buy the goods, and they get nothing emotionally meaningful from the work as they are limited to very regulated tasks. Finally, because capitalism is individualistic and fundamentally about profit, not collective good, capitalists aim to get the greatest work out of their workers for the least wages paid to them. Thus, the constant struggle for higher wages pits workers against each other in a competition. Indeed, a look at mass industrial production in the twentieth century would suggest Marx's observations were spot on. Workers were cogs in a wheel producing dozens upon dozens of the same product, to be shipped to consumers thousands of miles away, who are as ignorant of the producers as the producers are of them. As Gerscovich remarks of such products, "We have a term called 'orphan products' for things made by workers who have no idea what they are doing. Made by people who have no idea what they are doing, no history. One day they are making wallets and then they are making raincoats for Burberry. We don't want orphan products, that's just creating trash. [What we do] is like the opposite of alienated labor." Put simply, within this new breed of conspicuous producer, no matter whom I interviewed or what they made, their raison d'être remained the same: The basic ethos of conspicuous production is to fight alienated labor and to create a strong link between the producer and the consumer. As Bowman of Altadena Farmers Market remarked, "We are turning Karl Marx on his head. The farmer or the craftsman is now connected to his labor. We are connected to the good."

In fighting alienated labor (even if most of the conspicuous producers interviewed did not call it such, nor reference Marx), conspicuous producers give up another tenet of modern capitalism: profit maximization. In neoclassical economics, the general theory is that firms work to the goal of profit maximization above all others. Yet, every single one of the conspicuous producers I interviewed, from food to fashion to farmers' markets, admitted they are making very little profit (if any at all) or they are giving up the chance to make real money given the expense and time it takes to produce their socially conscious goods. Gerscovich of IOAN plainly admitted, "For our company, almost no profit." Or as Bowman remarked of the conspicuous production movement in general, "No one is doing it to get rich." Those at Intelligentsia explained that their business model inherently limits them from the bounties that companies like Starbucks or Peet's reap.

Conspicuous production has imbued a market economy with postmodern values, and those values take precedence over profit and economic growth. Put simply, their values are worth more than money.

"DON'T SELL OUT"

But what happens when the money does start to matter? In 1999, Garret John LoPorto had a plan to save the world via Ben & Jerry's ice cream.[53] When word got out that founders Ben Cohen and Jerry Greenfield were facing an acquisition by the international conglomerate Unilever, LoPorto, then a 23-year-old tech upstart, decided to fight back. His "Save Ben & Jerry's" grassroots campaign, involving Vermont governor Howard Dean, Congressman Bernie Sanders, and thousands of other activists, used the mantra "Don't Sell Out" and protested against the bullying by globalization and capitalism of a small Vermont-based company that (at least in their view) should stay that way.[54]

Cohen and Greenfield didn't want to sell. Founded in Burlington, Vermont in 1978, Ben & Jerry's ice cream operated locally and under a wider philosophy of social responsibility, environmental awareness, and bohemian sensibilities. Ben & Jerry's took well-known stances against practices they felt violated their code of ethics. In 2005, the company made a 900-pound Baked Alaska dessert and dumped it on Capitol Hill to express their criticism of a vote to open up the Alaskan Wildlife Refuge for drilling.[55] The company has widely shunned GMO produce, rGBH hormone dairy, and for a time, used only "eco-pint" unbleached cardboard packaging for all of its flavors.

These public stances against globalization and its negative impacts on the environment, not to mention their penchant for curious but delicious ice cream flavors (many of which also convey a social message), brought them many fans. Unsurprisingly, this local Vermont business looked pretty attractive to opportunistic big international companies—so much so that, despite the grassroots campaign, when Unilever stepped in to buy Ben & Jerry's, it was virtually impossible for the founders to turn them down. Unilever offered significantly more than what Ben & Jerry's was worth on the Nasdaq; declining the conglomerate's offer would actually do a disservice to the ice cream company's shareholders and would put Cohen and Greenfield in the position of a possible lawsuit. Ben Cohen described the day the deal went through as "Just about the worst day of my life."[56] Jerry Greenfield has remarked that preserving the values of the company remains a "constant struggle," as the small Burlington company's ethos runs almost antithetical to its global behemoth owner. Or, as Cohen explained more plainly, "We very carefully negotiated an acquisition agreement that was supposed to maintain the values of Ben & Jerry's. What we are learning is if you are owned by a corporation that, despite whatever words they might say, does not share those values, it's incredibly difficult to maintain those values."[57]

Ben & Jerry's isn't the only small, socially responsible company that has been subject to takeover. Burt's Bees, the natural, eco-friendly beauty product company established in 1984 in Maine, is devoted to "The Great Good." Like Ben & Jerry's, Burt's Bees' mantra is that of social responsibility, respect for the environment, and a commitment to natural ingredients. In 2004, the private equity firm AEA bought 80% of Burt's Bees for $173 million. In 2006, Unilever's John Replogle became the CEO of AEA. In 2007, with its eyes on the natural care market, Clorox, already generating $6 billion in sales a year with 9% growth annually, offered $925 million—in cash—to buy Burt's Bees.[58] AEA's powerful position in Burt's Bees' future, and the fact that the small-town company was already a step removed from the founders, made the sale to Clorox that much easier.

In 2006, for $100 million, Colgate-Palmolive purchased an 84% stake in Tom's of Maine, a small natural care company established in 1970 with a loan of $5,000. If possible, Tom's of Maine is an even crunchier and more eco-friendly enterprise than Burt's Bees or Ben & Jerry's; its logo looks like something from days of yore and fennel is its most powerful agent against plaque. One of the founders of the husband and wife team, Kate Chappell, sits on the board and makes sure that the hippy company's culture is preserved and its initial policies remain intact.[59] One such reinforcement seems to be that despite the Colgate-Palmolive takeover, Tom's of Maine packaging does not identify it as a Colgate subsidiary. That's probably a good thing, because it is unlikely that the bohemian shoppers who troll the aisles of Trader Joe's to pick up Tom's of Maine natural toothpaste and deodorant would be pleased to know of the Colgate connection. The irony is that Tom's of Maine is known as a natural and "cruelty-free company," while Colgate-Palmolive engages in animal testing and mass production of fairly chemically laden dish soap, among other products.[60]

These examples bring us to a problem that undoubtedly some other conspicuous producers may face fairly soon. Today, Burt's Bees, Tom's of Maine, and Ben & Jerry's can be found in Whole Foods and some small natural care companies, but also in Target, Walmart, and mass chain stores. Perhaps the democratization of natural, eco-friendly products is a good thing, but in what sense do the founders have any control over whether their product is sold in businesses that align with their core values, let alone have a say with the large multinationals that acquire them in the first place? Just as mass appeal for natural care products led to these takeovers, the increased desirability to a wide variety of consumers may create a situation in which companies like Intelligentsia and Industry of All Nations may have no choice but to sell out to bigger conglomerates (particularly if they become public companies). Even if the founders are personally less interested in profit than social values, the market, their shareholders, their board, and sheer capitalism may ultimately pull them into the mainstream, globalized economy and all of its mass-produced discontents. As they become indoctrinated into multinational companies, the products become patinas of the conspicuous production process from which they first emerged.

WHITHER INDUSTRY?

The final irony of conspicuous production is that much of the behavior of actually consuming these goods is not conspicuous at all. Sure, you can tote around your Whole Foods shopping bag or feel like you're part of the in-crowd at the farmers' market, but truthfully, when you're at home eating your heirloom tomatoes, no one but you knows where they were purchased—or that they are organic, for that matter. And that lovely gray cashmere sweater hand knit from Ireland may look fantastic, but nobody is thinking about the lady who knitted it. Despite being embedded in issues of status and class, such consumption is actually quite inconspicuous. Unlike conventional versions of conspicuous goods, where the production is anonymous but the good provides status to the consumer, the conspicuous bit of conspicuously produced goods is in how they're made and where they come from, which is the primary motivation for spending more money on them. Perhaps that is the point.

For all the good that this movement brings in terms of fair trade, localism, and anti-exploitation, and the noble values underpinning the whole process, there's something slightly naive about its anti-industrial, anti-globalization ethos. Globalization and the freedom of trade may have displaced some workers, but it has created jobs in many parts of the world that are desperately in need of economic growth. Whatever there is to say about the issues around labor exploitation (and there is plenty to say), there is something important in providing economic resources and possibility to countries that would otherwise not have participated in a capitalist market. And, the cheap clothes produced by free trade agreements and the rise of mass-produced goods have been helpful to middle-class families trying to keep clothes on the backs of their kids (again, not to say that consumers aren't also loading their closets with frivolity). Industry, mass production, and their consequences are the motivator for much of the conspicuous production movement and a good target for blame. But, while a member of the aspirational class is eating kale salad in his made-in-Brooklyn t-shirt, let's not lose sight of the fact that the current elite consumer ethos is only possible because of the economic growth and affluence that industry created and the luxurious postmodern values it allows us to possess.

Those made-in-Brooklyn t-shirts may not really matter, other than to signal, at least internally and to fellow members of the aspirational class, a particular ethos. They too, along with the rustic chalked signs advertising English cheddar, become a patina of conspicuous production and signifiers of one's membership within the aspirational class. But consumption of these subtle items is not simply indicative of our friends, income, or education level. Values have come to determine how we consume. Consumption suggests values and those values determine our consumption. But how we arrive at those values and internalize them is equally a part of the story. The geography of production matters, but our own geography plays a key role in consumption as well. Where we live has a huge effect on both our conspicuous and inconspicuous consumption choices and how we define ourselves. To what extent are the phenomena I write about in this book isolated to particular places? That is, to those particular places where most aspirational class members live and consume and thus transmit values and status to one another. To what extent does the story of the aspirational class resonate with all of America and to what extent is it actually the story of metropolitan America and its hinterlands? As the next chapter will show, cities have emerged as the central node where many of these choices, values, and tastes play out. Cities are the geography of the aspirational class and their consumption patterns.

CHAPTER 6

Landscapes of Consumption

The fundamental observation of twenty-first-century cities is that they have become what the sociologist Sharon Zukin has called "landscapes of consumption."[1] Cities are the geographical lens through which we can observe the consumption habits of the new elites. Through their shared values, ideologies, and consumption patterns, twenty-first-century cities connect more with one another than with towns and suburbs that may be more geographically proximate. Cities have become the ultimate consumption zone for the aspirational class, where many of the behaviors and practices I have discussed thus far play out. This rise in urban consumption is the result of an influx of elites—particularly wealthy members of the aspirational class—moving back into cities and cities, which in turn, cater to their needs and desires.

To be clear, urban centers are not just nodes for the upper-income members of the aspirational class; cities are intensely desirable to all the world's economic elite. Record-breaking apartment sales and rapid gentrification of once gritty neighborhoods are reported in newspaper headlines from New York to London to Berlin. The pushing out of dive bars and affordable housing for the influx of new condos and luxury retail is a standard trope in the twenty-first-century metropolis. In the building of this elite utopia, Western capitalist cities have become cultural and economic universes unto themselves. For every reasonably priced almond latte that an upwardly mobile member of the aspirational class purchases in Brooklyn, there is a multimillion-dollar apartment being sold to a Chinese oligarch on the Upper East Side. These two elite worlds collide in today's Western capitalist cities. Thus, understanding the important role of cities as they pertain to the aspirational class requires studying the role of urbanity as the spatial manifestation of much of the inequality and rise of the global economic elite that underpins the world economy. To understand today's cities is to understand what drives their desirability for the world's elite, aspirational and otherwise, and much of this allure can be found in what people consume.

The city was not always a desirable destination for the world's elite. Cities began as places of local trade, then export, and then with the Industrial Revolution, cities became the locus of production.[2] The Industrial Revolution and the manufacturing economy brought consumption to the masses, and its geographical home was the urban center. From Frederick Engels to Jacob Riis to Georg Simmel, sociologists and economists remarked upon the city's dire physical and social conditions as a result of factories, the tenements in which workers lived, and other elements of mass production.[3] Early twentieth-century cities were marked by a rapid influx of density never before seen in Western metropolises. This density was due to the rise in production—the manufacturing economy created the capability and the subsequent demand for mass-produced material goods, which brought forth immigrant workers and tenement housing. This expansion also made cities hard places to live. Cities became untenable by the mid-twentieth century (with the rise of public health problems, overcrowding, and pollution). Thus, unsurprisingly, when the federal government offered low-interest, amortized loans for suburban home ownership, those who could, fled urban centers.[4] The subsequent urban deindustrialization, commencing in the 1960s and continuing through the 1980s, left cities with no middle class and no jobs.

Those who study cities—economists, sociologists, urban planners— thought the demise would continue, that the city as we knew it would never recover. Indeed, they were partially right. Cities are no longer centers of manufacturing, and factories, which had gone to South America and Asia, did not reopen. There remains a massive plight of joblessness among unskilled, minority workers who had once been well-paid manufacturing workers. But the decline stopped. As early as the 1980s, a burgeoning advanced service economy took hold of major metro areas. While the actual production of goods left cities, an influx of firms that managed and ran the distribution of goods, services, and money began to move in. Headquarters and corporate management located in cities.[5] While the job of making things moved to cheaper locales in developing countries, the decisions around what to make, where to sell it, and how to value it, whether on the stock market or department store aisle, were made in major cities. In fact, the very cities that had been impacted by deindustrialization—Boston, New York, Chicago—were experiencing a resurgence due to the location of headquarters, financial services, law firms, and other highly skilled service industries. This revival of cities isn't a result of a rebirth of the industrial economy. As the London School of Economics geographer Michael Storper remarks in his book *Keys to the City*, "The decentralization of manufacturing essentially ended central cities' role in it. But [it] did not put an end to urban concentration."[6]

In fact, it's hard to say what tangible things educated, urban denizens actually create. Many work in a world of ideas, highly dependent on a formal, tertiary education. In her book, *Cities in a World Economy*, the sociologist Saskia Sassen documents the process by which cities evolved from centers of physical production to headquarters of knowledge and financial, nonphysical capital. A confluence of several different economic changes occurred. First, globalization affected all areas of business—the outsourcing of production to developing countries with cheaper wages and materials and the business deals and exchanges across major cities around the world. Part of these business deals were linked to the rise of financial markets as a key area of profit generation and their geographical concentration in major cities. These economic interactions were characterized by instantaneous exchanges among people and firms which required centralized, dense contact that emerged in a few major global cities, including New York, London, Hong Kong, and Tokyo. Finally, the financial industry required accompanying services (accounting, law, and public relations) in close proximity. While the rebirth of cities due to financial activities and what Sassen calls "high level producer services" occurred initially in the aforementioned centers, other cities were also experiencing the exodus of manufacturing and the influx of knowledge and innovation-driven industries, which also included technology (Boston, San Francisco) and creative industries (Los Angeles, New York).[7]

By the 2000s, cities were back in vogue. Part of what explains this phenomenon is that cities have become the nexus of the new global economic structure that prizes intangible skills, education, innovation, and creativity—Sassen's high level producer services are the underpinnings of what others have called the "knowledge economy," "symbolic

analysts," or the "creative class."[8] The restructuring of the global economy from widgets and factories to people and ideas most clearly impacted cities.[9] The need for proximity to exchange ideas and the desire
for instant access to the immaterial resources of density put a premium
on the dense urban geography. And as cities (and specifically the companies located within them) demand more skilled workers, these labor
market elites get paid more than others as a result of their education and
skills, and a highly clustered pattern of affluent, educated labor market
elite emerges. Around the world, the city is in the midst of a renaissance
as both companies and the people who work in them are flocking back
into the city.

This transformation has been rapid and profound. Stanford economist Rebecca Diamond found that between 1980 and 2000, the population of college-educated New Yorkers increased by 73%, while the population of non-college-educated decreased by 15%. This trend exists
across the country in highly skilled metros where the uptick in the educated is rapid and corresponds with an erosion of lower skilled workers.[10] Storper observes that from the late 1990s to early 2000s, cities in
general—old, cold, sprawling, or sunny—grew as a result of firm location and the skilled labor that followed. That cities as diverse as Atlanta,
New York, Los Angeles, and Chicago have all experienced significant
population growth suggests that it is not the specificity of cities but
rather the qualities of urbanity—density and diversity—that maximize
the work and profit-generation of the twenty-first century. Further,
labor market elites have the luxury of choosing to work close to where
they live, and many choose to minimize commuting time that impacts
their quality of life. Again, the attributes of the city most appeal to the
preferences of the new elites.[11] As Paul Krugman succinctly observed of
the phenomenon, "In general, this high-income elite gets what it wants,
and what it has wanted, since 2000, has been to live near the center of big
cities."[12]

Thus, the city has become the defining geography of the twenty-first-
century aspirational class and its distinctive ways of living. These elites'
desire to live close to their place of work has catalyzed cities and their
entrepreneurs to offer more restaurants, boutiques, cafés, and entertainment that reflect their values and consumer preferences. These days, people live in cities for reasons that are not simply financial or practical but

rather are related to what the city at large has to offer. Inspired by the successful rehabilitation of major metros, other smaller cities like Boulder, Pittsburgh, and St. Louis also undertook a renaissance—retrofitting industrial lofts for residential living, bringing more amenities into the city, paving bike paths and pedestrian-friendly walkways to attract members of the creative class (thought to be the lifeblood of the new economy).[13] Local politicians and developers advocate for active street life, coffee shops, and live music as a part of the new urbanity. Countless new-build developments around the country in both urban and suburban areas offer residential, shopping, and restaurants as a combined experience for the consumer. While some of these developments are in downtown (Zappos' founder Tony Hsieh's Las Vegas Downtown Project, Chicago's New City, or the Los Angeles Staples Center), many simply replicate the downtown experience with sidewalks, outdoor music, and cafés and apartments overlooking the "street life" (Santana Row in Silicon Valley, the Grove in Los Angeles, or the uber-luxury Bal Harbour shops in Florida). Some 150 years after the Industrial Revolution took hold of the metropolis, long after the last factory closed shop, the city has become the center of consumption, rather than production, of material goods.

Harvard economist Ed Glaeser has spent the last few decades trying to understand this relationship between consumption and city growth. The previous understanding of cities was that they were good for production but bad for consumption. As the Industrial Revolution and its aftermath spread wholly into western cities, urban centers became overcrowded (which increased the spread of disease), environmentally polluted, and essentially taken over by commerce and production processes. Cities became, in short, unpleasant places to live. One only has to glance at Frederick Engels's study of Manchester or read Kenneth Jackson's *Crabgrass Frontier* to get a sense of the horrors of the industrial metropolis. Those who could leave did so. Housing stock declined as the resources and people needed to maintain it were no longer there to do so. In the United States, this exodus was further catalyzed by the US government's FHA loans and GI Bill to support home ownership, which was primarily awarded to those purchasing homes in the suburbs. These efforts were implicitly racist through redlining and restrictive covenants, leaving out huge minority communities who were not given loans and were essentially trapped in a deteriorating urban core.[14] For several decades, starting in the mid-twentieth century, cities were replaced by suburbs as the desired place to live.[15]

This dynamic went on for decades. But Glaeser's work suggests the opposite is true today. Currently, the headquarters of the global economy are in major metros and their labor market elites are there too. These new elites desire dense, culturally rich neighborhoods that offer rich amenities and consumption options. Cities offering the greatest opportunities to consume are thriving. The dominant intellectual paradigm in urban economics is what is termed the New Neo-Classical Urban Economics (NNUE), which argues that individual and firm preferences around "amenity value," or quality of life, explain the location choices of companies and labor market elites. By way of example, one of the reasons that older, industrial cities experienced a rebirth is a result of consumption options and social interaction that was attractive to highly skilled workers.[16] Empirically, this theory has borne out in twenty-first-century cities: In work with fellow economists Jed Kolko and Albert Saiz, Glaeser finds that high amenity cities—those with parks, opera houses, an abundance of restaurants and retail—grew much faster than low amenity cities. In fact, the concentration of amenities in 1980 predicted subsequent population growth over the next decade. They also find that urban rents are much higher than urban wages, suggesting that the demand to live in cities can't be explained simply by the practicality of getting paid more. But the average city dweller is willing to put up with higher rents because of what urban life has to offer. What determines a city's success—and delineates the global urban hierarchy—is the extent to which a city offers consumption options to its inhabitants.[17] As cities become important sites of skilled human capital, those who run cities and own businesses within them generate amenities that make urban living worthwhile and interesting to these highly sought-after workers.[18] Thus the process of being a center of the global economy and an important consumption zone for the new elites goes in lockstep.

Glaeser and his colleagues break down amenities into four different types: local goods, aesthetics, public services, and speed. The latter three types of amenities are fairly straightforward: People like good schools and low crime and nice architecture, (reasonable) weather, and parks. People want good transportation systems like subways and bike paths and proximity to the central business district. So, on the surface, it's no surprise that Manhattan or London, with their sprawling public space, efficient subway systems, low crime, and strong schools (if you're in the right neighborhood) are so desirable. But it's more complicated when it comes to the local consumer options, and importantly, the eclectic mix that one city offers versus another.

Since the post-medieval period, we have witnessed a rise in real incomes and the emergence of a post-scarcity society.[19] These developments mean that, despite rising inequality, the general population in Western industrialized countries has more money and, specifically, more of it to devote to secondary and tertiary needs, after taking care of basic necessities. So the world over, most people are buying more goods. From a spatial perspective, this means that the most desirable places to live often have more desirable types of consumption. Big, "alpha" cities like New York, London, Hong Kong, San Francisco, Los Angeles, or Paris all offer many iterations of premium consumption options: a perfect cappuccino, a meal at a good restaurant, or a designer dress. And the local influence—good curry houses in London, great pizza in Chicago, baguettes in Paris—is what makes these cities distinct in what they produce alongside the endless string of cafés and boutiques. The concentration of different people, and lots of them, is what enables the curry houses to flourish—so many people skilled to produce a particular good and so many wanting to consume it.[20]

People themselves also become local goods that others want to be around, and their specificity and uniqueness in different cities make certain places desirable in different ways. We want to be around people with whom we can share ideas, culture, and stories, people who read the same books and watch the same movies. We are ultimately social animals and connect around a series of norms and shared identities. Part of this connectivity is an outcome of industry: those working in country music tend to live in Nashville and not only increase their productivity by working near each other and sharing ideas around composition notes or lyrics, but also tend to share an enjoyment in the same topics at dinner parties and bars. The clustering of people for work, whether finance or film or publishing, produces cohesive social groups that allow for shared identity. So, along with simply getting a job, people seek out places where the consumption of their social and personal lives is maximized.[21]

This social consumption is also how people end up meeting the people they want to date, marry, and create a family with, and with whom they form lifelong friendships. If you are a bachelor screenwriter, the prospects of your dating life are more interesting in Los Angeles than Miami; in the former, you will likely find more potential partners with whom you have things in common. Increasingly, as cities are sites of intellectual production (finance, technology, the arts) rather than industrial production, they are also the nexus where the very skilled end up meeting each other and having kids, thus becoming the ultimate power couples and producing children who grow up to become the same.[22] Much of the concern around inequality stems from the social and economic bifurcation between the skilled and the less skilled and the opportunities that exist for them and future generations. The roots of this phenomenon can be traced to the dating market of urban centers (particularly as people marry like, rather than marrying "up" or "down," a twenty-first-century trend economists term "assortative mating"[23]). Smart people want to be around other smart people not just for work, but also for friendships and romantic relationships, and over time that results in highly stratified hyper-educated affluent places where, as the economist Tyler Cowen remarked, "Money and talent become clustered in high-powered, two-earner families determined to do everything possible to advance the interests of their children."[24]

The social and economic interplay of urban inhabitants enables and promotes cities as the ultimate sites of consumption. A sizable number of the people in today's metropolis are more highly skilled and as a result more highly paid than most and they demand luxurious consumption options—whether art galleries, prestigious preschools, or cocktail bars. Niche entrepreneurs and multinational companies like Chanel and Cartier are responding to this desire in kind. Aside from high-end handbags and watches, the uptick in urban restaurants, bars, and even nail salons, gives people channels to spend their extra money, and makes cities all the more appealing to live in. Glaeser found that between 1998 and 2008, employment in Manhattan restaurants increased by more than 50%, suggesting that the demand for consumer options is being met with supply.[25]

Ironically, city living and all of its rich consumption options is a relative bargain for the wealthy (even if everyone else is struggling to pay the rent; more on this later). We know that taste varies with income. Part of this observation is simply a result of rich people having more money and therefore more disposable income to spend. But the fact that in a general sense, wealthy people might seek out similar basic goods to one another—free-range chickens, organic milk, nice restaurants, and massages—means that cities as home to the affluent tend to cater to their consumption needs specifically. One need only take a short stroll around Santa Monica to see an excess of day spas, organic tea houses, vegan restaurants, and other peculiarities of the rich in action. Jessie Handbury, a professor at Wharton, calls this phenomenon "income specific tastes." Handbury finds that wealthy people not only seek out variety in their luxury goods (for example, many may like gourmet cheese, but appreciate a selection from a variety of countries) but they also care very little about fluctuations in price. They are not paying attention to the rise in beef or milk prices that are reported in the nightly news. But by virtue of living in a city, these wealthy people are spending less on those nice goods anyway. Studying 40,000 American households and 500 food items, Handbury finds that the rich (those making more than $100,000 per year) spend 20% less on groceries in high per capita cities (New York, San Francisco) than if they lived in seemingly more affordable cities (like Detroit or Atlanta).[26] Manicures are cheaper in cities: New Yorkers spend $3 less on a manicure than any of the other top ten biggest cities.[27] The luxury of consumption offered by cities starts to look pretty lopsided: Not only do urban denizens have more consumer options but they also pay less for them.

Underpinning these findings are the basics of microeconomics: economies of scale and scope. Or, simply put, in urban centers there are plenty of people who will partake in the same types of consumption (economies of scale) to uphold amenities like baseball stadiums, opera houses, and theaters and will drive down fixed costs for expenditures such as massages, organic food, and happy hour. Simultaneously, there are enough people that the "long tail" of consumption (economies of scope)—ethnic restaurants, high-end boutiques, and avant-garde theater—will also be in demand. This interplay of significant demand for the same things and the large sum of idiosyncrasies that emerge from having so many people with diverse backgrounds and preferences in the same place is what propels so many choices in urban centers. The sheer number of diverse inhabitants both drives the endless options of city amenities to be produced and creates the lines around the corner for every noodle/cupcake/cronut shop in town. In short, demand meets supply irrespective of the product or service. The basic fact that many city women demand manicures means that salons open to respond to this demand, and those very same salons are competing and thus adjust their price accordingly. The same holds true for organic heirloom tomatoes—which are not sold at just one grocer, as might be the case in a small town in Kansas. Instead, one only needs to walk a few blocks to find five different grocery stores catering to this desire. The sheer volume of suppliers and demand is what makes luxury so much cheaper in affluent cities—an all-around unfair reality of the twenty-first-century consumer city.

When urbanites do bemoan the cost of living in New York or Los Angeles, they are actually demonstrating their detachment from the reality of the rest of America. Five dollars is a lot for a coffee, yes, but no one in small-town West Virginia or Pennsylvania is even considering that purchase, let alone the $500 pair of shoes—neither of which are uncommon urbanite purchases. Handbury explains that it's not so much that cities' basic consumer items are more expensive (according to her, items like milk are less expensive in cities), but rather that people's tastes become more expensive when they live in a city. And, as Rebecca Diamond finds, cities offer what she calls "hidden amenities"—access to (other) elites, lovely parks to stroll through, safe streets, diverse options for take-out—all of which improve well-being by 30% more than any standard-of-living index captures. The little prosaic things, not necessarily the designer shoes and expensive meals, make daily life more pleasant for the upwardly mobile and skilled.[28] In big and small ways, cities are the critical consumption zones for the global elite.

SCENES OF CONSUMPTION

Rich urban denizens may generally like the same luxuries, but they of course like them with modifications. Standing in line at a Starbucks listening to the order for a skinny "half-caf" latte with extra foam, and two squirts of sugar-free caramel, brings these bizarre permutations of the urbanite into sharp relief. Even neighborhoods cultivate their own version of the luxury urban consumption experience—whether Venice and its penchant for washable cashmere shirts or Beverly Hills's more standard Hermès approach to luxury. The same goes for Chicago's bohemian Wicker Park versus Gold Coast neighborhoods. Boston's moneyed Beacon Hill and intellectual Cambridge may be wildly different in taste, but both offer rich consumer options that distinctly cater to their respective inhabitants. University of Chicago sociologist Terry Clark believes these different amalgamations of consumption "scenes" comprise the "city as entertainment machine." "Quality of life is not a mere by-product of production," Clark writes with fellow sociologist Richard Lloyd, "it defines and drives the new processes of production."[29] The city is where the intangible and vague notion of quality of life materializes in specific goods and services that respond to the different preferences of the urban dweller. Clark's research tries to get at how these generalized dynamics of urban living play out in specific places. Rather than look at particular people, or particular locations, Clark looks at what people do and how they consume as a way to understand urban identities: glamour zones like Beverly Hills and Madison Avenue, with excessive conspicuous consumption and luxury goods; the Bohemian inclinations of Notting Hill, Soho, or Venice; or the more conventional behaviors of the middle class as found in the Upper West Side or Pasadena. But the same places can be different things to different people—Beverly Hills is at once home to a rich person, a place of semi-frequent conspicuous consumption to another, and a source of amusement and spectacle to yet another.[30]

CITIES ARE THE SAME, CITIES ARE DIFFERENT

Consumption may define the urban experience generally, but Los Angeles and San Francisco, despite both being Californian cities, couldn't be more different from one another, not just in the idiosyncrasies of their micro-scenes of glamour or grit, but also on a macro level. These cities are of course both great meccas of urbanity and all of its trappings—luxury coffee, great restaurants, museums, and big sports stadiums. But if you confused a San Franciscan with an Angelino, the former would be deeply insulted, priding himself on a bohemian intellectualism that the latter surely lacks. Angelinos find New Yorkers neurotic, New Yorkers find Chicagoans too Midwestern, and so forth. Herein lies a simple but important point about cities and their consumption: As New York is known for finance and fashion, San Francisco for technology, Detroit for automobiles, and Los Angeles for film and video games, the cities' consumption options are equally important in underpinning their identities.

Cities, when examined through consumption patterns, are no more similar to each other than they are to the average small town. In fact, most small towns have more in common with each other than two randomly chosen metros. This may seem obvious at first blush, but most of the research on cities has attempted to understand a larger pattern of urbanity—the way in which we understand cities as a unified whole. In his famous 1938 essay, *Urbanism as a Way of Life*, University of Chicago sociologist Louis Wirth set out to define the city through three criteria: size, heterogeneity, and density.[31] Many have followed suit: Henri Lefebvre, the French Marxist philosopher, argued that we are experiencing an "urban revolution" (indeed, 82% of the US population and more than half of the world are urban) and that the city needs to be studied as its own field, much like biology or physics. More recently, the Santa Fe Institute physicist, Geoffrey West, has constructed complicated equations and amassed big data to argue that regardless of size, density, or heterogeneity, deep, highly predictable structures uphold the city and urban patterns. West believes we can explain city functions and patterns through equations with 85% accuracy.[32] For example, a city's crime level, amount of waste, number of grocery stores, and so forth can be determined simply by knowing a city's population size. Other work by Marta Gonzalez of the Massachusetts Institute of Technology and her colleagues, finds that humans exhibit a generalizable mobility pattern. Studying 100,000 people's phone and text patterns from a six-million-person sample, Gonzalez and her colleagues find that a majority of people spend most of their time in four distinct locations. Even if most of us live and work in different locations, our spatial pattern is roughly predictable. In fact, the researchers went on to break out the individuals into three different groups to see if any differences might emerge, and found the behavior to be exactly the same. The groups were "largely indistinguishable" from one another.[33] The entire studied population tended to mainly make four stops to the same places and made those stops on a daily basis. So while the stops themselves were to different locations, the pattern of behavior is the same irrespective of where one lives, one's race, occupation, or any other demographic or economic characteristics. They therefore conclude that it is possible to predict where people are at particular points in time with great accuracy and understand their movement, irrespective of where they are in a city or the city in which they reside.

As impressive as such approaches are in construction, execution, and findings, this new wave of research doesn't tell us anything substantive about what it really means to be human, to live in a city, and what are the qualitative differences between those four different locations for one person versus another. For example, the four stops for a man who lives in Chicago might be leaving his four-bedroom house in the affluent Gold Coast in the morning to go for a run, stopping at a café for a coffee, heading to his finance job in downtown Chicago, and stopping at some organic café after work to pick up a dinner of wild salmon and organic broccoli. These four stops are meaningfully different from those of an hourly worker, single mom who might be battling the DC Beltway on her way to drop off one of her kids at daycare, and the other at elementary school, who then travels many more miles to a job that doesn't pay the bills, to a harried after work pick-up of her kids, to a much less salubrious grocery store experience with limited fruit and vegetable options, before going to her perhaps much less safe, smaller apartment. Both days can be described in four stops, but the lives described are so incredibly different, and the data tell us nothing about these very different experiences of people living in the same city, let alone the millions of other people who also live in a city.

These data do not really describe the people who live there and what their lives are actually like. Generalizable patterns of city life are only superficial. Even Geoffrey West himself, after looking at all the models and data, remains puzzled by the ongoing mysteries of cities—why do we put up with them and what makes them so compelling (despite their high rent, cockroaches, and overzealous, cutthroat competition)?[34]

What's clear is that cities as a whole are often understood only in broad strokes—those key criteria Wirth outlined some 75 years ago, to which we've made small additions in more recent research. Yes, cities are big and dense and diverse, just as villages are small, often racially homogeneous, and offer a more physically sprawling living experience of farmland or ample backyards. But what does that tell you about growing up in a small town in Missouri versus one in Mississippi? Yes, cities offer more amenities, but someone who likes a daily bike ride and the outdoor life isn't going to necessarily appreciate the half cream, half coffee specialty of sidewalk vendors and the Barney's Warehouse Sale as amenities; he may instead view these staples of the New York City identity as a nuisance. What makes urban life meaningful are the small components that ultimately define and vastly differentiate the city experience in San Francisco, Paris, Hong Kong, or Chicago.

THE SUM OF CITY LIFE

It's hard to get at the small stuff, for sure. Some of it, the peculiarities of architecture, the history, the types of books people read and then discuss at dinner parties and book clubs, is almost impossible to articulate with any precision on a macro scale. But how we consume suggests particular values, preferences, and in turn what we might be talking about at those dinner parties in different cities. And that's something we can track. When my doctoral student Hyojung Lee and I consulted the Consumer Expenditure Survey to see the thousands of things that Americans consume and parsed out the data by city, we found that part of our qualitative understanding of city difference can be understood through the lens of what the people in them consume.

Through the lens of detailed consumption patterns, cities appear to have very little in common with one another, other than those broad generalizations. This single observation explains why, whether Dodgers versus Giants fans or Chicago versus New York pizza, we see such antagonism between particular metropolises, and their respective urbanites, and why we can't make sense of cities as a cohesive unit and must look at each of them individually. Rather, city dwellers are an amalgamation of people just as different from one another as they are from other countries or villages. When we look at consumption data, inhabitants of Los Angeles really do appear to have come from a different planet from those in Miami or Dallas. In the next section, I will break down these differences by how we eat, drink our coffee, drink alcohol, decorate our homes, and date, among other things that form the days of our urban lives.[35]

WHAT WE EAT

In some basic ways, we can see that some cities are healthier than others, and the data show that Los Angeles, New York, Miami, and San Francisco are home to the biggest fruit and vegetable consumers. Angelinos consistently spend 30–40% more of their total expenditures on fresh vegetables and between 10% and 40% more on fruit than any other city, except San Francisco.

Miami rivals Los Angeles in its fruit consumption. New Yorkers and San Franciscans aren't quite as health-conscious, but they too spend significantly more on fruit and vegetables. On the one hand, some of these findings make sense. Miami and Los Angeles are located in two of the most agriculturally rich states in the country, and unsurprisingly, the produce tastes better, and as a result of abundance, is less expensive than in other cities. But there is also a cultural dynamic at play: These cities are home to people who care a lot about health and looking good. New York City has long been the capital of Tom Wolfe's "social x-rays," and the warm weather and beach scenes typical of Los Angeles and Miami put pressure on everyone to care at least a little bit about looking good without much clothing on.

Conversely, it should come as no surprise that Dallas, Houston, Philadelphia, and Baltimore rank as the lowest consumers of fresh vegetables and fruit. One could make the geographical argument that they are simply farther away from fresh produce, but so is New York City. These are also cities known for steak, barbeque, beer, and comfort foods. Philadelphia cheesesteak sandwiches may not be a daily habit but they do reflect a culture that is more meat than kale. The cattle ranches in Texas offer an abundance of good beef. The culture of these cities and the best of their offerings propel consumer habits. However, for some cities the explanation is economic: Baltimore and Philadelphia are home to a greater share of low-income population. As has been long documented, grocery stores in poorer neighborhoods often do not provide fresh fruit and vegetable options, creating what sociologists and urban planners call "food deserts." Low-income inhabitants often must rely on processed and high-fat foods to feed their families.

Candy, chewing gum, cola, and artificial sweeteners are popular in the Midwest but for the most part are avoided in coastal cities. Northeast cities consistently spend less than the national average by a significant amount. In 2010, for example, New Yorkers spent about half as much as most cities spend on artificial sweeteners and 55% less on candy and chewing gum. (The only exception is Boston, which spends about 60% more than the national average on artificial sweeteners and about 15% more on candy and chewing gum.) In general, city dwellers do not consume these items as compared to the rest of the country.

Non-metro areas consume a lot of artificial sweeteners, cola, fats, oils, and fresh milk and cream—exactly the items that city dwellers don't buy. They also buy more frozen and canned vegetables and fruit rather than fresh. These are items that are, across the board, rarely bought in cities. This difference may simply be a matter of practicality; most people living in cities don't have big freezers and pantries, and affluent city neighborhoods offer easy access to fresh produce. Those living outside of cities and their suburbs also dine out a lot less than city dwellers, who have access to the other foodstuffs (like butter and cream) in their restaurant and take-out consumption.

WHAT WE DRINK

We often think of coffee as a distinctly urban drink—frenzied neurotic city dwellers consuming it by the gallon. Yet, interestingly, other than a few cities, urban dwellers are not drinking or spending more on coffee than everyone else in the country. In fact, New York City, home to what we thought was the crazed, coffee-addicted urbanite, actually consumes less than the national average by about 30%. The real urban coffee drinkers are not Seattle or San Francisco either—but Boston, Detroit, Philadelphia, and the suburbs of Los Angeles, where share of total expenditure on coffee is up to 20% higher than the national average expenditure share. Where Seattle spends the most is in roasted coffee—which is of course part of the city's culture and export market. Insofar as there is a trend in caffeine consumption, city inhabitants generally consume more tea than the rest of the country, particularly in the Northeast in New York City and Philadelphia. Could this be a vestige from the days of Edith Wharton? Possibly, although true to New York's reputation as a pioneer of cultural trends, equally it could be the next best thing and the one that other places haven't caught on to yet. When it comes to bottled water, Los Angeles inhabitants spend up to 75% more than the rest of the country. This appears to be one of the defining consumption products of the city, as no other city even comes close to its numbers.

As a whole, urban dwellers have something in common when it comes to nonalcoholic beer, dining out, and drinking wine. They consume none of the country's nonalcoholic beer (and I mean none of it) and universally spend more money on dining out and drinking wine—social activities that go hand in hand. San Francisco, San Diego, New York, and Boston have been known to spend more than twice as much on wine, in total expenditure, than the national average. And for those cities that are less likely to drink wine—Philadelphia and Detroit—they make up for it in beer and cocktails. Generally, beer is less of an urban drink than wine or cocktails, although Boston and Minneapolis are overachievers in all areas of alcoholic consumption. Only Miami is a teetotaler across the board, spending about 40% less than the rest of the country on alcoholic beverages.

HOME IS WHERE THE MONEY IS

Cities may offer cheaper goods, but when it comes to homeownership and running a household, urbanites spend significantly more for the privilege of location. Parks, an abundance of museums, coffee shops on every corner, and ample shopping—all of those "hidden amenities" and consumption options—are factored into the cost of homeownership and rent in cities. Across most major cities, inhabitants devote significantly more of their share of expenditures to housing than the national average. By share of expenditure, I mean that, of a household's outgoing costs, the greatest percentage (or share) is devoted to housing. By this measure, New York City spends the most—about 50% more than the national average share of expenditure—this includes renters and owners (an important distinction I will explain below). The most expensive housing market overall, in terms of average annual spending, is in San Francisco. Severely hit by economic hardship, Detroit and Cleveland have lower housing expenses than the national average. The housing markets in these cities have not rebounded, which may account for cheaper housing and an overall depressed urban economy (less employment means fewer people can afford to buy houses which further drives down demand which impacts housing prices)—both of which detract from these cities' desirability and competitiveness in the housing market. But housing can also be cheaper when there is a lot of available space on which to build. Houston and Dallas, with their more relaxed zoning and love of sprawl, are home to those who devote significantly less of their overall expenditures on owning a home than the national average (that's including less expensive rural areas). In short, owning or renting a home in a depressed housing market or in one where there is more land and thus more housing means that housing prices are cheaper and generally mortgages are a smaller part of a household's overall expenditures.

Despite the multi-million-dollar price tag of houses in their cities, what may give San Franciscans and New Yorkers pause is that they spend a remarkably small amount and share of their total expenditures on *homeownership* (as opposed to renting, which shows very different trends that I will discuss shortly). For San Francisco, arguably the hottest real estate market in the country, housing expenditure shares on owning a home are only 20% more than the national average. In 2012, San Franciscans spent less than the national average in their share of expenditures devoted to owning a home (11.8% of total expenditures nationally versus 11.5% for San Franciscans). New Yorkers (as in those who live in one of the five boroughs) consistently spend 20–25% less than the national average on homeownership and in 2009 spent a third less than everyone else. These last two numbers may surprise both those living in these cities and anyone aware of the high cost of housing associated with them as well. But remember, the calculation is share of total expenditures—not absolute dollars. Homeowners in San Francisco or New York are those who earn much more sizable incomes and can more comfortably afford the high prices. So even if New York or San Francisco houses or apartments sell in the millions, those who can afford them are already making so much more than everyone that, as a share of total outgoing costs, housing takes up less of a proportion than it would with a less wealthy group of home buyers (in Orlando, Florida or Atlanta, Georgia, for example). Also, homeownership in New York is less common than renting, which may bring the overall average down. When you consider absolute dollars devoted to homeownership, New Yorkers still spend less than everyone else, in terms of average annual expenditures on owned dwellings, while San Francisco's housing market is one of the most expensive in the country, behind Washington, DC (in 2007 average absolute spending in San Francisco was more than two times that of New York City). Yet here, too, as a share of expenditures, housing does not dominate, confirming that people in San Francisco generally have sufficiently high incomes that, for those who buy rather than rent homes, homeownership does not dominate their spending.

The way to understand the impact of these cities' housing costs on the average city dweller is to examine expenditures on housing for those who *rent*, where New York City, San Francisco, and Miami households devote huge amounts of their spending. No matter how comfortable a local housing market is, for most people, a mortgage is often a huge chunk of total expenditures. Even for a home in a reasonably priced housing market, thousands of dollars may be devoted to a mortgage every month. Rent, however, fluctuates wildly from $550 a month for a luxury one bedroom, 600-square-foot apartment in Cleveland to more than $2,500 for the same space in Manhattan. Because more urban dwellers rent than own, rent is a good measure of what's really going on for the majority of people living in cities. As both a share of expenditures and in absolute dollars, the rent in major cities is very expensive. New Yorkers spend 300% of the national average on rent (an average of more than $8,000 per year, which is almost four times more than Minneapolis, twice as much as DC, and more than twice as much as Chicago, Boston, Seattle, or Phoenix). According to StreetEasy, the average rent in New York City was predicted to be $2,700 in 2015—that's almost 60% of median income in the city (the rule of thumb is that a household should be spending 30% or less of before-tax income on housing). Between 2000 and 2013, New York City rental prices grew almost two times the pace of income, with this trend impacting low-income neighborhoods the most.[36]

The second most expensive rental market is San Francisco, where the average household spends anywhere from 50% to 80% more than the national average (but double the rent for smaller, less expensive cities like Phoenix, Houston, Dallas, or Philadelphia). As a share of their total outgoings, Los Angeles and San Diego households spend more than twice the national average on rent expenditures. There are a few ways to look at these numbers. First, these are some of the most desirable places to live, but many people cannot afford to buy a home so the rental market is very heated and rentals are in short supply. Second, in some cities those who rent rather than buy have less total income and thus a greater share of their income and expenditures is devoted to housing as well as food and clothes. Finally, some of these cities—New York, San Francisco, and DC, for example—are experiencing an influx of uber-luxury apartment complexes that are really an option only for the superrich. This type of building is essentially creating a "two-tier" rental market between the superrich and everyone else.[37] As those luxury apartments absorb the housing demand of the superrich, and as people who would have been owners stay in the rental market, the share on housing may seem lower than expected in New York and San Francisco (which may explain why San Francisco's share of expenditures on rent is lower than that of San Diego—the former city simply has many more richer tenants who pull down the average share of income devoted to rent). Other cities around the country are experiencing almost the inverse trend: In Minneapolis, Chicago, and Baltimore, people spend slightly more than the national average in share of expenditures devoted to homeownership, but they spend significantly less on rent.

Another unique aspect of the urban housing market is the vacation home—something most Americans never consider as a purchase. The vacation home is a hallmark of urban spending—again reflecting the general affluence of those living in cities compared to those living elsewhere. New York, Philadelphia, San Francisco, and Chicago take the lead here: On average, New Yorkers spend 242% of the national average on vacation homes, Philadelphians spend 175%, San Franciscans 164%, and Chicagoans spend 152%. In 2008, New Yorkers spent up to 436% of the national average in share of expenditures on vacation homes.

(Incidentally, after the Great Recession, New Yorkers reined in spending on vacation homes. In 2012, they spent "just" 213% of the national average, while Washington, DC and Boston both increased their vacation home expenditures to 205% of the national average. Philadelphia, San Francisco, and Chicago all significantly reduced their spending on vacation homes, spending just 14–41% more than the average American household.) You might think that New Yorkers buy expensive vacation homes given that they devote greater percentages of their expenditures to vacation homes than anywhere else in the country (from 2007 to 2012 they spent on average 1.3% of total expenditures on vacation homes compared to the national average of 0.6%), and that might be true— vacation homes in the Hamptons cost many millions of dollars. But it's also the case that New Yorkers appear to spend so much more than everyone else because just a very slim margin of the population purchases a vacation home, which is in itself a luxury consumer choice far removed from the normalcy of milk and eggs and owning *one* home.

NANNIES, HOUSEKEEPERS, AND THE PRICE OF TIME

Similarly, child care in the form of nannies over daycare is an urban luxury and reality especially in Washington, DC, and the Connecticut and New Jersey suburbs.[38] Without question, nannies cost more in cities, but people in cities tend to work more, too, and those labor market elites tend to have the money to afford nannies versus daycare. Again, in the case of New York, there is a self-selection bias: Those who can afford nannies tend to make enough money that the expenditure makes only a tiny dent in overall expenditures.

Housekeeping services are also a remarkably urban phenomenon, with New York, Los Angeles, and San Francisco spending almost double the rest of the country (whereas housekeeping supplies is a disproportionately non-metro purchase). Most city households spend more than the national average, reflecting both the abundance of such services in cities (making it easy to find a regular housekeeper) but also the need for outsourcing because of the work schedules of urban workers. Much like nannies and daycare, housekeeping buys back time, allowing people to work the hours they need to be productive in high-pressure careers, but also to use their free time for activities other than washing the dishes and vacuuming.

KEEPING UP WITH THE JONES'S IN DIFFERENT WAYS

When I was a graduate student in New York City, I lived in a 400-square-foot studio, I slept on a twin bed, ate a breakfast of a muffin and a coffee on the go while walking to the library, and I wrote my dissertation and first book at a small Target-purchased imitation wood desk squashed next to a bookcase crammed with Marx, microeconomics textbooks, and most of my literary fiction collection, stacked high with journal articles atop those books. The desk was a mere two feet from my bed. I remember near the end of my time in graduate school, my best friend walked into my Upper West Side studio one winter day, looked around, and said, "You'd better finish up that doctorate soon because your apartment looks like that of a serial killer." I graduated that May.

Inside those stuffed closets (I had two that were so small it was hard to even fit a winter coat) and under that small bed, I had literally mountains of expensive clothing I had no business owning. The clothes, heaped on my coffee table or stuffed into one of those tiny closets, were the entire collections of Intermix and Barney's Co-op, and yet most nights I subsisted on cold Chinese takeout or pizza, eaten standing up over the kitchen sink before I headed out for an evening of fun adventures with my friends.

What was paradoxical was that I could have used at least some money on reasonable furniture from Ikea, or perhaps spent a little less time shopping and going out with my friends and more on tidying up my apartment, but the incentives weren't there—no one came over anyway. No one really hosted dinner parties or had people over for coffee. People did everything outside of their home in the cafés and bars located on all corners of the city. Working on my first book, I remember interviewing Ingrid Sichy, editor of *Interview* magazine at the time, and she said the same thing, unprompted by me—that the city was one's dining room, living room, and extended home—rather than the apartment, which is just where we went to sleep at night. Sichy, friend of Andy Warhol, glamorous cultural icon on the New York City scene, was, just like the rest of us, merely paying rent to actually live and be entertained in the city at large.

Thus it is no surprise at all to see that many urban households seem to have similar priorities. Across all cities, urbanites reveal remarkably less expenditure share than the national average on household textiles, bathroom and bedroom linens, furniture, and silver serving pieces—all the trappings of the tidy, beautifully maintained home. As a whole, their expenditure share on televisions is lower than the national average and non-metro areas. New York City, Philadelphia, Detroit, DC, and Atlanta spend the least of all cities on TVs. Sure, there are some exceptions— New York City likes its decorative pillows. Houston and Dallas like textiles and furniture, and Chicagoans consistently spend just above average on TVs—but the trend is clear. Urban folks spend their money on things outside of the material goods of the home. They may outsource labor to make their home lives easier, but they are not spending money on the material aspects of their homes. This decision is in part because they eat and entertain outside the home. It may also be due to the transient nature of many people's urban experience—people live in cities for some parts of their lives, then they get married, have kids, and move to the suburbs, which is when they start to care about sofas and bathroom towels.

Yet, another important aspect of this pattern is that urbanites spend so much time outside of their homes that their materialism is devoted to their own external physical appearance, rather than that of their internal world, thus encapsulating Georg Simmel's early-twentieth-century observation of eccentric urbanites who use clothing as a quick signal of identity and individuality.[39] When we look at both men's and women's apparel and footwear we find exactly this trend: People in cities spend more on shoes and clothes. Certain cities are acutely emblematic of this trend. As a share of their outgoing expenditures, New York City women spend two times more on shoes than everyone else. As far as women's clothes go, Dallas and New York City are home to the biggest spenders, unsurprising given the ostentatious need-to-be-seen nature of both cities' cultures. New York City and Washington, DC are home to the biggest spenders on men's shoes—likely a result of being the epicenters of two male-dominated industries: finance and politics. While most cities spend an average amount on watches, New York City and Los Angeles spend more by a large margin. In fact, in 2010, New Yorkers spent about 27 times more on watches as a share of total expenditures than everyone else—no city even compares. In absolute dollars, New Yorkers spent more than $1,300 on average on a watch in 2010, while Los Angeles is significantly more modest at $105. While watches can cost many tens of thousands, and $105 isn't so unreasonable, remember the number is an average, so plenty of households are reporting spending nothing at all and still New Yorkers spent in excess of a thousand dollars on watches per household. Even though LA is ranked second in terms of share devoted to watch-buying, it's but a tenth of New York's spending.

Watches may price out most people, even city folks, but those inexpensive manicures (and massages and facials) are a lure for urbanites across the board. New Yorkers, Miamians, and the DC set are the biggest spenders on personal care services, but pretty much everyone except the crunchy bohemians of Seattle are a part of the trend. Yet, for all the money spent on massages, trainers, exercise classes, and haircuts, urbanites actually spend very little of their total expenditures on beauty products like hairspray, makeup, and other accoutrements (Boston least of all). One explanation could simply be that they are spending so much energy and money on their ongoing self-care—exercise, skincare, and hair—that products like mascara are less necessary. City dwellers have sculpted themselves to some version of a natural perfect. Keep in mind, however, that exercise classes and nice haircuts cost significantly more than any tube of mascara. Another explanation for the differences in beauty and personal grooming care in cities versus non-urban areas comes down to options. Many of the self-care services are simply not on offer outside of major cities. If massages, Pilates, or meditation classes can be found in a small town, there are unlikely to be many competitors, so these services are far more expensive (remember the economies of scale for luxury urban goods). While the non-metro household is unlikely to be spending much money on Pilates instructors or weekly manicures, one can barely walk down a city block without passing an exercise studio or nail salon. Thus, relative to the urbanite, non-metro households spend much less on services but more on products, which are far more democratic and withinin their reach. Most anyone can get a tube of good mascara, but it's pretty hard to find a regular yoga or Zumba class outside of a major city. Finally, it could simply be the aesthetic culture of cities: As ostentatious as they are in some respects, there is a subtlety to many city dwellers' beauty habits. Makeup rarely looks obvious, manicures are often clear or a pale pink. The exceptions to this trend are Houston and Dallas (and Seattle, of all places), where there is more of an inclination to spend on beauty products, including wigs and hairpieces.

THE HIDDEN AND NOT-SO-HIDDEN AMENITIES OF CITIES

Irrespective of these intercity differences, there are distinct qualities of urbanity that connect cities to one another. Earlier in this chapter I discussed how cities offer experiences that are not entirely material and yet often explain the compelling nature of city living and why so many people are willing to put up with the general mayhem of city life. As previously noted, Rebecca Diamond calls these things hidden amenities.[40] Edward Glaeser sees social interaction and density as a means for city dwellers to be more productive in their work lives and maximize their potential in the marriage market.[41] Personally and professionally, people thrive when they are close together and have access to many options and resources, in much the same way that biotech research scientists or artists are most creative in concentration and socialization with others like them. Most of us enjoy being around others—we make more friends, we attain more knowledge about current trends, we meet our future spouses, and so forth. And of course a greater concentration of people provides more opportunities for these interactions to occur. We can quantify the importance of such urban social capital by studying the ways in which people spend money to attain social capital. When we want to make friends, country clubs and social clubs are a swift way to become part of a particular group of people. When we want to influence those in power, political contributions are the most direct route, and when we want to meet a boyfriend, girlfriend, husband, or wife, dating services provide us access to many other single people. All of these options are essentially monetized mechanisms for interacting with other people, and they provide an effective and efficient system in an otherwise complicated social scene. All of these things cost money, and in this realm, city dwellers spend significantly less than their suburban counterparts.

The same is true for dating services, where cities spend significantly less shares of their total expenditures than the national average. Boston, Cleveland, San Diego, and the Connecticut and New Jersey suburbs take the prize for the least interest. Perhaps those who live there feel that the city offers them all they need in their romantic life—or they're not dating at all. (Recent data indicate that in many cities, 40% to almost 50% of residents are single.)[42] More generally, whether for platonic or romantic reasons, free versions of social networks like Meet-Up, OK Cupid, and their ilk work so efficiently in big cities that costly services are less imperative. The only two exceptions to this trend are New York City and Detroit, where inhabitants spend up to 150% above the national average on dating services. While it's hard to pinpoint exactly who is spending on finding their soul mate, one might suspect that in New York City, wealthy New Yorkers might seek out their ideal mate through high-end services like Kelleher International. These types of matchmaking services (which are more old-fashioned than online dating) require entrance fees of $15,000. Some soul mate searchers will pay $150,000 to launch an international search.[43] Detroit is a bit more challenging to understand: In 2010, Detroit spent about nine times the national average on dating, which is nine times the national average spending share. Detroit's affection for Match.com and its online brethren might be explained as a result of the overall decline in population and hemorrhaging of the urban economy. Many of the "free" social benefits of living in a dense city may have eroded.

While most urbanites don't invest in dating, they do spend a lot of time on free dating services like Grindr and Tinder, which are social media apps that allow users to essentially have a geographical sense of where other potential mates are located. In a somewhat disconcerting case in point, I was eating in a Mexican restaurant in Pasadena with my friend Eric (an avid Grindr user, if only in the passive, trolling sense). While I was eating tacos, he was doing a Grindr search; it turned out that a potential mate was at a table a mere 10 feet away, as indicated by the location button on his app flashing incessantly. Since the Grindr app has to be open for a location to be traced, this guy also would also had to have his app open and would thus be aware of Eric's whereabouts, making for a rather awkward situation when neither of them made an effort to speak (or would it have been worse the other way round?). Apps like Grindr and Tinder work very well in dense urban environments because their effectiveness (and array of options) relies on proximity to others to make flash decisions about meeting up, efficiently illustrating the hidden amenities of living in cities.

In 1956, in his book *The Power Elite*, the sociologist C. Wright Mills wrote about an echelon of society he called the "Metropolitan 400," an elite set of individuals born from historically prestigious families.[44] Individuals in this group, whom Mills believed were intertwined with political, military, and corporate elite, were part of a larger conspiracy (whether conscious or not) to firmly solidify their positions as the major decision makers in all aspects of society, further separating them from what can only be called the "have-nots," thus having detrimental consequences for those not a part of this group. While Mills spends a great deal of time discussing the elites in all parts of society, the Metropolitan 400 were defined by their city address and by their membership to the Social Register, a list of local elites in particular major cities around the United States. The Metropolitan 400 was a Mills construct with acute descriptions of Brooks Brothers suits, Ivy League pedigree, and memberships to social clubs. So perturbed by the rise of democratic wealth, Mills argued, American aristocracy or "old money" looked for ways to distinguish themselves from the simply rich, and one such way was through the Social Register and its accompanying social practices and memberships.

Some 60 years later, the Social Register still exists, and the use of social clubs to create in-crowds (primarily defined by their economic status) is alive and well. Boston, San Francisco, Washington, DC, and the affluent New York suburbs of Connecticut and New Jersey spend a good 40% or more than the national average on social clubs. But there are also changes in the landscape. Some cities like Detroit, Cleveland, Dallas, and, surprisingly, New York are completely disengaged from this elitist practice. Part of this difference can be explained by what social clubs are actually about: the formalization (and monetization) of being a part of a particular group, exactly what Mills found problematic. Whether WASP high society of Boston, the elite financers of Connecti-

cut, or the political inner circles of Washington, making friends still remains hard, but in such circles writing checks to enter elite groups lubri-
cates the process. While all cities possess elites, some younger cities
don't have a lineage of old-money high society and are more egalitarian
in general—Los Angeles, Miami, and Atlanta, for example, all of which
spend less or just on average with the rest of the country on social
memberships.

CONSPICUOUS CONSUMPTION IN CITIES

Mills, like his contemporary John Kenneth Galbraith, and Thorstein Veblen before, was concerned about the social ramifications of concentrated wealth and its various signals. The pernicious and less obvious
examples are those of secret social clubs, particular accents revealing
where one studied or grew up, and the subtle cues of prestige. These
types of behaviors and practices were particularly exclusive because obvious signs of status were becoming so commonplace—lots of people
were beginning to spend on conspicuous consumption. If everyone
could afford to look rich by donning Ralph Lauren, or buying automobiles (even luxury ones), the classic material signals of wealth were less
a demarcation between the rich and the rest. No one cared who had a
nice car or wore golf shirts—these signals of affluence evolved into signals of the egalitarian American Dream. Real elitism was far more subtle
and relied on symbolic capital and social cues that were acquired in
more exclusive milieus, whether the beach houses of Cape Cod or the
Hamptons, the Ivy League or social clubs.

This phenomenon is never so obvious as it is in metropolitan America.
In studying the status goods that are a part of conspicuous consumption
—watches, jewelry, shoes, clothes, and so forth, what one might call "socially visible goods"—it's apparent that people in cities spend much more
on conspicuous consumption than anyone else—even controlling for
age, income level, education, race, occupation, and marital status.[45] Particular cities—New York City, Dallas, Los Angeles, and San Francisco—
influence their inhabitants' spending more than others. What I mean
is that, just by virtue of living in one of these cities, you will spend on
conspicuous consumption more than if you lived elsewhere. The city

itself becomes an influence on how one spends. For example, New Yorkers—regardless of how old they are, how much they earn, or whether they are black or white, married or single—spend 50% more on conspicuous consumption goods than those living outside of cities and 40% more than the nation as a whole. The other three aforementioned cities influence status spending by just under 20% more than those living outside of a city. You might think that such spending is a function of living in expensive locations, but a look at these cities' overall expenditures reveals that they spend essentially what the rest of the country does on other, more normal, less conspicuous consumption items.

Why do we see such patterns? Here we come full circle to those early urban sociologists like Louis Wirth and Georg Simmel. It is precisely the density, heterogeneity, and high visibility of city life that make status goods more worthwhile to purchase (everyone sees them, after all). When we see other people wearing nice jewelry, great shoes, or designer handbags on the subway, at the museum, on the sidewalk, there is a peer effect driving us to do the same. But equally, we purchase ostentatious and conspicuous goods as a way to show our differences. Christian Louboutin's five-inch heels are a sign of being a part of an elite fashion set while also screaming "look at me" with their bright red soles. The shoes become both a tool for fitting in and standing out, much as a Rolex, a Chanel handbag, or Porsche does as well. As the great German sociologist Georg Simmel remarked some 90 years ago in his essay "The Metropolis and Mental Life," when people move to cities, they become more eccentric, more visually individualistic, as a way to distinguish themselves from the throngs of others living there.[46] Such individuality and distinction must occur instantaneously as we walk past each other on the street, thus clothing becomes one of the most efficient ways to do so.

Much of conspicuous consumption rests on our relationship to our neighbors and peers and thus city life plays a significant role in how we consume. In a 2006 article in the *Quarterly Journal of Economics*, Dartmouth professor Erzo Luttmer found that our neighbors' wealth inversely affected our well-being. In fact, while living next to rich people makes us unhappy, it's worse to be friends with them.[47] Thus, in New York City, where making $500,000 is "middle class,"[48] it's no surprise that its inhabitants feel the pressure to keep up with their friends who make

$5 million a year, or to at least appear as though they are on par. In New York City, just like San Francisco, everyone feels poor (even the well-to-do) because the density of the city forces close and frequent contact with others, including those with great wealth. This density puts further pressure on inhabitants to be status-conscious, and reminds them of their social and economic position vis-à-vis everyone else. In general, cities have this effect on us—we are both pressured and rewarded by conspicuous, status-oriented consumption.

One area of conspicuous consumption where urbanites feel a lesser need to impress is car purchases. Other than Detroit, Minneapolis, and Seattle, urban dwellers spend less than the national average on cars as a result of good public transportation and walkability in cities (even in Los Angeles), and the use of sidewalks and subways further propels us to interact with the rest of the city. But the lack of cars as status symbol is the corollary to the increased pressure to acquire those other socially visible goods like shoes and watches.

The raison d'être of cities is that they are centers of human civilization, whether production, as they were during the Industrial Revolution, or the consumption of apparel, restaurants museums, and nightlife, as they are now. They have always been great centers of people, and with that come the signals and their trappings that allow us to both distinguish and assimilate ourselves with others. That those in cities spend more on conspicuous consumption is a result of what it is like to live in a city—a dense, frenzied place where we are both trying to fit in and strike out on our own at the same time. But it is the localized interpretation of status and consumption and the appropriation and re-appropriation of meaning that is imbued upon particular objects, some of which I have parsed out and attempted to quantify, that is most fascinating.

In his book *Distinction*, the French sociologist, Pierre Bourdieu, wrote about the means by which status was attained across different classes. Bourdieu argued that the working class didn't simply want what the rich already had, but rather each class's values reflected their respective social position. In essence, they wanted different things altogether. The working class prized new over vintage or antique, American football rather than tennis, ostentatious weddings rather than small, quiet affairs.[49] To use Max Weber's term, the rich, middle class, and working class embody and prioritize different "styles of life."[50] Consumer behavior becomes one of the key elements in demonstrating status, and thus different cities, with their diverse populations in terms of race, income, industry, and educational levels, have dramatically different consumption patterns. Their social lives, and the environment in which they form tastes, or what Bourdieu called "habitus," is reflected in their distinct consumption patterns.[51] The everyday patterns of life play into these choices.

Empirically, we can see the extent to which the unique characteristics of a city might influence consumer behavior and thus why different cities express different levels of conspicuous consumption. With my colleague Gary Painter and student Hyojung Lee, we quantified and measured how cities shape consumption habits. Holding everything else equal (for example, age, income level, education, and race), particular urban characteristics influence how inhabitants spend on status goods. As would be expected, the denser the city (as defined by number of thousand persons per square mile), the more conspicuous consumption. When there are more people around, there is greater pressure to reveal status and also a greater social bump from conspicuous consumption. Because young people likely have fewer obligations in other areas of their lives and enjoy a highly social lifestyle, the younger the population, the greater the level of conspicuous consumption. Given that they provide more opportunities for their clientele to flaunt their status, greater numbers of drinking establishments and restaurants are also associated with conspicuous consumption.[52]

Conversely, more expensive rental markets (and thus less discretionary income) are associated with less conspicuous consumption, as are rainy days, given the greater likelihood that bad weather encourages us to stay at home. Counterintuitively, cities with a higher population of the top 1% also spend less on conspicuous consumption. While this latter result may seem contradictory, consider that if there are a lot of people with a lot of money, many more people can conspicuously consume and so such goods are less powerful in conveying status among a group of people who are already elite. Like the great sociologists of the early twentieth century and Veblen himself, we find that people engage in status-suggestive behavior when they are in social environments and around many other people where there is a premium and incentive to stake out one's position. Consider the spread between cities' conspicuous consumption versus "nonconspicuous" spending (which we define as total expenditures minus conspicuous consumption): We find that the difference in conspicuous consumption spending between the highest spending city (Detroit) and the least spending city (Boston) is a whopping 32%. For nonconspicuous spending, the spread between San Diego and Detroit narrows to just 4.4%. This stark discrepancy suggests that nonconspicuous consumption is not socially or geographically specific; rather, consumers exhibit a generalizable pattern in buying basic goods and services. Conspicuous consumption, on the other hand, appears highly dependent on particular variables and particular places. Overall, conspicuous consumption is a distinctly "urban feature."[53]

When I think about city differences, I am often reminded of a more contemporary, albeit quirky, example—that of the surfer menorah. As its namesake would suggest, this item is a menorah fashioned with a surfboard placed on the stem between the candelabrum's branches and its foot. New York University sociologist Harvey Molotch wrote in great detail about its popularity on the beaches of Laguna Niguel in Southern California and the impossibility of selling it anywhere else. It is the hybrid culture specific to Southern California that allows such an item to be ironic (even literal for some) rather than offensive. But such an item only exists as a result of the great beaches that enable surfing and the rise of auto design, which brought lots of new acrylics and materials that allowed surfboards to advance along with a liberal Jewish population. Along with surfboards came the "high-jinks" surfer culture that inspired the irreverent art scene of the 1960s which influenced the production of that surfer menorah many decades later. The surfing wouldn't be possible without the beach and the ocean, but those surfboards were a result of materials spawned from aerospace and cars. So the surfer menorah becomes place-specific due to the confluence of artistic materials, culture, and demographics that are found only in the peculiarities of Southern California.[54] More generally, little things influence how people in particular cities live their day-to-day lives. Those little things become the big differences that make Boston and San Francisco and everything in between such distinctive places to live and define oneself, much of which we accomplish through what we consume.

But different cities (and their cultures) also find different means to a similar end. By way of anecdote, after moving from New York to California, I found that within five or six years I wore less black, ate more vegetables, learned how to cook quinoa (even though I still find its appeal mystifying)—all of which were antithetical to my New York City modus vivendi and identity. Perhaps these differences can be explained by the cold weather of New York, the city's position as the fashion industry capital, and thus the penchant to wear black. Juxtapose this milieu to the good life, good weather, and sense of well-being for which Los Angeles has always prided itself. Los Angeles' history of television emphasizes women appealing to mainstream America rather than the avant-garde aesthetic of runway fashion. But in both examples, I (like many women before and after me) was responding to a prevailing female aesthetic. There are countless examples. Our consumption patterns often reflect the dominant culture in which we are immersed: New York fashion and the social x-rays of high society, Los Angeles' television and film stars, Portland's bohemian intellectuals, or San Francisco's anti-fashion tech entrepreneurs (or what *New York Times* fashion writer Guy Trebay dubbed, "the land that style forgot").[55] Most of us are none of the above, but when we live somewhere we tend to reflect it somewhat in how we look and what we consume to look that way. Through the accretion of history, geography, industry, and even weather, cities offer particular and idiosyncratic options that build upon and influence one another—an overabundance of yoga pants in Los Angeles, pink chinos in Boston, backyard vegetable gardens in Portland, coral nail polish in Orlando, or the active unfashionable San Francisco style. As Molly Young writes in *New York Magazine*, "If culture is partly a result of who is attracted to a given locale, it makes sense that those enticed by San Francisco's temperate climate would likewise gravitate toward soft, moisture-wicking zip-ups."[56]

Yet despite these little differences, cities are fundamentally connected to one another through their positions as nodes of consumption and inhabitation for the twenty-first-century elite. Twenty-first-century cities may not possess the Metropolitan 400, but through skyrocketing rent, expensive preparatory schools, and exorbitant cost of living, they exist as figurative and literal citadels of elite living. The Metropolitan 400 of C. Wright Mills's time was exclusive but limited to a small cast of characters who were economically and socially rare even to other urban denizens. Today's cities house a far bigger elite and one that reinforces their position not simply through high society but through the trappings of their day-to-day lives. Living among other elites allows them to ignore the vast inequality between their urban utopia and even their nearby suburbs, let alone the rest of the world. As Ross Douthat remarked:

> [Global elites] have their own distinctive worldview ... their own common educational experience, their own shared values and assumptions (social psychologists call these WEIRD for Western, Educated, Industrialized, Rich and Democratic) and of course, their own outgroups (evangelicals, Little Englanders) ... like any other tribal cohort they seek comfort and familiarity: From London to Paris to New York, each Western "global city" (like each "global university") is increasingly interchangeable so wherever the citizen of the world travels he already feels at home ... they can't see that what feels diverse on the inside can still seem like aristocracy to the excluded.[57]

Covered by an invisible tissue of urbanity, cities are able to offer many versions of themselves to those who self-select into one metropolis versus another and consume accordingly.[58] We respond to these options and in the process they shape us. But as we are shaped by our cities, we simultaneously shape them, and the world at large, too. That cities are becoming centers of what Douthat has termed "elite tribalism" means that, despite their many options and seeming diversity, they too are reinforcing inequality and the class divisions of the twenty-first century.

CHAPTER 7

"To Get Rich Is Glorious"? The State of Consumption and Class in America

Is a family with a car in the driveway, a flatscreen television and a computer with an Internet connection poor?
—Annie Lowrey, "Changed Life of the Poor: Better Off, but Far Behind," *New York Times*, Economy sec. (April 30, 2014)

The surface of American society is covered with a layer of democratic paint, but from time to time one can see the old aristocratic colours breaking through.
—Alexis de Tocqueville, *Democracy in America* (1835)

That money can't buy happiness is a truism older than Edith Wharton's *The House of Mirth* or Charles Dickens's *A Christmas Carol*. But this axiom is oversimplified. It fails to take into account research that suggests that money can buy happiness up to $75,000 annual income. Or, as the Nobel Prize–winning psychologist Daniel Kahneman and his colleague Angus Deaton found, if you're divorced and make less than $1,000 a month, you are more than twice as likely to be sad than if you're divorced and make more than $3,000 a month. Similarly, they found that if you have asthma, you are twice as likely to be sad if you are within the poorer income bracket.

Kahneman and Deaton find that those who were wealthier experienced feelings of accomplishment and being in the right place in their life journey. In other words, possessing financial resources is correlated with satisfaction but not necessarily with the true sense of contentment or joy that happiness brings.[1] Why? Wealth and the consumption avenues it opens become an effective means for comparing one's success and achievement to others but are not necessarily in and of themselves a source of happiness.

Similarly, in dramatic longitudinal studies of both developed and developing countries, a team of researchers found that increases in per capita income and GDP do not translate into durable life satisfaction. In some cases, increases in wealth actually result in declines in happiness. Known as the "happiness-income paradox" or the "Easterlin paradox" (after the economist Richard Easterlin who discovered the phenomenon), the researchers conclude that although in the short term economic expansions increase happiness, over the long term there is no significant relationship.[2]

American consumers know this irony only too well. In what has been termed the "anxious middle"[3] by Larry Summers, or what Juliet Schor calls the "cycle of work and spend,"[4] America has cultivated a consumption-driven lifestyle and subsequently stretched itself to achieve it. Many Americans, aligning consumerism with the American Dream, continue penniless along this track. As countless news articles have documented, other than the top economic echelons of society, everyone is struggling and unable to achieve the American Dream—whatever that is these days—without massive amounts of debt. And yet, your average citizen still believes in the ideas of Horatio Alger (not realizing perhaps that Alger was a writer of fictional heroes).

As this book has shown, America's consumerism—particularly conspicuous consumption—hides the vast inequality within this new America. In the twenty-first century, America's aspirational class has rejected many of the material means by which status has been historically revealed. They have eschewed materialism, aspiring to what they believe is a higher social and cultural platform. In these efforts, the aspirational class utilizes new means to demonstrate its class position. Rather than simply conspicuous consumption, this dominant cultural elite prefers to engage in conspicuous production, conspicuous leisure, and inconspicuous consumption, all of which produce much greater class stratification effects than the acquisition of material goods.

Thorstein Veblen believed that conspicuous leisure would decline while conspicuous consumption would increase at a rapid pace among the rich and nouveau riche. He could not have anticipated the significant rise of the manufacturing economy, or that the middle class would not only become huge spenders but would also have access to material goods like cars, closets full of clothes, televisions, and easy credit, that were not even attainable by the rich at one point. By material standards, even the poor today have more than the rich did during Veblen's time. Conspicuous consumption has become omnipresent, but—as the data on our spending patterns illuminate—not as Veblen would have predicted. Veblen's leisure class no longer exists. Mobility is a result of knowledge, not birthright. Today's cultural hegemony is dominated by the aspirational class who are not idly sitting around but productively acquiring physical and metaphysical benefits for themselves and their offspring. As such, their consumer behavior has shifted from material displays of status to more implicit and tacitly coded means of showing social and economic position and reproducing their position of wealth for future generations. The aspirational class has disdain for mass market material goods, or the "Walmart effect" of democratizing consumerism, and they have the luxury to do so, further distinguishing themselves from everyone else. The falling prices of manufactured consumer goods have simultaneously made them more accessible across class lines while exposing the human and environmental costs of their inexpensiveness: exploitative labor practices, dangerous chemicals, and destruction of rain forests.

In response, conspicuous production has triumphed. Where the product comes from and how it is made matter far more than what it looks like. In more recent years, members of the aspirational class have sought more subtle signs of status—made-in-LA t-shirts, organic food, woven leather bags with no label, and labor-intensive coffee makers. Using the case of the Swiss mechanical watchmaking industry, Harvard Business School professor Ryan Raffaelli calls "re-emergence in technologies" the resurgence of market demand for what was once thought to be a moribund good. Similarly, other artisanal and made-to-order items are experiencing somewhat of a renaissance.[5] According to the *Economist*, independent bookshops are growing for the first time in decades; fountain pens, discarded in the 1950s for the Bic ballpoint and its brethren, are back in fashion; and Swiss watches are in greater demand than ever before. The heart of their revival lies in the attention to craftsmanship, tradition, and history. "People do not just buy something because it provides the most efficient solution to a problem," writes the *Economist*'s Schumpeter column, "They buy it because it provides aesthetic satisfaction—a beautiful book, for example, or a perfectly made shirt—or because it makes them feel good about themselves."[6] These new consumer choices reflect abhorrence toward the standardization and accessibility of mainstream consumer goods.

The consumption practices of the new elite are not simply a response to middle-class conspicuous consumption (and a further differentiation from ordinary America). In some instances, such as college education and full-time nannies, they also cost a lot more than a nice car or Coach handbag and have broader ramifications than merely serving as material signals of status. But these consumer choices have social costs too. The aspirational class members make decisions and establish norms that have far more pernicious outcomes for society than did previous leisure-class consumerism. Rather than buying silver spoons and going on long holidays, their investments in education, health, retirement, and parenting ensure the reproduction of status (and often wealth too) for their offspring in a way that no material good can. Through this reproduction of cultural capital and its trappings we see the emergence of what Charles Murray has called the "New Upper Class" and "New Lower Class," which is not simply an economic divide, but is also a deep cultural divide that has never existed with such distinction as it does today.[7] Even the cultural differences around the more nebulous norms of mothering, knowledge, and environmental consciousness are underpinned by economic position, and these symbolic boundaries are far from costless.

What is most concerning about today's elites is that behaviors that appear to be moral or value-laden choices are deeply embedded in socioeconomic position and many of these decisions are quotidian, not grand material signifiers. In fact, the media's obsession with financial elites, oligarchs, and plutocrats' extravagant lifestyles distracts from some of our far more pressing issues of cultural, social, and economic stratification. The lives of the superrich may be interesting, but these people have always existed and they do not make a significant impact on most of our lives. But the aspirational class, many of whom exist in the top 1%, 5%, and 10% income brackets, are a much larger force. Their decisions and investments, which are increasingly inconspicuous, reproduce wealth and upward mobility in a way that leaves out the middle class in detrimental ways. When it comes to conspicuous leisure and inconspicuous consumption—that is, education, health care, child care, and time to spend with one's family—the freedom to engage in these investments genuinely affects the "life chances," to use sociologist William Julius Wilson's term, of the aspirational class as compared to the rest. Investing in a child's secondary education, being able to afford fruits and vegetables and regular health checkups, even having the time to breast-feed, all give the next generation a leg up. Having "arrived" used to mean the minivan and the suburban house, but those don't get the kids into a good university, and that university (and being able to write the tuition check) is increasingly what divides the rich from everyone else. The aspirational class may not be the 0.01%, but they live in an entirely different and more privileged cultural universe than almost everyone else. As one commentator observed, "Is it possible that those who have enough disposable income [are] so caught up in fitness and food trends—Zumba and kale, CrossFit and juicing—that they've become inured to deeper, pervasive wellness issues facing the less wealthy?"[8]

At this point, I would like to focus on some of the general concerns around economic inequality, which are not exclusive to the aspirational class but are in lockstep with the larger problems American society faces as different cultural, social, and economic classes become more and more estranged from one another. The inverse of the aspirational class is the current state of America's middle class. While this book is about the dominant elite and their consumer habits, it would be remiss to not address the other side of the story. Just as the top income groups are spending significantly more on education for their children, alarmingly the middle class is spending less. As this book and other research have shown, for the middle class, the good life is not in the inconspicuous consumption so exalted by the aspirational class; they simply cannot afford it. Instead, today's middle-class mobility has become more about stuff and less about life, which is to say, to purchase the material goods that suggest social position requires more working hours, less leisure time, and less time to spend with one's family.[9] Given that the middle class has suffered tremendous job loss, decline in their housing values, and wage stagnation, purchasing this material version of the good life is not as easy as it was previously.

First, the paradox of all of those cheap goods that make status goods so accessible to the middle class is that they are being created at the expense of good middle-class jobs, which are both moving to developing countries with cheaper labor forces and being replaced by computers. Globalization and standardization, the hallmarks of modern consumer goods, took those remaining middle-class factory jobs to Brazil and India.

The 2008 housing bust eroded almost all of the economic gains of the middle class, or what the Pew Research Center has called "the lost decade of the middle class." In fact, even though many blame the financial industry and its titans for much of the global economic collapse, the middle class was the most affected by the Recession. Middle-class jobs and wages dried up, never to recover fully. The middle-class housing market has regained some of its momentum but not to its mid-2000 highs, whereas the top tier of housing has never been more expensive. Eighty-five percent of middle-class households say their lifestyle is more difficult to maintain today than in 2000.[10]

Simultaneously the rich have gotten substantially richer. The Great Recession, perhaps significantly brought on by the titans within the top 1%, actually hurt the bottom 90% the most.[11] Their home values haven't recovered, their wages (already stagnating before the Recession) haven't improved, and their jobs are lost. While everyone generally agrees that inequality is a problem, there are a multitude of explanations for what has caused the unwinding of the middle class and America's upward mobility, and many of them are tied up in the general observation that we buy too much and that material goods (and the social position they are to imply) are too heavily counted on for happiness.

In a stunning and stark portrait of the new America, *Financial Times* reporter Edward Luce follows the lives of Americans who are experiencing the erosion of the middle class and its accompanying good life. In an essay entitled "The Crisis of Middle Class America," Luce portrays the Freemans, a quintessential American family living in Minneapolis. They have just a small mortgage, earn $70,000 a year, and are fit with A/C, plenty of food, beer, and evenings sitting on the porch. Mark Freeman works in a warehouse, Connie is an anesthesia supply technician. Their son Andy, who is autistic, is their major expense, and they paid a huge fee to get him on their health insurance (Mark's sleep apnea machine also packs a financial punch). Yet their house, purchased at $53,000 in 1989, once valued at $105,000 and now worth $73,000, was almost repossessed a few years ago. Materially, they seem fine on the surface, but they are not. Mark works two extra jobs—karaoke on Wednesday evenings and managing the local liquor store on Saturdays. As Mark explained, "We need all four jobs to keep our heads above water."[12]

As the middle class has declined, so too have the social structures that ensured its capacity for upward mobility. George Packer argues in *The Unwinding* that this is the "new America."[13] The decline of the middle class and its implicit social contract defines life in America from the late twentieth century to the present day. Even just 30 years ago, one could become a well-paid member of the middle class, and consumer items such as TVs, cars, and home ownership aligned closely with upward mobility. Today, because consumer items are so cheap (as is credit), material goods tell us very little about the economic success of a household. As Packer himself put it in a PBS interview, the "unwinding" is that of America's "contract that said if you work hard, if you essentially are a good citizen, there will be a place for you, not only an economic place, you will have a secure life, your kids will have a chance to have a better life, but you will sort of be recognized as part of the national fabric."[14]

Despite earning seemingly good paychecks and owning their homes in pleasant suburbs, much of America is victim to "median wage stagnation": for the past 40 years, everyone but the top 10% has experienced flat annual incomes, with paychecks no better in real dollars than they were in 1973. As Luce writes, "That means that most Americans have been treading water for more than a generation."[15] Even more alarming, Paris School economist Thomas Piketty argues in his runaway 2014 hit *Capital in the Twenty-first Century* that the period of relative equality between World War I and the early 1970s was an anomalous period of capitalism. Using detailed data from countries around the world across a 200-year period, Piketty makes a compelling case that for the years between 1914 and 1973, a series of government policies and global crises flattened out the gap between rich and poor and prevented the rich from getting greater returns on capital. Piketty believes that the inequality that is so profound in the current day is actually inherent to capitalism's basic structure, and that the six-decade stretch of greater income equality observed in the middle of the twentieth century is not to occur again.[16] What these statistics mean is that most Americans can no longer afford to engage in the conspicuous consumption that has underpinned their "happiness." Normal middle-class Americans have had their homes repossessed, their credit ratings slashed, and their ability to establish their identity through consumption almost entirely eradicated. We need to find a new way to live.

These observations on America coincide with what is known by economists and policymakers as the Great Stagnation—the alarming finding that the median wage hasn't grown since 1973, rising only by 10% in real terms over the past 37 years. In short, 90% of America hasn't gained a penny over the past four decades.

The numbers show it: Median income for the middle class dropped from $73,000 in 2000 to $69,500 in 2011, while median net worth of this household plummeted to $93,150, from almost $130,000 in 2000 and a high of $152,000 in 2008 (all figures are in 2011 dollars).[17] Goods may be cheaper, but that doesn't mean much if you don't have a paycheck to cover them (and must rely on credit cards instead). In their parallel universe, the rich have recovered and then some. In her book *Plutocrats*, Crystia Freeland observes that post-Recession the division between the superrich and the rest is even greater than before the financial collapse.[18] Or, in what the Century Foundation calls "A Tale of Two Recoveries," every dollar and more of gains in household wealth in the post-Recessionary period (2009–2011) went to the top 7% of households. This top group saw its net worth grow almost 30% during this time, while everyone else saw their net worth fall by 4%.[19]

Simultaneously, the things that really affect quality of life and upward mobility cost much more than a flat-screen TV or a minivan. Inconspicuous consumption—education, health care, child care, and college tuition—are the items that truly impact quality of life and upward mobility, and these are the items the rich spend on and through which they further stratify themselves from everyone else. As this book has shown, inconspicuous consumption becomes more and more expensive and a practice reserved to the richest members of the aspirational class.[20] The erosion of middle-class jobs and the expense of inconspicuous consumption bifurcate the rich from the rest in a profound way that suggests future generations may never catch up with today's rich and their children. This divide also amplifies the alienation and inequality between the rich and poor on a social and cultural level. The problems are so much deeper than the material goods that used to be clear status markers. Today, the division between the aspirational class and the rest is defined by college degrees, health, well-being, mortality rates, and time spent with one's children. The cultural elites (let alone the economic elite) in this country are so removed from the day-to-day hardships of the middle- and lower-income classes, that they may become unable to even imagine (let alone solve) the pervasive problems of their poorer fellow citizens.

The problem with the new American economic landscape is profound on a number of levels. There is an intense sociological impact to the erosion of the middle class and rising inequality. What Evergreen State College professor Stephanie Coontz calls "the new instability" is the increasing tenuousness of married life for those who are not highly educated or highly paid. As she points out, in 1970, marriage rates were largely indistinguishable by education levels (and for a while so were divorce rates). Today, if you're educated and rich, you're also more likely to get married than those who are neither, and you are much less likely to get divorced. While 60% of this upper-income group is still in their first marriage at the age of 40, almost 60% of those without a bachelor's degree are no longer in their first marriage at the same age. At the same time that the upper classes are putting their children through private schools and university, 25% of men 30–35 years of age are barely able to support a family of four above the poverty line (in 1969, just 10% of men 30–35 years of age were in the same dilemma). In 1969, 75% of men aged 25 were able to support that same family. In 2004, the age threshold for men who were able to support a family moved up to 30 years old. Further, while marrying one's secretary seemed the secret to a man's blissful marriage in the Mad Men days, today the secret to stability is marrying a woman with earning power and even more education than her husband.[21]

The decline of America's middle class is profound for the global economy as well. Americans have never been savers, and yet, we are worse now than we were 30 years ago—personal saving declined from 10% in the early 1980s to virtually zero in 2014.[22] The money that Chinese workers put under their mattress (indeed this is literally what they do) is what Americans pump into consumer goods.[23] But these days, not only do American households have less money and save less, for rich households the money they do have is being redirected into education, health care, and pensions.

THE MIDDLE CLASS GOES GLOBAL

Globalization has often been the villain in conversations around mass consumerism and the decline of America's middle class. But something else is afoot as well. As much as the global rich are infiltrating elite Western markets (as documented in books like *Plutocrats*, and in the frenzy around New York, San Francisco, and London property markets), a larger group is also becoming increasingly important to the world economy. Those factory jobs that left the United States are aiding in what economists are now calling the "global middle class."[24] Just as the Industrial Revolution brought the United States and UK a new class of reasonably paid workers who then returned this income to the consumer economy, there is a growing population that, as a result of developing world industrialization and globalization, has moved out of poverty and into a middle-class quality of life. But what do we mean by a global middle class? Even America's poor are doing better materially and financially than many of the reasonably well off in developing countries. Thus, is the term global middle class absolute—we have a fixed minimum and maximum income level—or relative—the median of each individual country? There is much speculation here, and drawbacks to each approach. For example, some use a relative approach (like that of New York University economist William Easterly), defining middle class as the 20–80% income bracket in the United States. However, what is middle in America is rich in most other places: The three middle quintiles in the United States would certainly be the top brackets in India or Venezuela, for example. More accepted definitions of the global middle class revolve around an absolute criterion. The Brookings Institution, the United Nations, and OECD define a member of the global middle class as someone who earns, spends, or has the purchasing power of $10–$100 per day.[25] This approach has been largely accepted, as it means that an individual can consume more than basic necessities, purchasing extra apparel, perhaps going out to dinner, and buying a car. In other words, the global middle class is defined in part by its participation in the global consumer market. This purchasing power is critical to major international companies selling anything from brand-name food to cars. It also means the American middle class, which long supported the world economy with its consumption habits, is less essential.

Let's consider the numbers. According to Brookings Institution scholars Homi Kharas and Geoffrey Gertz, the impact of the global middle class on the world economy has only just begun. By 2021, the number of Asian middle-class consumers, an estimated 2 billion, will far outpace their Western counterparts. Kharas's and Gertz's analysis of the emerging global middle class uses the $10–$100 spending power range and studies 145 countries, capturing 98% of the world's population. Their projections suggest that by 2020, 54% of the world's middle class will come from Asia Pacific, while North America's and Europe's global share will decline to just 10% and 22%, respectively (from 18% and 36%, respectively, in 2009). Kharas and Gertz believe that from 2009 to 2030 there could be a sixfold increase in the Asian middle class, while North America and Europe decline significantly in their global share (and North America also declines in its absolute number of people). By 2022, Kharas and Gertz believe more people in the world will be middle class rather than poor.[26]

When it comes to share of global consumption, this new global middle class will take over the role that the North American and European consumers currently hold. In 2009, North America accounted for 26% of middle-class consumption (some $5,600 billion) and Europe accounted for 38% of middle-class consumption (roughly $8,000 billion).[27] Kharas and Gertz believe that by 2020, the Asian Pacific market will generate 42% of global middle-class consumption (to North America's 17% and Europe's 29%). While the United States is currently the biggest middle-class consumer economy (followed by Japan and Germany), by 2020, China is projected to become number one and by 2030, India and China will hold the top two slots (generating 23% and 18%, respectively) with the United States significantly farther behind in third, generating 7% of global middle-class consumption. In one generation, almost half of global middle-class consumption may shift to an entirely different part of the world, with entirely different aesthetics, culture, and social dynamics.

Already, car sales and mobile phone sales are greater in China than in the United States. In 2000, the United States market accounted for 37% of worldwide car sales, while China accounted for just 1%. Fifteen years later, China is the world's largest car economy, accounting for almost 14 million vehicles in 2009, compared to the United States' 10.4 million. As early as 2008, the cell phone manufacturer Nokia generated more than three times more revenue in China than in the United States.[28]

It's worth noting that massive income inequality, access to education, and the great political and cultural divides between the Chinese rural and urban populations may impact these estimates. Yet, by the sheer size of their populations alone, it seems nearly inevitable that the Asian Pacific middle-class consumer will take over where Western influence and power was once held. "If this transpires, the world will see a new global middle class—an Asian middle class," write Kharas and Gertz. "There will be a cross-over from the West to the East in the products, fashions, tastes and designs oriented to the mass middle class."[29]

Another, perhaps simpler way to capture the global middle class is by looking at car purchases. In *Foreign Policy*, Shimelse Ali and Uri Dadush argue that while there is no fully agreed upon measure for capturing the global middle class, perhaps the single greatest sign of entering the middle class is buying an automobile. For Ali and Dandush, the income range ignores the fact that someone making $2 a day can still purchase a mobile phone and that what people earn doesn't tell you about what they'll actually buy. Owning a car is a signal of the ability and inclination to purchase a luxury good. This approach suggests that places like China, India, and Russia are growing even faster than the income analysis would suggest. In the emerging BRICs (Brazil, Russia, India, and China), new passenger car sales were six times larger in 2010 than they were in the 1990s.[30] The United States experience is antithetical: In 2000, there were more than 17 million car purchases; in 2015, that figure had barely budged.[31]

There are a lot of reasons we should care about the global middle class.[32] From a strictly economic perspective, the decline of present-day developed industrialized countries' middle classes would suggest that the world economy will suffer a massive blow as a significant portion of the United States' and Europe's consumers begin to spend less. Both population and income have stagnated in advanced economies, and the "middle class" as a concept is misrepresentative of the current, highly constrained economic situation of this population in Western countries. Second, as Ronald Inglehart has pointed out, economic development is an important step on the way to fairer, more democratic societies. Thus, as Ali and Dadush conclude, a rising middle class may mean more equitable governments and populations that demand more from their leaders, whether environmental standards or basic services.

Companies obviously care for their own purposes. In a 2010 *McKinsey Quarterly* report, David Court and Laxman Narasimhan argue that finding out where the "emerging middle class" is coming from will set the stage for brand loyalty for years to come. As they observe, "early winners" remain brand leaders. They found that in 17 consumer product categories in the United States, the leaders in 1925, such as Kraft, Del Monte Foods, and Wrigley, remained the leaders for the rest of the twentieth century. Court and Narasimhan also find that emerging markets resemble developed markets—they have affection for particular brands, idiosyncrasies with regard to price points and what they will spend money on, but also great aspirations for certain products.[33] The Chinese in particular tend to shop for more hours per week than the average American and include shopping as a favorite leisure activity. Global retailers, whether Chanel or Walmart, count on these cultural tendencies. Chanel is China's number one favorite luxury brand, while Walmart already has some 270 stores in China. The future is happening now.

If the United States offers the archetype of the middle class, then there are lessons to be learned by the global middle class that may take its place. As the US experience has demonstrated, the tendency toward consumerism and material goods is good for the world's economy, but it is hardly good for the consumers themselves. Material aspirations create great pressures on society to work excessively and to focus on external markers of achievement. Further, the cycle of material attainment only compounds itself. Each generation believes it needs more than the generation before to feel comfortable or live the good life. In reality, that belief cannot possibly be true. We confuse the pressure to keep up with our peers as the key to success—and by extension happiness. Status is a movable feast, and once the middle class catches on, as this book has shown, the dominant elites find new ways to illustrate their status.

Most of us know that material goods—consumption—buy us only a small amount of happiness if any at all. Research shows that if we are going to spend money, we actually ought to spend it on others, if we are to attain any meaningful satisfaction from it. No matter how the tide of material goods ebbs and flows, the interpersonal means of happiness remains constant—strong family life, falling in love, stability, and our close ties to friends. For America and its fellow consumer-oriented Western countries and emerging consumer economies, we need to figure out how to redirect our lives toward these goals rather than toward attaining the latest consumer good. Or as the great economist Richard Easterlin himself put it to me when I interviewed him for this book, "I hope that the progress of knowledge will be such that we can bring under control the forces of economic growth that are misdirecting our efforts of wellbeing."

No country better exemplifies the disconnect between happiness and income than China, where, since 1990, the rise of the free market is correlated with a decline in happiness that has been equally profound. China is the world's second largest economy, the Chinese are 400% wealthier than they were some 30 years ago, and their consumption and GDP have doubled (twice). Mao's communism has been replaced by middle-class urban denizens with TVs and refrigerators. Easterlin describes China as "one vast extension of Orange County, California."[34] Yet, as Easterlin explains, the decline in the safety net, social welfare, and jobs, has made people less satisfied than in the pre-1990 communist economy, even if they now have more wealth and more consumer products to buy. One study coined the term "frustrated achievers" to describe those who felt that even if they are doing well, someone else is always doing even better.[35] Deng Xiaopin, the leader of the Communist Party of China, who led the country to a market economy, (supposedly) famously said, "To get rich is glorious!"[36] Not so much, it turns out.

Buying goods is never going to make us happy. Not in the late 1800s, as the Industrial Revolution gave us a middle class and the beginnings of mass consumerism, not in the early 1900s with Henry Ford's Model T, not in the 1950s with dishwashers, fridges, and A/C for all, and not in the twenty-first century's mass luxury business. In some respects, our constant quest for the meaning of life (which becomes more possible in a post-scarcity society where we have time to ponder and pursue more existential questions because we know we have food for dinner) has confused matters even more. For the aspirational class, post-scarcity society has allowed them to invest in practices that at first seem constructive: motherhood, exercise, acquisition of cultural capital. Ostensibly, these activities should make people happier, but they too have become status markers and signs of achievement, and in that process have created more pressure and less happiness, not so dissimilar from material signifiers of social position.

Even the seemingly worthy consumption practices of the aspirational class set up destructive ingroup/outgroup distinctions across social and economic classes. Yes, paradoxically, we want to be different from others while we simultaneously seek to fit in. Consumption is a simple and effective way to create these distinctions and identities. But our desire to fit in or show our social position is structurally flawed because it always involves leaving others out. The creation of an "us" necessarily creates an "other." And consumption, in its various forms, becomes the conduit for showing these distinctions, or more precisely, class lines. If we are constantly finding ways to differentiate from others, to show our social and economic position, once any group catches up, we are quick to find new means to reestablish our uniqueness. Today's status markers are particularly pernicious because they involve practices and goods far more significant than material goods. Our parenting, cultural knowledge, choices in food become moral choices when they are really about economic constraint or freedom. Society frowns upon those who make inferior decisions on such matters, willfully ignorant that many of these decisions, veiled in morality, are practical and realistic outcomes of socioeconomic position.

This book has examined American culture and consumption in the twenty-first century and in particular the norms and practices of a new cultural formation, the aspirational class. The practices and behaviors that I observe can be seen in the local section of Dublin supermarkets that offer almond butter and quinoa, in the mothering practices (and pressures) in London, and the boutiques of Paris. The limitations of my landscape are due to the data at hand, but the expanse of these phenomena is in evidence worldwide. Thorstein Veblen's view of consumption in the nineteenth century still applies today, but society and class are far more complicated. Many of us have access to the items that were then status markers of only the rich. Acquiring those status markers does not indicate one's financial well-being, let alone happiness or fulfillment. Status itself, always present and always changing, has since permeated many other aspects of life. The question I leave you with is this: Does being different from others, being better than others at acquiring possessions or the perfect heirloom tomatoes, or making the decision and investment to breast-feed or feed your family organic produce really advance society at all? Perhaps this seems a rhetorical question, but I do not mean it as such. In some ways, the choice to be a better, more involved parent, exercise more, read more newspapers, probably does make us healthier, happier, and more engaged members of society.

But we cannot lose sight of the extent to which these practices are not even an option for huge segments of society. They are obviously not choices for the poor, the near-poor, and even huge swathes of the middle class. But even for the aspirational class, these status markers become points of peer pressure. As the sociologists Sarah Bowen, Sinikka Elliott, and Joslyn Brenton observe in a recent essay, "The Joy of Cooking?," all of this burden to perfect things on a superficial level just leaves us overwhelmed anyway. This does not mean that all of our consumption practices are off base: Caring about where things come from, supporting local farmers, making home cooked meals, investing in education rather than handbags are certainly more constructive and establish better value systems than the flashy consumer culture of the 1980s and early 2000s. But even the aspirational class consumer gestalt reflects a frenzy and status-consciousness that not only leaves many out, but also stresses us out. In all of our consuming—conspicuous and inconspicuous—we may be missing out on living our lives, entirely.

Irrespective of one's opinion on the merits or otherwise of how society chooses to consume in the twenty-first century, one thing is clear: Consumption is more than just buying things. Consumer habits reveal who we are and who we aspire to be. Our choices around what we consume simultaneously connect us and estrange us from different groups within society. To quote the great anthropologist Dame Mary Douglas and Baron Isherwood, "Goods ... and consumption have been artificially abstracted out of the whole social scheme."[37] As I hope this book has

198 • CHAPTER 7

shown, our consumption habits reveal something much deeper and more complicated than what material objects ostensibly suggest. In its summation of things big and small, consumption is a process and positioning of conveying information and identity. As we understand what motivates how and why we consume, we also learn more about humanity, how and where it organizes itself, the implications and limitations to these decisions, and, finally, what matters to us as individuals and society as a whole.

Appendix

CONSUMER EXPENDITURE SURVEY

The Consumer Expenditure Survey (CE) is an annual survey of American consumer behavior, conducted by the US Census Bureau under contract with the Bureau of Labor Statistics. The history of the dataset goes back to the late nineteenth century, though the modern and annual-based survey began in 1980. One of the major goals of the survey is to update a cost-of-living index, known as the Consumer Price Index (CPI); however, given its comprehensive and accurate information on consumers' spending behaviors and their socioeconomic characteristics, it has long been used by researchers to analyze and explain consumer behaviors.

The CE comprises two independent surveys: the Diary Survey and the Interview Survey. The Diary Survey collects expenditure data on small and frequently purchased items and is reported by a self-administered diary, while the Interview Survey is designed to collect data on expenditures that are relatively large (e.g., durable goods) or that are regularly bought (e.g., rent, insurance). Given the superior performance of the Interview Survey found in Bee et al. (2012), this book mainly used the Interview microdata for analyzing certain consumer groups' behavior.

The microdata not only provide individual household-level information on purchased items, specified by hundreds of Universal Classified Codes (UCC), but also contain information on demographic and socioeconomic characteristics of the household. Since the quarterly Interview Survey covers approximately 7,000 households across the country (nationally representative), the sample size of the annualized dataset is about 35,000 consumer units. All the analyses are weighted using sampling weights to represent national estimates and are performed through statistical package Stata version 11.1.

Table A.1. Average household income and expenditures, 1996–2014 (in 2015 dollars)

	1996	1997	1998	1999	2000	2001
Unweighted counts of consumer units	20,251	20,850	21,549	27,262	26,947	28,339
Weighted number of CUs (in thousands)	82,629	84,991	84,115	81,692	81,454	88,735
Average income before taxes	57,190	58,766	60,280	62,271	61,246	63,426
Average annual expenditures	50,163	50,346	51,205	52,439	51,567	51,826
Food	7,129	7,189	7,148	7,066	7,024	6,922
Alcoholic beverages	427	426	431	426	417	452
Housing	15,221	15,561	15,859	16,245	15,942	16,332
Apparel and services	2,057	2,063	1,966	1,994	1,914	1,800
Transportation	9,887	9,730	9,774	10,178	10,327	10,470
Health care	2,555	2,572	2,634	2,682	2,711	2,766
Entertainment	2,624	2,577	2,552	2,722	2,542	2,583
Personal care products and services	436	435	428	425	432	314
Reading	249	252	247	240	214	197
Education	690	737	783	769	796	779
Tobacco products and smoking supplies	395	397	402	443	455	433
Miscellaneous	1,231	1,161	1,198	1,175	1,019	985
Cash contributions	1,645	1,600	1,798	1,906	1,848	1,790
Personal insurance and pensions	5,616	5,646	5,982	6,168	5,926	6,003

	2002	2003	2004	2005	2006	2007
Unweighted counts of consumer units	30,398	31,820	36,168	35,625	33,261	31,945
Weighted number of CUs (in thousands)	92,388	97,391	116,282	117,356	118,843	120,171
Average Income before taxes	64,999	65,734	68,495	71,131	71,145	71,969
Average annual expenditures	52,364	51,507	51,091	53,135	53,789	54,396
Food	6,876	6,779	6,978	6,962	7,049	8,080
Alcoholic beverages	449	401	400	428	446	381
Housing	16,439	16,369	16,336	17,185	18,089	18,078
Apparel and services	1,747	1,563	1,518	1,567	1,495	1,452
Transportation	10,404	10,257	9,687	10,063	9,837	9,712
Health care	2,969	2,980	3,018	3,062	3,059	3,079
Entertainment	2,667	2,575	2,621	2,694	2,676	2,747
Personal care products and services	340	341	341	335	332	332
Reading	191	171	163	153	137	135
Education	941	943	1,047	1,089	978	1,025
Tobacco products and smoking supplies	436	394	358	383	382	368

	2002	2003	2004	2005	2006	2007
Miscellaneous	1,062	806	796	892	917	849
Cash contributions	1,798	1,876	1,765	2,016	2,195	2,079
Personal insurance and pensions	6,048	6,052	6,065	6,307	6,197	6,076

	2008	2009	2010	2011	2012	2013	2014
Unweighted counts of consumer units	32,238	32,936	32,883	31,541	31,480	30,315	30,173
Weighted number of CUs (in thousands)	120,770	120,847	121,107	122,287	124,416	125,670	127,006
Average income before taxes	70,017	69,471	67,826	67,086	67,399	64,750	66,762
Average annual expenditures	52,919	51,617	50,109	49,963	50,867	49,637	50,816
Food	7,833	7,654	7,533	7,519	7,631	7,470	7,607
Alcoholic beverages	358	376	369	373	375	369	398
Housing	17,640	17,523	16,971	16,668	16,361	16,390	16,788
Apparel and services	1,305	1,238	1,205	1,140	1,182	1,093	1,138
Transportation	9,172	8,173	8,085	8,514	9,070	8,731	8,582
Health care	3,096	3,281	3,237	3,291	3,469	3,499	4,097
Entertainment	2,691	2,614	2,435	2,367	2,322	2,185	2,354
Personal care products and services	331	332	311	308	313	292	299
Reading	128	120	107	120	99	104	103
Education	1,098	1,124	1,098	1,051	1,191	1,091	1,083
Tobacco products and smoking supplies	344	417	389	366	339	328	307
Miscellaneous	872	824	789	756	807	618	558
Cash contributions	1,910	1,901	1,773	1,811	1,973	1,864	1,788
Personal insurance and pensions	6,142	6,039	5,805	5,680	5,736	5,602	5,715

Source: 1996–2014 Consumer Expenditure Interview Survey Public-Use Microdata, Bureau of Labor Statistics

Table A.2. Conspicuous and inconspicuous expenditure categories

Conspicuous consumption	UCC Code
Food away from home	
Meals at restaurants, carry-outs, and other	790410
Catered affairs	190902
Food on out-of-town trips	190903
Alcoholic beverage away from home	
Alcoholic beverages at restaurants, taverns	790420
Alcoholic beverages purchased on trips	200900
Household textiles	
Bathroom linens	280110
Bedroom linens	280120
Kitchen and dining room linens	280130
Curtains and draperies	280210
Slipcovers, decorative pillows	280220
Other linens	280900
Household furniture (excluding mattress and springs)	
Mattress and springs	290110
Other bedroom furniture	290120
Sofas	290210
Living room chairs	290310
Living room tables	290320
Kitchen, dining room furniture	290410
Infants' furniture	290420
Outdoor furniture	290430
Wall units, cabinets, and other occasional furniture	290440
Floor coverings, nonpermanent	320111
Refrigerator and oven	
Refrigerators, freezers (renter)	300111
Refrigerators, freezers (owned home)	300112
Cooking stoves, ovens (renter)	300311
Cooking stoves, ovens (owned home)	300312
Housewares	
Plastic dinnerware	320310
China and other dinnerware	320320
Flatware	320330
Glassware	320340
Silver serving pieces	320350
Other serving pieces	320360
Household miscellaneous	
Window coverings	320120
Infants' equipment	320130
Outdoor equipment	320150
Lamps and lighting fixtures	320220
Clocks and other household decorative items	320233
Office furniture for home use	320901

Conspicuous consumption	UCC Code
Indoor plants, fresh flowers	320903
Computers and computer hardware for nonbusiness use	690111
Cellular phone service	270102
Men's clothing	
Men's suits	360110
Men's sport coats, tailored jackets	360120
Men's coats and jackets	360210
Men's hosiery	360312
Men's accessories	360330
Men's sweaters and vests	360340
Men's active sportswear	360350
Men's shirts	360410
Men's pants and shorts	360513
Men's costumes	360902
Boys' clothing	
Boys' coats and jackets	370110
Boys' sweaters	370120
Boys' shirts	370130
Boys' hosiery	370213
Boys' accessories	370220
Boys' suits, sport coats, vests	370311
Boys' pants and shorts	370314
Boys' active sportswear	370904
Boys' costumes	370902
Women's clothing	
Women's coats and jackets	380110
Women's dresses	380210
Women's sport coats, tailored jackets	380311
Women's vests and sweaters	380312
Women's shirts, tops, blouses	380313
Women's skirts	380320
Women's pants and shorts	380333
Women's active sportswear	380340
Women's hosiery	380430
Women's suits	380510
Women's accessories	380901
Women's costumes	380903
Girls' clothing	
Girls' coats and jackets	390110
Girls' dresses and suits	390120
Girls' shirts, blouses, sweaters	390210
Girls' skirts, pants, and shorts	390223
Girls' active sportswear	390230
Girls' hosiery	390321
Girls' accessories	390322
Girls' costumes	390902

Table A.2. (*continued*)

Conspicuous consumption	UCC Code
Infants' clothing	
Infant coat, jacket, snowsuit	410110
Infant dresses, outerwear	410120
Infant accessories	410901
Footwear	
Boys' footwear	400210
Women's footwear	400310
Girls' footwear	400220
Watches, jewelry, and luggage	
Watches	430110
Jewelry	430120
Luggage	430130
Vehicle	
New cars	450110
New trucks	450210
Used cars	460110
Used trucks	460901
New motorcycles	450220
Used motorcycles	460902
Automobile finance charges	510110
Truck finance charges	510901
Motorcycle and plane finance charges	510902
Other vehicle finance charges	850300
Auto rental	520511
Auto rental, out-of-town trips	520512
Truck rental	520521
Truck rental, out-of-town trips	520522
Motorcycle rental	520902
Motorcycle rental, out-of-town trips	520905
Aircraft rental	520903
Aircraft rental, out-of-town trips	520906
Car lease payments	450310
Cash down payment (car lease)	450313
Termination fee (car lease)	450314
Truck lease payments	450410
Cash down payment (truck lease)	450413
Termination fee (truck lease)	450414
TV and audio	
Televisions	310140
Personal digital audio players	310314
Sound components and component systems	310320
Boat and motors	
Boat without motor and boat trailers	600121
Purchase of boat with motor	600132
Outboard motors	600110

Conspicuous consumption	UCC Code
Personal care products	
Wigs and hairpieces	640130
Funeral	
Funeral expenses	680140
Cemetery lots, vaults, maintenance fees	680901

Inconspicuous consumption, labor-intensive	UCC Code
Property management and security	
Property management (owned dwellings)	230901
Management and upkeep services for security (owned dwellings)	340911
Property management (owned vacation homes)	230902
Management and upkeep services for security (owned vacation homes)	340912
Household services	
Babysitting and child care in your own home	340211
Babysitting and child care in someone else's home	340212
Care for elderly, invalids, handicapped, etc.	340906
Adult daycare centers	340910
Daycare centers, nursery, and preschools	670310
Housekeeping services	340310
Gardening, lawn care service	340410
Household laundry and dry cleaning, sent out	340520
Home security system service fee	340915
Legal and accounting fees	
Legal fees	680110
Accounting fees	680902

Inconspicuous consumption, experience-driven	UCC Code
Alcoholic beverage at home	
Beer, wine, other alcohol	790330
Lodging on trips	210210
Mattress and springs	
Mattress and springs	290110
Repair of clothing, watch, etc.	
Shoe repair and other shoe service	440110
Alteration, repair, and tailoring of apparel and accessories	440130
Watch and jewelry repair	440150
Apparel laundry and dry cleaning not coin-operated	440210
Automobile service clubs	
Automobile service clubs	620113
Airline, taxi, and ship fares	
Airline fares	530110
Taxi fares and limousine services on trips	530411
Taxi fares and limousine services	530412
Ship fares	530901

Table A.2. (*continued*)

Inconspicuous consumption, experience-driven	UCC Code
Medical services	
Physicians' services	560110
Dental services	560210
Eyecare services	560310
Fees and admissions	
Recreation expenses, out-of-town trips	610900
Social, recreation, health club membership	620111
Fees for participant sports	620121
Participant sports, out-of-town trips	620122
Movie, theater, amusement parks, and other	620211
Movie, other admissions, out-of-town trips	620212
Admission to sporting events	620221
Admission to sports events, out-of-town trips	620222
Fees for recreational lessons	620310
Other entertainment services, out-of-town trips	620903
Musical instruments and other entertainments	
Musical instruments and accessories	610130
Rental and repair of musical instruments	620904
Rental of video cassettes, tapes, films, and discs	620912
Pets, toys, hobbies, and playground equipment	
Pet purchase, supplies, medicine	610320
Pet services	620410
Vet services	620420
Toys, games, arts and crafts, and tricycles	610110
Stamp and coin collecting	610140
Playground equipment	610120
Rental noncamper trailer	520904
Boat and trailer rental out-of-town trips	520907
Rental of campers on out-of-town trips	620909
Rental of other vehicles on out-of-town trips	620919
Rental of boat	620906
Rental of motorized camper	620921
Rental of other RV's	620922
Docking and landing fees	520901
Athletic gear, game tables, and exercise equipment	600210
Bicycles	600310
Camping equipment	600410
Hunting and fishing equipment	600420
Winter sports equipment	600430
Water sports equipment	600901
Other sports equipment	600902
Rental and repair of miscellaneous sports equipment	620908
Other entertainment	
Film	610210
Photo processing	620330
Repair and rental of photographic equipment	620905
Photographic equipment	610230

Inconspicuous consumption, experience-driven	UCC Code
Photographer fees	620320
Live entertainment for catered affairs	680310
Rental of party supplies for catered affairs	680320
Personal care services	
Personal care services	650310
Reading	
Newspaper, magazine by subscription	590310
Newspaper, magazine non-subscription	590410
Books through book clubs	590220
Books not through book clubs	590230
Encyclopedia and other sets of reference books	660310
Tuitions	
College tuition	670110
Elementary and high school tuition	670210
Miscellaneous	
Dating services	680904
Vacation clubs	680905
Credit card memberships	620112
Shopping club membership fees	620115
Cash contributions	
Cash contributions to charities and other organizations	800821
Cash contributions to church, religious organizations	800831
Cash contribution to educational institutions	800841
Cash contribution to political organizations	800851

Table A.3. Regression results

Expenditure regression model with MSA dummies, 2012

	Coef.	Std. err.	z	P > z	95% conf. interval	
Age of householder (ref: 35 to 44)						
16–24	0.273	0.032	8.5	0.000	0.210	0.336
25–34	0.143	0.022	6.5	0.000	0.099	0.186
45–54	−0.047	0.022	−2.2	0.028	−0.089	−0.005
55–64	−0.134	0.024	−5.6	0.000	−0.180	−0.087
65–74	−0.102	0.040	−2.5	0.012	−0.181	−0.023
75 and older	−0.238	0.045	−5.3	0.000	−0.327	−0.149
Income class (ref: P45 to 55)						
P0–5	−0.584	0.038	−15.5	0.000	−0.658	−0.510
P5–15	−0.702	0.031	−22.8	0.000	−0.762	−0.642
P15–25	−0.504	0.029	−17.1	0.000	−0.562	−0.446

Table A.3. (*continued*)

	Coef.	Std. err.	z	P > z	95% conf. interval	
P25–35	−0.286	0.029	−10.0	0.000	−0.342	−0.230
P35–45	−0.177	0.028	−6.3	0.000	−0.233	−0.122
P55–65	0.133	0.028	4.8	0.000	0.078	0.188
P65–75	0.261	0.028	9.3	0.000	0.206	0.317
P75–85	0.435	0.029	15.2	0.000	0.379	0.492
P85–90	0.611	0.035	17.6	0.000	0.543	0.679
P90–99	0.839	0.030	27.6	0.000	0.779	0.898
P99–100	1.420	0.063	22.5	0.000	1.296	1.544
Gender of householder						
Female	−0.068	0.013	−5.2	0.000	−0.094	−0.043
Race/ethnicity of householder (ref: non-Hispanic white)						
African American	−0.091	0.021	−4.4	0.000	−0.132	−0.050
Asian	−0.057	0.029	−1.9	0.052	−0.115	0.001
Hispanic	0.030	0.021	1.4	0.160	−0.012	0.072
Other	−0.001	0.049	0.0	0.991	−0.097	0.096
Marital status of householder (ref: married couple)						
Widowed	−0.142	0.030	−4.8	0.000	−0.201	−0.084
Divorced	−0.124	0.023	−5.5	0.000	−0.168	−0.079
Separated	0.022	0.041	0.5	0.595	−0.059	0.102
Never married	−0.056	0.023	−2.5	0.014	−0.101	−0.011
Composition of earners (ref: single-earners)						
Dual-earner household	−0.031	0.020	−1.6	0.117	−0.070	0.008
Education attainment of householder (ref: high school dropouts)						
High school graduate	0.078	0.024	3.3	0.001	0.032	0.124
Some college and Associate's degree	0.141	0.023	6.1	0.000	0.096	0.187
Bachelor's degree	0.270	0.025	10.6	0.000	0.220	0.320
Masters degree or higher	0.253	0.028	8.9	0.000	0.198	0.309
Household size						
Number of children under 18	0.029	0.007	4.1	0.000	0.015	0.042
Number of seniors age 65 and over	0.006	0.022	0.3	0.799	−0.037	0.048
Homeownership (ref: renter)						
Owner household	0.123	0.016	7.5	0.000	0.091	0.155
MSA dummies (ref: household in non-MSA areas)						
New York, NY	0.397	0.039	10.2	0.000	0.321	0.474
New York, Connecticut suburbs	0.057	0.041	1.4	0.161	−0.023	0.136
New Jersey suburbs	0.154	0.041	3.8	0.000	0.074	0.234
Philadelphia MSA, PA NJ DE MD	0.129	0.040	3.2	0.001	0.050	0.207
Boston-Brockton-Nashua, MA NH ME CT	0.052	0.041	1.3	0.209	−0.029	0.132

	Coef.	Std. err.	z	P > z	95% conf. interval	
Chicago – Gary – Kenosha, IL – IN – WI	0.132	0.034	3.9	0.000	0.065	0.198
Detroit – Ann Arbor – Flint, MI	0.128	0.048	2.7	0.007	0.035	0.221
Cleveland – Akron, OH	0.130	0.062	2.1	0.038	0.007	0.252
Minneapolis – St. Paul, MN – WI	0.131	0.059	2.2	0.025	0.016	0.246
Washington, DC – MD – VA – WV	0.062	0.046	1.4	0.178	–0.028	0.152
Baltimore, MD	0.091	0.062	1.5	0.144	–0.031	0.213
Dallas – Ft. Worth, TX	0.213	0.044	4.9	0.000	0.127	0.299
Houston – Galveston – Brazoria, TX	0.159	0.048	3.3	0.001	0.064	0.254
Atlanta, GA	0.169	0.048	3.5	0.000	0.074	0.264
Miami – Ft. Lauderdale, FL	–0.029	0.060	–0.5	0.634	–0.147	0.089
Los Angeles – Orange, CA	0.150	0.032	4.7	0.000	0.088	0.212
Los Angeles suburbs, CA	0.198	0.049	4.1	0.000	0.102	0.293
San Francisco – Oakland – San Jose, CA	0.172	0.040	4.4	0.000	0.095	0.249
Seattle – Tacoma – Bremerton, WA	0.106	0.050	2.1	0.036	0.007	0.205
San Diego, CA	0.188	0.056	3.4	0.001	0.079	0.298
Phoenix – Mesa, AZ	0.039	0.059	0.7	0.510	–0.076	0.153
Constant	7.622	0.038	198.8	0.000	7.546	7.697

Expenditure regression model, 1996–2012

	ln(veblen)		ln(inconspicuous)		ln(other)	
	Coef.	Std. err.	Coef.	Std. err.	Coef.	Std. err.
Age of householder (ref: 16 to 24)						
25–34	–0.120	0.008	–0.169	0.009	0.220	0.003
34–44	–0.255	0.009	–0.225	0.009	0.259	0.003
45–54	–0.315	0.009	–0.217	0.009	0.278	0.003
55–64	–0.388	0.009	–0.181	0.010	0.239	0.003
65–74	–0.476	0.013	–0.094	0.014	0.126	0.005
75 and older	–0.813	0.014	–0.049	0.015	0.040	0.005
Income elasticity						
ln(income before taxes)	0.146	0.004	0.135	0.004	0.164	0.001
Income elasticity × Income class (ref: P40–60)						
P0–P20	–0.054	0.001	–0.041	0.001	–0.029	0.000
P20–P40	–0.023	0.001	–0.020	0.001	–0.011	0.000
P60–P80	0.022	0.001	0.023	0.001	0.011	0.000
P80–P90	0.039	0.001	0.045	0.001	0.021	0.000
P90–P95	0.051	0.001	0.061	0.001	0.030	0.000
P95–P99	0.062	0.001	0.079	0.001	0.036	0.000

Table A.3. (*continued*)

	ln(veblen)		ln(inconspicuous)		ln(other)	
	Coef.	Std. err.	Coef.	Std. err.	Coef.	Std. err.
P99–P100	0.079	0.001	0.102	0.002	0.044	0.001
Race/ethnicity of householder (ref: non-Hispanic white)						
African American	−0.111	0.006	−0.180	0.006	−0.048	0.002
Asian and Pacific Islander	−0.144	0.009	−0.324	0.009	−0.057	0.003
Hispanic	0.044	0.006	−0.310	0.007	−0.036	0.002
Other	−0.022	0.015	−0.139	0.016	−0.019	0.006
Marital status of householder (ref: Married couple)						
Widowed	−0.216	0.008	−0.106	0.008	−0.122	0.003
Divorced	−0.145	0.006	−0.208	0.006	−0.114	0.002
Separated	−0.110	0.011	−0.128	0.012	−0.082	0.004
Never married	−0.175	0.006	−0.223	0.006	−0.202	0.002
Education attainment of householder (ref: high school dropouts)						
High school graduate	0.181	0.006	0.315	0.006	0.051	0.002
Some college and Associate's degree	0.295	0.006	0.630	0.006	0.078	0.002
Bachelor's degree	0.353	0.007	0.880	0.007	0.139	0.002
Master's degree or higher	0.349	0.008	1.038	0.008	0.165	0.003
Household size						
Number of children under 18	0.016	0.002	0.085	0.002	0.055	0.001
Number of seniors age 65 and older	0.015	0.006	0.044	0.007	0.033	0.002
Homeownership (ref: renter)						
Owner household	0.143	0.004	0.318	0.005	0.062	0.002
Region (Ref: South)						
Northeast	−0.066	0.005	0.017	0.006	0.015	0.002
Midwest	−0.011	0.005	0.059	0.005	−0.008	0.002
West	−0.004	0.005	0.190	0.005	0.075	0.002
Metro size (Ref: less than 125,000)						
More than 4 million	0.140	0.006	0.150	0.006	0.187	0.002
1.2–4 million	0.105	0.006	0.119	0.006	0.124	0.002
0.33–1.19 million	0.115	0.007	0.124	0.007	0.080	0.002
125–329.9 thousand	0.063	0.006	0.122	0.006	0.049	0.002

Table A.4. Average annual expenditures by metropolitan area and year (in 2015 dollars)

1. Fruits and vegetables

	US	NY	CT	NJ	PHI	BOS	CHI	DET	CLE	MIN	DC
2007	598	668	846	677	530	704	725	698	575	835	825
2008	653	664	952	686	648	895	724	657	613	640	761
2009	654	664	991	821	718	827	808	686	577	692	857
2010	677	653	965	787	632	1,045	943	733	543	855	821
2011	711	769	1,182	843	618	994	866	831	605	739	926
2012	728	679	932	852	759	1,215	857	829	589	731	987

	BAL	DAL	HOU	ATL	MIA	LA	LA SUB	SF	SEA	SD	PHX
2007	625	580	578	600	866	904	718	852	605	474	656
2008	531	605	574	460	755	925	846	979	914	832	552
2009	682	610	621	451	806	842	768	863	776	744	661
2010	599	666	653	573	797	832	832	973	658	690	570
2011	856	833	770	610	681	850	950	1,008	688	622	729
2012	705	645	715	850	774	938	1,034	1,007	1,007	822	717

2. Artificial sweeteners

	US	NY	CT	NJ	PHI	BOS	CHI	DET	CLE	MIN	DC
2007	6	5	7	4	4	8	4	10	2	3	11
2008	6	5	11	5	9	12	7	8	6	3	7
2009	6	3	11	0	6	10	7	5	2	5	14
2010	5	1	3	4	1	6	6	4	1	1	4
2011	6	3	7	4	5	10	4	7	2	3	4
2012	5	2	5	2	4	9	3	4	2	0	4

	BAL	DAL	HOU	ATL	MIA	LA	LA SUB	SF	SEA	SD	PHX
2007	5	5	10	5	5	9	3	1	7	4	9
2008	10	7	5	6	8	4	13	5	9	5	1
2009	13	6	5	3	3	5	2	12	5	5	6
2010	3	4	3	6	8	6	3	10	4	0	2
2011	1	9	5	10	1	7	27	3	4	2	4
2012	7	6	5	6	2	6	19	4	5	3	2

3. Candy and chewing gum

	US	NY	CT	NJ	PHI	BOS	CHI	DET	CLE	MIN	DC
2007	80	58	107	78	75	69	89	130	79	101	55
2008	80	42	101	66	75	88	95	66	97	85	88
2009	86	47	115	67	68	85	108	84	95	138	74
2010	78	33	78	63	79	104	97	82	128	96	78
2011	87	56	107	88	70	96	86	78	95	170	91
2012	88	52	85	84	77	124	104	90	72	130	91

Table A.4. (*continued*)

	BAL	DAL	HOU	ATL	MIA	LA	LA SUB	SF	SEA	SD	PHX
2007	95	62	85	94	47	67	87	142	104	37	74
2008	64	96	64	48	31	73	108	87	115	47	78
2009	72	61	86	67	47	59	97	83	123	84	103
2010	58	69	61	67	32	60	87	75	71	21	140
2011	112	72	82	53	51	57	110	108	101	57	91
2012	133	62	62	88	46	88	88	144	135	86	117

4. Coffee

	US	NY	CT	NJ	PHI	BOS	CHI	DET	CLE	MIN	DC
2007	51	46	62	47	53	43	72	51	95	51	66
2008	51	35	58	46	68	74	51	57	40	55	65
2009	58	36	87	57	53	86	51	84	67	62	68
2010	60	43	100	57	78	88	65	64	53	42	113
2011	75	56	114	69	82	127	78	89	78	87	104
2012	86	51	113	71	115	149	71	78	75	81	55

	BAL	DAL	HOU	ATL	MIA	LA	LA SUB	SF	SEA	SD	PHX
2007	75	37	42	42	55	78	97	87	31	45	68
2008	28	43	46	38	52	45	68	45	90	103	42
2009	25	30	42	60	67	69	82	86	64	74	55
2010	45	38	43	48	55	62	82	96	78	49	52
2011	59	75	68	52	58	72	80	97	117	75	51
2012	83	67	64	73	83	110	83	117	120	90	119

5. Roasted coffee

	US	NY	CT	NJ	PHI	BOS	CHI	DET	CLE	MIN	DC
2007	32	34	38	33	39	30	53	34	46	30	38
2008	34	21	42	29	44	55	34	36	31	37	43
2009	39	23	54	36	38	60	36	56	41	40	46
2010	37	26	67	33	59	55	42	35	32	32	69
2011	47	32	70	43	50	85	52	58	42	60	63
2012	53	32	67	34	73	97	37	44	44	45	33

	BAL	DAL	HOU	ATL	MIA	LA	LA SUB	SF	SEA	SD	PHX
2007	56	22	29	29	31	40	58	59	18	29	48
2008	18	31	31	23	28	29	45	34	62	76	32
2009	15	21	29	43	43	50	51	58	55	56	38
2010	25	25	24	29	30	37	52	67	57	34	29
2011	43	45	44	28	25	46	60	64	91	53	31
2012	62	42	34	39	42	65	47	76	80	62	81

6. Tea

	US	NY	CT	NJ	PHI	BOS	CHI	DET	CLE	MIN	DC
2007	29	26	41	34	33	31	33	39	30	25	36
2008	32	25	44	39	42	52	40	40	31	18	71
2009	29	27	56	44	39	43	34	32	19	18	38
2010	29	29	48	29	45	44	34	30	26	40	51
2011	31	35	39	32	61	38	34	34	35	41	36
2012	30	32	32	45	35	47	45	22	40	12	33

	BAL	DAL	HOU	ATL	MIA	LA	LA SUB	SF	SEA	SD	PHX
2007	28	23	34	21	46	48	27	35	33	25	29
2008	19	20	30	13	24	39	21	29	37	56	15
2009	45	32	28	18	25	27	17	31	24	36	28
2010	27	30	15	20	24	23	17	33	22	34	33
2011	31	36	36	24	22	34	27	26	37	23	40
2012	23	22	48	17	20	35	35	59	26	41	17

7. Bottled water

	US	NY	CT	NJ	PHI	BOS	CHI	DET	CLE	MIN	DC
2007	60	70	85	85	49	93	78	86	52	58	100
2008	61	51	91	87	57	87	74	64	76	31	57
2009	57	57	86	73	63	67	69	84	49	53	68
2010	52	61	77	57	56	63	65	47	25	33	75
2011	53	55	90	88	51	78	58	65	55	40	72
2012	57	65	68	87	65	67	58	34	37	64	78

	BAL	DAL	HOU	ATL	MIA	LA	LA SUB	SF	SEA	SD	PHX
2007	79	93	65	53	36	109	85	70	55	54	67
2008	33	62	94	46	52	129	105	85	88	99	63
2009	43	52	91	39	35	90	90	55	55	100	63
2010	44	64	64	69	27	87	77	51	35	58	60
2011	57	67	75	58	30	90	64	59	30	77	55
2012	50	66	86	78	61	86	114	51	70	84	57

8. Wine

	US	NY	CT	NJ	PHI	BOS	CHI	DET	CLE	MIN	DC
2007	97	58	117	180	50	135	101	26	108	247	258
2008	87	70	101	128	90	181	103	52	103	123	163
2009	100	89	214	213	73	189	97	62	80	129	203
2010	87	82	371	138	113	122	79	57	32	119	205
2011	104	67	101	130	178	113	114	83	52	88	179
2012	103	72	178	125	150	200	69	125	36	155	145

Table A.4. (*continued*)

	BAL	DAL	HOU	ATL	MIA	LA	LA SUB	SF	SEA	SD	PHX
2007	202	98	123	86	94	111	73	417	81	55	187
2008	51	94	94	45	98	113	87	194	239	276	43
2009	181	111	219	81	99	104	123	182	189	201	150
2010	93	54	78	101	38	116	56	131	256	119	44
2011	68	85	149	84	96	165	143	259	189	151	244
2012	267	74	104	109	87	101	228	166	176	193	95

9. Other alcoholic beverages

	US	NY	CT	NJ	PHI	BOS	CHI	DET	CLE	MIN	DC
2007	456	346	698	590	390	559	575	464	353	1,098	796
2008	442	292	602	529	539	646	576	381	412	628	774
2009	433	413	662	470	360	635	446	349	439	739	573
2010	412	453	895	443	507	652	375	372	357	813	599
2011	455	368	469	534	478	813	496	520	429	629	875
2012	450	262	553	529	605	813	510	413	294	696	706

	BAL	DAL	HOU	ATL	MIA	LA	LA SUB	SF	SEA	SD	PHX
2007	553	314	570	446	233	549	436	840	367	230	547
2008	291	386	685	300	375	528	458	712	862	714	391
2009	436	426	732	347	322	481	547	715	818	588	608
2010	332	321	367	384	154	528	373	640	859	574	411
2011	412	447	484	479	303	859	429	757	582	746	681
2012	734	447	464	350	282	418	697	654	673	685	483

10. Housing

	US	NY	CT	NJ	PHI	BOS	CHI	DET	CLE	MIN	DC
2007	16,925	17,804	26,262	24,725	19,771	20,330	21,028	15,708	17,772	19,906	26,070
2008	17,102	19,462	27,752	25,163	21,828	20,598	20,771	15,960	16,010	19,652	26,326
2009	16,887	18,853	25,378	25,718	20,183	20,919	20,595	16,704	14,910	18,607	25,083
2010	16,555	18,725	27,056	24,389	19,026	21,261	20,448	16,236	14,681	18,001	25,756
2011	16,813	18,431	25,952	25,635	20,365	21,170	20,510	16,161	14,852	17,333	25,330
2012	16,856	19,937	27,012	24,425	19,799	20,001	19,780	15,817	15,704	18,804	29,379

	BAL	DAL	HOU	ATL	MIA	LA	LA SUB	SF	SEA	SD	PHX
2007	20,279	17,855	18,254	17,478	19,285	22,867	22,081	25,221	20,733	21,890	19,652
2008	20,549	17,805	17,820	16,863	17,712	22,334	23,328	26,080	22,110	23,081	19,504
2009	21,004	18,668	19,963	17,306	19,990	21,755	19,374	25,686	22,117	20,712	17,620
2010	20,061	17,737	18,559	18,416	16,379	20,580	18,859	26,818	21,367	22,018	15,254
2011	21,251	18,851	17,979	18,415	15,494	21,002	19,722	27,032	21,877	21,368	17,979
2012	20,668	18,897	19,097	17,684	15,838	20,804	21,409	24,885	19,453	22,358	19,401

11. Owned dwellings

	US	NY	CT	NJ	PHI	BOS	CHI	DET	CLE	MIN	DC
2007	6,733	4,531	13,195	11,406	7,681	8,733	9,697	6,649	6,603	8,169	12,596
2008	6,760	4,895	12,914	12,785	9,831	8,709	9,049	6,359	6,351	8,913	12,259
2009	6,542	3,868	11,662	11,777	8,562	8,146	9,733	6,878	5,135	8,205	10,649
2010	6,271	4,578	12,386	11,253	7,709 ·	8,445	9,128	6,491	5,539	7,423	10,607
2011	6,147	4,515	12,125	12,409	8,575	8,231	8,467	6,439	5,747	7,355	10,814
2012	6,059	4,224	12,262	11,468	7,747	7,267	8,007	5,610	6,233	7,468	12,169

	BAL	DAL	HOU	ATL	MIA	LA	LA SUB	SF	SEA	SD	PHX
2007	9,769	6,405	7,277	7,542	8,720	8,835	11,210	10,629	8,937	9,316	7,267
2008	9,360	6,423	6,485	7,099	6,380	8,041	10,771	10,828	8,822	8,578	8,442
2009	9,768	6,102	8,269	7,564	7,757	7,841	7,590	11,131	8,660	7,004	6,872
2010	8,255	6,530	6,704	7,316	6,013	7,184	6,849	11,277	8,476	8,669	5,599
2011	9,520	6,326	6,265	7,239	4,490	6,481	6,768	10,576	8,796	7,512	6,180
2012	7,844	6,395	7,234	5,889	5,891	6,218	8,713	8,255	7,369	8,678	7,156

12. Rent

	US	NY	CT	NJ	PHI	BOS	CHI	DET	CLE	MIN	DC
2007	2,491	6,725	2,320	3,033	2,603	3,132	2,433	1,977	2,676	1,997	3,514
2008	2,616	7,172	2,726	2,889	2,572	2,983	2,774	2,147	1,777	2,435	3,860
2009	2,733	8,043	2,644	3,676	3,076	3,441	2,632	2,094	2,402	2,382	4,417
2010	2,776	8,217	2,777	4,154	2,857	3,652	2,691	2,169	2,268	2,209	4,213
2011	2,904	7,844	3,144	3,966	3,013	3,074	3,366	2,032	2,239	1,928	4,280
2012	3,061	8,588	3,536	4,264	2,945	3,578	3,476	2,327	2,244	2,302	4,283

	BAL	DAL	HOU	ATL	MIA	LA	LA SUB	SF	SEA	SD	PHX
2007	2,205	2,911	2,496	2,752	3,583	6,283	2,819	5,780	3,155	6,111	3,386
2008	3,496	3,256	2,837	3,028	4,192	6,773	3,565	6,516	4,057	6,323	2,734
2009	2,951	3,691	2,440	2,545	4,310	6,646	4,130	6,378	3,744	6,390	2,755
2010	2,752	2,898	2,841	2,989	4,045	6,362	4,559	6,639	3,633	6,436	2,548
2011	2,643	3,692	2,587	2,475	5,119	6,880	4,794	6,559	3,491	6,548	2,790
2012	3,868	3,566	2,843	3,314	4,003	7,053	4,158	7,358	3,979	6,095	3,241

13. Owned vacation home

	US	NY	CT	NJ	PHI	BOS	CHI	DET	CLE	MIN	DC
2007	288	928	504	625	491	479	456	346	479	287	359
2008	296	1,136	744	680	754	574	529	297	505	151	539
2009	300	513	556	623	812	354	389	454	238	349	413
2010	277	181	708	128	389	340	583	359	154	466	460
2011	263	361	589	259	368	587	650	111	421	142	913
2012	229	440	679	138	344	595	296	229	295	465	757

Table A.4. (*continued*)

	BAL	DAL	HOU	ATL	MIA	LA	LA SUB	SF	SEA	SD	PHX
2007	50	69	289	129	62	96	304	647	368	118	465
2008	124	91	193	273	296	81	254	449	501	179	157
2009	472	150	379	102	907	269	172	882	433	102	215
2010	1,010	188	219	121	283	381	352	609	546	199	284
2011	493	103	181	156	130	242	310	781	497	186	290
2012	84	188	214	202	295	36	140	425	188	153	346

14. Babysitting and child care in own home

	US	NY	CT	NJ	PHI	BOS	CHI	DET	CLE	MIN	DC
2007	52	21	98	147	87	97	79	16	7	13	294
2008	47	37	169	69	43	123	49	63	3	86	197
2009	47	225	126	304	16	88	63	49	51	17	33
2010	53	31	245	112	45	294	147	55	57	43	13
2011	51	55	217	283	117	40	75	21	0	104	162
2012	54	129	186	118	41	55	121	21	4	48	587

	BAL	DAL	HOU	ATL	MIA	LA	LA SUB	SF	SEA	SD	PHX
2007	28	87	51	19	57	62	56	130	22	113	19
2008	0	5	17	3	5	150	131	105	16	275	107
2009	5	32	155	14	0	81	20	114	27	189	62
2010	291	38	76	16	5	103	58	51	183	150	9
2011	25	28	30	52	11	83	32	127	207	19	1
2012	34	76	51	116	18	80	53	72	66	35	14

15. Housekeeping services

	US	NY	CT	NJ	PHI	BOS	CHI	DET	CLE	MIN	DC
2007	118	171	219	216	122	147	198	44	96	95	241
2008	119	202	188	209	205	164	176	131	92	82	213
2009	112	108	199	110	73	161	203	181	14	90	341
2010	112	165	281	149	109	206	128	123	45	143	326
2011	105	100	159	174	89	182	160	95	27	58	329
2012	132	284	220	141	175	153	141	204	93	84	469

	BAL	DAL	HOU	ATL	MIA	LA	LA SUB	SF	SEA	SD	PHX
2007	104	102	110	89	179	307	136	313	125	289	140
2008	71	82	88	110	107	275	141	257	113	198	134
2009	184	185	214	99	270	262	108	217	232	223	83
2010	113	153	159	109	129	242	202	247	129	113	138
2011	210	145	137	129	57	290	188	386	80	94	122
2012	106	109	148	98	112	272	321	528	81	235	281

16. Televisions

	US	NY	CT	NJ	PHI	BOS	CHI	DET	CLE	MIN	DC
2007	162	222	107	207	130	201	241	143	110	104	256
2008	164	131	303	160	203	113	195	102	132	125	218
2009	140	95	157	124	105	147	211	115	144	91	133
2010	119	83	112	147	122	128	179	99	151	132	169
2011	113	106	182	180	46	108	141	114	105	143	145
2012	102	83	143	112	97	121	126	96	160	93	160

	BAL	DAL	HOU	ATL	MIA	LA	LA SUB	SF	SEA	SD	PHX
2007	187	264	94	181	166	175	195	200	252	94	135
2008	236	226	259	119	298	187	258	230	255	62	216
2009	128	160	289	81	202	148	164	146	163	105	95
2010	208	193	217	113	87	93	38	129	115	65	186
2011	81	128	230	108	161	142	116	129	108	129	75
2012	180	96	92	110	48	131	92	90	92	117	122

17. Women's footwear

	US	NY	CT	NJ	PHI	BOS	CHI	DET	CLE	MIN	DC
2007	160	259	212	264	181	123	458	137	1	158	231
2008	138	210	221	174	136	195	105	110	101	222	237
2009	149	245	362	98	108	181	145	101	97	121	349
2010	146	324	209	123	199	96	246	101	232	85	192
2011	151	343	217	141	94	259	179	157	94	206	238
2012	159	277	121	161	213	154	198	205	74	64	298

	BAL	DAL	HOU	ATL	MIA	LA	LA SUB	SF	SEA	SD	PHX
2007	111	169	168	161	140	213	147	144	118	152	266
2008	41	174	125	72	52	162	214	209	27	89	133
2009	283	273	260	147	122	133	194	437	345	298	266
2010	138	247	80	291	100	166	104	139	218	118	133
2011	55	167	329	192	94	158	162	93	119	495	130
2012	207	195	73	261	145	187	278	84	118	198	168

18. Women's clothes

	US	NY	CT	NJ	PHI	BOS	CHI	DET	CLE	MIN	DC
2007	626	934	1,008	941	472	546	1,200	651	1,235	923	934
2008	594	555	1,037	883	690	535	817	481	1,185	765	702
2009	558	550	876	544	492	645	602	510	307	574	1,129
2010	565	737	768	472	738	538	703	477	614	415	753
2011	600	977	757	804	462	647	614	429	720	782	1,067
2012	571	540	706	594	775	564	633	589	433	889	767

Table A.4. (*continued*)

	BAL	DAL	HOU	ATL	MIA	LA	LA SUB	SF	SEA	SD	PHX
2007	338	449	667	469	497	608	693	629	1,043	740	1,056
2008	420	725	500	538	526	654	330	987	709	518	367
2009	606	878	827	576	523	466	914	870	875	1,437	648
2010	543	691	584	446	166	839	723	526	953	546	1,954
2011	580	925	833	547	400	625	587	772	342	569	614
2012	672	908	412	848	461	723	803	1,013	599	774	736

19. Men's clothes

	US	NY	CT	NJ	PHI	BOS	CHI	DET	CLE	MIN	DC
2007	353	515	263	464	454	342	327	383	331	529	518
2008	345	485	517	362	356	200	431	233	180	374	572
2009	304	376	392	327	318	408	299	406	258	264	432
2010	304	535	520	426	512	368	251	228	201	394	701
2011	323	462	423	424	370	302	410	240	227	282	509
2012	318	442	527	379	337	312	363	235	225	361	424

	BAL	DAL	HOU	ATL	MIA	LA	LA SUB	SF	SEA	SD	PHX
2007	502	407	241	426	118	470	261	784	551	493	330
2008	312	277	290	300	147	469	375	387	697	626	329
2009	382	350	437	176	245	276	1,341	259	446	379	322
2010	412	276	218	217	152	371	449	632	365	269	156
2011	414	505	528	283	194	434	443	385	423	180	340
2012	316	446	335	418	245	481	286	516	566	357	255

20. Personal care products and services

	US	NY	CT	NJ	PHI	BOS	CHI	DET	CLE	MIN	DC
2007	587	591	746	798	594	534	725	468	574	694	749
2008	616	582	855	608	687	650	726	562	481	761	920
2009	595	536	797	733	620	662	696	671	439	700	1,017
2010	581	515	884	618	633	756	709	528	625	650	967
2011	634	611	705	769	569	716	741	633	626	702	1,127
2012	629	664	685	732	724	703	614	679	516	857	925

	BAL	DAL	HOU	ATL	MIA	LA	LA SUB	SF	SEA	SD	PHX
2007	511	740	804	487	578	732	697	852	641	510	761
2008	596	776	714	570	628	765	820	1,009	879	689	641
2009	715	698	708	651	618	627	686	812	796	682	1,080
2010	687	745	796	667	580	664	612	753	958	679	454
2011	605	911	774	624	503	766	780	823	746	647	566
2012	1,028	691	913	655	633	708	650	830	726	703	678

21. Dating services

	US	NY	CT	NJ	PHI	BOS	CHI	DET	CLE	MIN	DC
2007	0.39	0.34	0.13	1.04	0.00	0.00	0.20	0.48	0.00	0.00	0.54
2008	0.26	1.05	0.27	0.00	0.00	0.00	0.00	0.73	0.00	0.00	0.00
2009	0.38	1.28	0.02	0.00	0.28	0.47	0.28	0.31	0.00	0.00	0.00
2010	0.32	0.86	0.21	0.00	0.45	0.00	0.00	3.05	0.00	0.00	0.34
2011	0.44	0.77	0.00	0.00	1.01	0.06	0.53	2.19	0.00	0.00	1.11
2012	0.50	0.13	0.00	0.43	0.00	0.12	0.59	1.33	0.00	1.51	0.82

	BAL	DAL	HOU	ATL	MIA	LA	LA SUB	SF	SEA	SD	PHX
2007	0.00	0.00	0.44	0.16	0.00	0.27	0.38	0.14	0.33	0.00	0.53
2008	0.00	0.00	0.26	0.00	0.00	0.00	0.67	0.16	1.18	0.00	0.89
2009	1.04	0.00	0.00	0.00	0.00	0.39	0.00	0.22	0.00	0.00	0.30
2010	0.00	0.00	0.00	0.00	0.00	0.30	0.00	0.16	0.00	0.00	0.00
2011	0.00	0.17	0.00	0.93	0.36	1.53	0.00	0.00	0.00	0.00	0.00
2012	0.00	2.26	0.00	0.35	0.00	0.00	0.00	0.35	6.05	0.00	0.00

22. Social, recreation, health club membership

	US	NY	CT	NJ	PHI	BOS	CHI	DET	CLE	MIN	DC
2007	123	133	194	117	186	278	203	59	79	127	220
2008	127	104	395	158	169	281	199	94	86	280	158
2009	115	95	238	165	209	215	147	197	42	196	271
2010	121	50	208	237	143	208	124	106	55	139	307
2011	122	117	312	185	115	124	164	139	92	151	246
2012	127	110	187	167	100	144	316	121	225	198	322

	BAL	DAL	HOU	ATL	MIA	LA	LA SUB	SF	SEA	SD	PHX
2007	100	58	136	59	48	94	303	253	118	115	101
2008	154	87	216	70	40	111	110	256	188	124	225
2009	109	63	187	105	39	141	56	231	192	108	83
2010	100	98	86	102	40	130	35	163	322	93	87
2011	92	157	115	181	29	218	68	252	215	187	114
2012	98	85	101	113	89	162	65	317	185	191	233

NOTES

CHAPTER 1.
THE TWENTY-FIRST-CENTURY "LEISURE" CLASS

1. The "lady tasting tea test" is a now famous study of one of the first statistical experiments, and the foundation of what statisticians call the "null hypothesis," or the assertion that two or more observed phenomena are not related—in this case, the lady's ability to determine the composition of the tea and the reality of milk in first or last. In Fischer's experiment, the null hypothesis (that the lady could not determine the composition of the tea) was rejected (because in fact she did). I first came across this story and Fischer's formulation of the null hypothesis in David Salsburg's 2002 book, *The Lady Tasting Tea: How Statistics Revolutionized Science in the 20th Century.*

2. Fortnum and Mason 2014.

3. I must thank the writer and historian Kate Berridge for this information.

4. Douglas and Isherwood 1996.

5. Ibid.

6. While Veblen was always careful to point out that status emulation occurred in all strata of society, he was most critical of the leisure class.

7. Menken 1920, p. 72.

8. Hutchinson 1957.

9. As the great twentieth-century public intellectual John Kenneth Galbraith observed of Veblen, he practiced what he wrote: Veblen's house was a sty, his bed unmade, and he was agnostic at a time when most of his colleagues espoused Christianity and divinity degrees. Veblen never really fit in. In a 1957 essay in *The Listener*, the famous economist T. W. Hutchinson called him "an economist outsider" but also "something of a major American prophet" who studied and understood the social and economic matters of the human condition.

10. Galbraith remarked it is one of the only books written by an economist in the nineteenth century that is still read today.

11. Veblen's concerns about status also revolved around a number of other key concepts, ranging from the subjection of women, to the argument that all of society remains tribal (and by extension barbarian), to his work on the practices and objects that demarcate status. This latter focus is perhaps the most damning of current society, particularly his study of conspicuous leisure (education, intellectualism, sporting activities) and nonpecuniary practices (etiquette and manners), conspicuous waste (such as unnecessary house help or burning blankets like the Kwakiutl), and, of course, conspicuous consumption.

12. Vaizey 1975; Seckler 1975.

13. Capitalism dates back to the fourteenth century with tensions between English

aristocracy and agricultural producers, but modern-day capitalism, also known as merchant capitalism, can be traced to sixteenth- to eighteenth-century England.

14. For example, he believed all of social hierarchy had much to do with Darwinism and predatory behavior rather than simply class.

15. Wallace-Hadrill 1990, pp. 145–192.

16. Again I must thank Kate Berridge for this example.

17. Wallace-Hadrill 1994; Berridge 2007.

18. Berridge 2007.

19. Interview with Kate Berridge.

20. Wallace-Hadrill 1994, p. 166.

21. Wallace-Hadrill 1990.

22. Price 2014.

23. Richards 1991, p. 8.

24. Charles et al. 2009.

25. Richards 1991.

26. A/X data: https://en.wikipedia.org/wiki/Armani#Armani_Exchange. J.Crew data: http://www.vault.com/company-profiles/retail/j-crew-group,-inc/company-overview.aspx. Ralph Lauren data: http://www.vault.com/company-profiles/general-consumer-products/ralph-lauren-corporation/company-overview.aspx. The Gap data: http://www.gapinc.com/content/gapinc/html/aboutus/keyfacts.html.

27. http://www.economist.com/node/17963363.

28. Ibid., and http://www.dailymail.co.uk/femail/article-2822546/As-Romeo-Beckham-stars-new-ad-Burberry-went-chic-chav-chic-again.html.

29. Ewing 2014.

30. Frank 2012.

31. The study uses education as a proxy for wealth as the two variables tend to correlate.

32. Gershuny 2000; Lesnard 2003.

33. http://www.statista.com/statistics/184272/educational-attainment-of-college-diploma-or-higher-by-gender/.

34. Please see Piore and Sabel 1984.

35. http://www.economist.com/node/4462685.

36. Wilson 1987.

37. Reich 1992.

38. Florida's understanding of economic restructuring includes all sectors and occupations that are responsible for generating "meaningful new forms," which includes a whole host of other workers including artists, musicians, writers, scientists, engineers, and other members of the "creative class." See Florida 2002.

39. Brooks 2000, pp. 85–94.

40. Trentmann 2016.

CHAPTER 2.
CONSPICUOUS CONSUMPTION IN THE TWENTY-FIRST CENTURY

1. Galbraith 1958.

2. In Vance Packard's *The Status Seekers*, he argues that material goods do not

actually reveal status. Many of the trappings of social behavior rely on hidden behaviors and norms such as choice of word or accent.

3. Johnson 1988.

4. As the historian Donna Loftus told me, Victorian England middle classes had a somewhat fraught relationship with conspicuous consumption. On one hand, they were extremely frugal and proclaimed the importance of thrift and austerity and eating porridge, yet others buy fancy houses with highly decorated interiors.

5. The numbers in this chapter are mainly from the Consumer Expenditure Interview Survey Public-Use Microdata. They may be slightly different from those from Consumer Expenditure Diary or Integrated Survey, but the overall trend is consistent.

6. 1996 is the earliest data that allow us to undertake this analysis in detail.

7. The consumption ratio is defined here as the ratio of (a) the amount of dollars spent on conspicuous consumption of a certain subpopulation over the US average conspicuous consumption expenditures, to (b) the earnings/income of a certain subpopulation over the US average income. [consumption ratio = (the amount of money spent on conspicuous consumption of group i / the US average amount of money spent on conspicuous consumption) / (the income of group i / the US average income)].

8. Low-income families spend 38% more than their income ratio would suggest, but 4 points less than they did in 1996.

9. "The higher the education, the higher the cremation rate. The higher the income, the higher the cremation rate. Asian populations cremate at a higher rate. Urban communities cremate at a higher rate. African-American populations have a lower cremation rate." http://connectingdirectors.com/articles/3220-cremation-by-the-numbers-cana-projections-are-in#sthash.Ol9aUPLC.dpuf.

10. Charles et al. 2009.

11. Heffetz 2011.

12. For a complete breakdown of all variables studied and regression results, please see the appendix to this book.

13. In more recent analysis my colleagues and I included total expenditure as one of the control variables. Taking into account total expenditures we find that more education corresponds with a lesser total share of expenditure on conspicuous consumption. See Currid-Halkett et al. 2018. To examine how consumption behavior differs across different population groups, this research estimates the following equation:

$$y_{ijt} = X_{ijt}\beta + \alpha_j + \tau_t + \varepsilon_{ijt}$$

where y_{ijt} is the log of consumption of household i in metropolitan area j in year t. We compare regression coefficients with different types of consumption, such as conspicuous consumption, inconspicuous consumption, and other expenditures. X_{ijt} is a vector of demographic and socio-economic characteristics of an individual household, α_j is a metropolitan area characteristic, and τ_t is a year fixed effect. The sampling weights are used in the regression to account for sampling design, and robust standard errors are used to correct for heteroscedasticity. For more detailed information, see the appendix, as well as the table "Consumption by Income Class," which is available online.

CHAPTER 3.
BALLET SLIPPERS AND YALE TUITION: INCONSPICUOUS
CONSUMPTION AND THE NEW ELITES

1. Bourdieu 1984.

2. Zukin and Macguire 2004.

3. Packard 1959, chapter 10, p. 85.

4. The term inconspicuous consumption has been used by others to describe other consumption phenomena. See for example Postrel 2008. In his 1957 essay on fashion, the German sociologist Georg Simmel observed that once the middle classes began to imitate the elites' form of dressing, the elites re-configured their style to again distinguish themselves, which he believed explained why fashion changed so much and so quickly. If not for class, Simmel argued, fashion would not exist. Fashion's raison d'être is to essentially reaffirm existing class lines through visual cues. And the same can be applied to mannerisms and styles of life. Along Simmel's lines, the increasing ostentation and public display of wealth present in middle-class life has made the upper middle classes revert from the baroque affectation of Veblen's time to more subtle signifiers of social status. The WASPs have always prized discretion and in-the-know forms of status symbols (bulky Barbour coats, vacationing in the Hamptons when they were rustic and rural), but this more subtle form of class identification has spread across the new elites.

5. Gershuny 2000.

6. Fussell 1983.

7. Khan and Jerolmack 2013.

8. Holt 1998.

9. Khan 2012.

10. Packard 1959, chapter 10, pp. 89–90.

11. Johnston and Baumann 2007.

12. Khan 2012.

13. Ibid., p. 16.

14. Moore 2012.

15. Bennhold 2012.

16. U = upper class and non-U = non-upper class.

17. Cooke 2012.

18. Fussell 1983.

19. Weber 1978.

20. Bourdieu called the milieu in which we gained this information and capital the "habitus," or the environment and larger system in which tastes were formed and were different from other habitus.

21. Lamont 1992.

22. Gill 2014.

23. Khan and Jerolmack 2013.

24. Gershuny 2000.

25. Please see the appendix for a detailed breakdown of the consumption categories and items collected from BLS Consumer Expenditure data.

26. Frank 2015.

27. Sayer, Bianchi, and Robinson 2004.

28. Bianchi 2000.

29. Bianchi, Milkie, Sayer, and Robinson 2000.

30. Sullivan 2014.

31. Kurtzleben 2013.

32. Work by Miles Corak shows that those societies where education provides the greatest benefits are also far less mobile. Corak 2013.

33. Gunderman 2014.

34. Lee and Painter 2016.

35. Mills 1956.

36. Khan 2015.

37. Dale, Krueger, and National Bureau of Economic Research 2011.

38. The only exception to the Dale and Krueger paper is for racial and ethnic minorities (black and Hispanic) and for students with parents who have little education. Dale and Krueger believe this result may be due to highly selective colleges providing good access networks for these more disadvantaged students, and as such they leave university with greater social and cultural capital than they entered it, which is not the case for the wealthy, elite students.

CHAPTER 4.
MOTHERHOOD AS CONSPICUOUS LEISURE IN THE
TWENTY-FIRST CENTURY

1. Health and Human Services has aimed for the goal that 50% of women breast-feed exclusively through 6 months and 75% partially breast-feed through 12 months (most babies start to eat solid food at 4–6 months).

2. Sacker et al. 2013.

3. CDC Breastfeeding Report Card 2013.

4. Arora et al. 2000.

5. CDC Breastfeeding Report Card 2014.

6. Racial discrepancies exist as well, with 80% of non-Hispanic whites breast-feeding versus 65% of blacks. Among those who do breast-feed, Asians and non-Hispanic whites are the most likely to follow the guidelines precisely: Almost 16% of Asians and 13% of non-Hispanic whites exclusively breast-feed through 6 months, while 76% of all non-Hispanic white women at least initiate breast-feeding. Age matters too. Seventy-seven percent of mothers giving birth over the age of 30 breast-feed, while younger mothers are less likely to do so.

7. McDowell, Wang, and Kennedy-Stephenson 2008.

8. Heck, Braveman, Cubbin, Chávez, and Kiely 2006.

9. Robinson 2011.

10. Barthes 2012.

11. Ibid., pp. 79–82.

12. Barthes 2012.

13. Ibid., p. 82.

14. Barthes 2012, pp. 84–84.

15. Barthes 2012, p. 129.

16. Barthes 2012.

17. McCann, Baydar, and Williams 2007.

18. Langellier, Chaparro, Wang, Koleilat, and Waley 2014.

19. Guendelman et al. 2009.

20. http://www.pewresearch.org/fact-tank/2014/05/07/opting-out-about-10-of -highly-educated-moms-are-staying-at-home/.

21. Cohen 2014.

22. Sandberg 2013.

23. Kendall 2013.

24. For further fascinating research on the topic of low-income mothers and their barriers to breast-feeding, please see Chin and Dozier 2012.

25. For a review of some of the key research in this area, please see: http://fivethirty eight.com/features/everybody-calm-down-about-breastfeeding/.

26. Groskop 2013.

27. Bakalar 2014.

28. http://www.theatlantic.com/magazine/archive/2009/04/the-case-against -breast-feeding/307311/. Rosen 2009.

29. http://www.theguardian.com/commentisfree/2011/apr/01/france-breast -breastfed-baby-death.

30. Sussman 1975, p. 313.

31. Ibid.

32. Sussman 1975.

33. Ibid., p. 313.

34. Golden 1996.

35. Ibid.

36. Wright and Schanler 2001.

37. Druckerman 2012.

38. Wright and Schanler 2001.

39. Roth and Henley 2012.

40. Gould, Davey, and Stafford 1989.

41. Shapiro 2012, p. MM18.

42. Many people might think home birth is a curious choice given the pain and lack of a medical doctor, but a surprising number of women would prefer this option. Marian MacDorman, a statistician with the CDC and an expert on home births, suggested, "Maybe these [minority, poor] women are less interested in home births. But as a midwife pointed out to me, 'Maybe they just don't have the access.'" MacDorman continued, "Recent survey data supports the second hypothesis. Black women were interested at the same rate as whites ... [While] the cost of a home birth is about a third of a hospital birth but most insurance doesn't cover it."

43. Garcia-Navarro 2013.

44. http://www.slate.com/articles/double_x/doublex/2012/01/cesarean_nation _why_do_nearly_half_of_chinese_women_deliver_babies_via_c_section_.html.

45. Diamond 2012.

46. Weber 1905.

47. Veblen even went on to point out that much of the staff in a wealthy household was somewhat unnecessary, suggesting that they too were sitting around and being unproductive, an observation he coined "conspicuous waste."

48. Guryan, Hurst, and Kearney 2008.

49. Ramey and Ramey 2010.

50. http://static1.squarespace.com/static/54694fa6e4b0eaec4530f99d/t/55102730e
4b0bc812283d0ed/1427121968182/Investing+in+Children-+Changes+in+Parental
+Spending+on+Children%2C+1972%E2%80%932007.pdf.

51. Linder 1970.

52. Brooks 2013; Klinkenborg 2013. For a more expanded look at the issue, see
American Academy for Arts and Sciences 2013.

53. http://observer.com/2005/04/lotte-berk-in-last-stretch/#ixzz3fnrZvF13.

54. http://observer.com/2005/03/battle-of-the-butts/#ixzz3ftn8Qx9B. My interview
with Jennifer Williams was also very helpful on the history of the Lotte Berk studio and
the origin of cardio barre classes.

55. http://observer.com/2005/03/battle-of-the-butts/.

56. Greif 2016.

57. http://www.economist.com/news/united-states/21660170-sweating-purpose
-becoming-elite-phenomenon-spin-separate.

58. Druckerman 2012.

59. Greenfeld 2014.

60. Bell 1976.

61. Trentmann 2016, p. 18.

62. Daniel 2016.

CHAPTER 5.
CONSPICUOUS PRODUCTION

1. Fair Trade is a large organization involving many different actors (farmers, import-
ers, exporters, and roasters) that aims to offer a living wage and sustainable production on a
wide scale. By meeting minimum standards put forth by Fair Trade, farmers gain access to
a larger market for their goods and are given funds to further help their business. These efforts are laudable, but there are significant drawbacks: Coffee can be sold for much higher
prices to consumers, but those profits are not returned to the original farmers; quantity
matters more than quality (farmers are not compensated for better quality beans); and the
local distribution centers (offering the relationships and discretionary funds) can be poorly
run. There are a number of upsides to the alternative Direct Trade model: there's no middleman (so that it is just a relationship between the farmer and the roaster); smaller crops that
allow for diversification of beans; a negotiated discussion between the farmer and the roaster
on the appropriate price for a particular batch of beans (farmers are paid an accurate price
based on value of the beans); and an emphasis on quality over quantity. See Keller 2015.

2. Greif 2016, p. 47.

3. If you are confusing my point with that of Brooks's "bobos," allow me to clarify.
Bobos are bohemians who grew up and got rich and wrestle with their bohemian sensibilities and bourgeois paychecks. The rise of conspicuous production actually brings
together those who still don't have any money (hipsters, bohemians) with those who
have lots of it, because they share the same values and at the price point of coffee, tomatoes, and organic cotton t-shirts they can both actually afford.

4. http://reason.org/news/show/whole-foods-health-care.

5. http://www.newyorker.com/magazine/2006/05/15/paradise-sold.

6. See Molotch 2002; Zukin and Kosta 2004.

7. http://www.ers.usda.gov/data-products/chart-gallery/detail.aspx?chartId=48561&ref=collection&embed=True.

8. Haughney 2013.

9. http://www.statista.com/statistics/282479/sales-revenue-of-farmers-markets-in-the-united-kingdom-uk/.

10. Haughney 2013, p. B1.

11. Alkon 2008.

12. Johnston 2008.

13. Alkon and McCullen 2011.

14. Greif 2016, pp. 50–52.

15. Daniels did note, however, that one of the biggest road blocks still today is labor practices. While there has been a lot of attention devoted to the food production, labor is still an unresolved issue. As she put it, "There is a great deal of strength in local economy, sustainability, and animal welfare groups but labor is often still behind in the public consciousness." There have been important strides: For example, the tomato laborers in Immokalee, Florida formed a coalition and convinced buyers of the tomatoes to pay an extra penny per pound and devote that penny to their coalition to support more fair labor practices. (For an in-depth look at the tomato industry, please see Barry Estabrook's *Tomatoland* [2012].) In February 2016, President Obama signed the Trade Facilitation and Trade Enforcement Act, which prohibits the purchasing of food that has been produced by child labor or forced labor (as is the case with shrimp sold in the United States, much of it coming from Thailand, which is notorious for such exploitative labor practices). At the time 350 items, including Thailand shrimp, were on the list. The original Tariff Act of 1930 was created to prevent such violations but has only been used 39 times in the past 86 years because of a loophole around "consumptive demand." If there was great demand for a particular import, it was allowed to be sold in the United States regardless of production practices. (See Mendoza 2016.)

16. Keynes 1920.

17. Moltoch 2002.

18. IOAN company website: http://www.industryofallnations.com/About-Industry-Of-All-Nations-ccid_55.aspx.

19. http://www.ecommercebytes.com/cab/abn/y11/m01/i11/s01.

20. "Artisanal Capitalism: The Art and Craft of Business." *The Economist*. January 4, 2014.

21. Clifford 2013a.

22. Sirkin, Zinser, and Manfred 2013.

23. Clifford 2013c.

24. Segran 2016, Clifford 2013b.

25. 15 facts that can't be ignored about U.S. manufacturing 2016.

26. Gittleson 2015.

27. Clifford 2013c.

28. Ibid.

29. Clifford 2013b.

30. Clifford 2013a.

31. Bajaj 2012.

32. Yardley 2013.

33. Barboza 2008.

34. "Made in the USA" Matters to Shoppers 2012.

35. Gittleson 2015.

36. www.worldwildlife.org.

37. www.worldwildlife.org.

38. Engels 1845.

39. For some thorough summaries of the environmental movement, key events, literature, and legislation, please see the following websites: http://www.pbs.org/wgbh /americanexperience/features/timeline/earthdays/; http://www.encyclopedia.com/earth -and-environment/ecology-and-environmentalism/environmental-studies/environ mental-movement; https://en.wikipedia.org/wiki/Environmental_movement_in_the _United_States; https://www.minnpost.com/earth-journal/2013/07/25-classics-environ mental-writing-help-your-summer-reading-list.

40. Inglehart 2000, p. 223.

41. Inglehart 2000.

42. http://abcnews.go.com/GMA/story?id=6225503.

43. Doherty and Etzioni 2003. Please see http://simplicitycollective.com/start-here /what-is-voluntary-simplicity-2 for general overviews on the movement and its history.

44. Etzioni 2004.

45. Taylor-Gooby 1998.

46. Grigsby 2004.

47. I must thank Harvey Molotch for his observation here.

48. Obniski 2008.

49. "Artisanal Capitalism: The Art and Craft of Business." *The Economist*. January 4, 2014.

50. Barber 2013.

51. I must thank Joan Halkett for her knowledge on this topic.

52. Marx, K. (1980; Originally 1844). *The economic and philosophic manuscripts of 1844*. New York: International Books; and SparkNotes, "The Economic and Philosophic Manuscripts of 1844" Summary: First Manuscript "Estranged Labor." Retrieved from http://www.sparknotes.com/philosophy/marx/section1.rhtml.

53. Rapoza 1999.

54. Ibid.

55. http://www.cnn.com/2005/TECH/science/04/22/anwr.protests/

56. Rosenberg 1999; Goldberg 1999.

57. Roberts 2010.

58. Farrell 2007.

59. "Colgate expands reach into quirky toothpaste," 2006.

60. http://voices.yahoo.com/top-5-cosmetic-companies-test-animals-today -5584883.html.

CHAPTER 6.
LANDSCAPES OF CONSUMPTION

1. Zukin 1993.

2. North 1955; Jacobs 1969; Glaeser 2005.

3. Engels 1845; Simmel 1903; Riis 2009.

4. Jackson 1985.

5. Christopherson and Storper 1986; Sassen 2012.

6. Storper 2013, p. 72.

7. Saxenian 1994; Scott 2005; Storper 1997.

8. See Florida 2002; Drucker 1993; Bell 1973; Reich 1991.

9. Storper 2013.

10. Diamond 2016.

11. Storper 2013.

12. Krugman 2015.

13. Florida 2002.

14. Please read Kenneth Jackson's *Crabgrass Frontier* (1985) for a fascinating account of the evolution of American cities and suburbs and the government policies that facilitated these outcomes.

15. Jackson 1985; Kunstler 1993.

16. Storper 2013.

17. Glaeser, Kolko, and Saiz 2001.

18. Diamond 2012. See also Berry and Glaeser 2005.

19. Sadler 2010; 2016.

20. Glaeser has a great discussion of this interplay in chapter 5 of his book *Triumph of the City* (2011).

21. Glaeser 2011.

22. Costa and Kahn 2000.

23. http://www.nytimes.com/2016/02/23/upshot/rise-in-marriages-of-equals-and-in-division-by-class.html.

24. Ibid.

25. Glaeser 2011.

26. Handbury 2012.

27. Rampell 2013.

28. Diamond 2012.

29. Lloyd and Clark 2001.

30. Silver, Clark, and Yanez 2010.

31. Wirth 1938.

32. Leher 2010.

33. González, Hidalgo, and Barabási 2008.

34. Leher 2010.

35. Please see the appendix for detailed comparative consumption patterns across cities; and the table "Consumption Patterns by Cities," which is available online at press.princeton.edu/titles/10933.html.

36. http://streeteasy.com/blog/new-york-city-rent-affordability/.

37. Dewan 2014.

38. New Jersey suburbs: Counties of Bergen, Essex, Hudson, Hunterdon, Mercer, Middlesex, Monmouth, Morris, Ocean, Passaic, Somerset, Sussex, Union, Warren. New York suburbs: Counties of Dutchess, Nassau, Orange, Putnam, Rockland, Suffolk, Westchester. Connecticut suburbs: Counties of Fairfield, Hartford, Litchfield, Middlesex, New Haven, Tolland.

39. Simmel 1903.

40. Diamond 2012.

41. Glaeser 2011.

42. Kleinberg 2012.

43. http://www.nytimes.com/2013/10/13/fashion/the-high-end-matchmaking-service-for-tycoons.html.

44. Mills 1956.

45. Please see the appendix for detailed regression results.

46. Simmel 1903.

47. Luttmer 2005.

48. Salkin 2009.

49. See also Holt 1998 and Lamont 1992.

50. Weber 1978.

51. Bourdieu 1984; Lamont 1992; Holt 1998.

52. Currid-Halkett, Lee, and Painter 2016.

53. Ibid.

54. Molotch 2003.

55. http://www.nytimes.com/2010/09/02/fashion/02Diary.html?pagewanted=all&_r=0.

56. Young 2014.

57. Douthat, R. (2016, July 3). "The Myth of Cosmopolitism." *Sunday Review: New York Times.* Retrieved from http://www.nytimes.com/2016/07/03/opinion/sunday/the-myth-of-cosmopolitanism.html?_r=0.

58. I must thank Saskia Sassen for helping me think through the connectivity of cities around global elite consumption. One cloudy summer afternoon in London, Saskia and I met for coffee and spoke about this idea and she came up with the concept of an "invisible tissue of urbanity."

CHAPTER 7.
"TO GET RICH IS GLORIOUS"? THE STATE OF CONSUMPTION AND CLASS IN AMERICA

1. Kahnemon and Deaton 2010.

2. Easterlin, Angelescu-McVey, Switek, Sawangfa, and Zweig 2010.

3. Summers 2006.

4. Schor 1991.

5. Raffaelli 2015.

6. "Second Wind" 2014.

7. Murray 2012.

8. http://www.zocalopublicsquare.org/event/is-healthy-living-only-for-the-rich/#.Va0cPWfslzI.facebook.

9. Schor 1998.

10. http://www.pewsocialtrends.org/2012/08/22/the-lost-decade-of-the-middle-class/.

11. Lewis 2010.

12. Luce 2010.

13. PBS NewsHour 2013.

14. Ibid.

15. Luce 2010.

16. Piketty 2014.

17. http://www.pewsocialtrends.org/2012/08/22/the-lost-decade-of-the-middle
-class/.

18. Freeland 2012.

19. http://www.tcf.org/work/workers_economic_inequality/detail/a-tale-of-two
-recoveries.

20. Lowrey 2014.

21. Coontz 2014.

22. http://www.foxbusiness.com/personal-finance/2014/05/14/median-american
-savings-0/.

23. Kharas and Gertz 2010.

24. Pezinni 2012.

25. Yueh 2013; "Who's in the Middle?" 2009; and Kharas and Gertz 2010.

26. Kharas and Gertz 2010.

27. Kharas 2011.

28. Kharas and Gertz 2010.

29. Ibid.

30. Ali and Dadush 2012.

31. www.statista.com/statistics/199983/us-vehicle-sales-since-1951/.

32. As much discussion as there is around the global middle class, there are a number of critiques suggesting that it is not nearly as omnipresent or well-to-do as some suggest. See for example Burrows 2015 and Bremmer 2016.

33. Court and Narasimhan 2010.

34. Easterlin 2007.

35. Graham and Pettinato 2001.

36. There is much debate around whether Deng Xiaoping actually made this statement, although it is regularly attributed to him. In fact, there is no documented proof he actually uttered these words, although they have become synonymous with his role in opening the floodgates of capitalism in China. See also Iritani 2004.

37. Douglas and Isherwood 1979.

REFERENCES

15 facts that can't be ignored about U.S. manufacturing. (2016, May 15). *MP Star Financial*. Retrieved from https://www.mpstarfinancial.com/15-facts-thatcant-be-ignored-about-us-manufacturing/.

Ali, S., & Dadush, U. (2012, May 16). The global middle class is bigger than we thought. *Foreign Policy*. Retrieved from http://www.foreignpolicy.com/articles/2012/05/16/the_global_middle_class_is_bigger_than_we_thought.

Alkon, A. H. (2008). From value to values: Sustainable consumption at farmers markets. *Agriculture and Human Values 25*(4): 487–498. doi:10.1007/s10460-008-9136-y.

Alkon, A. H., & McCullen, C. G. (2011). Whiteness and farmers markets: Performances, perpetuations ... Contestations? *Antipode 43*(4): 937–959. doi:10.1111/j.1467-8330.2010.00818.x.

American Academy for Arts and Sciences (2013). The heart of the matter: The humanities and social science for a vibrant, competitive and secure nation. Cambridge, MA: American Academy for Arts and Sciences.

Arora, S., McJunkin, C., Wehrer, J., & Kuhn, P. (2000). Major factors influencing breastfeeding rates: Mother's perception of father's attitude and milk supply. *Pediatrics 106*(5): e67.

Bagwell, L. S., & Bernheim, B. D. (1996). Veblen effects in a theory of conspicuous consumption. *American Economic Review 86*(3): 349–373.

Bajaj, V. (2012, November 25). Fatal fire in Bangladesh highlights the dangers facing garment workers. *New York Times*. Retrieved from http://www.nytimes.com/2012/11/26/world/asia/bangladesh-fire-kills-more-than-100-and-injures-many.html.

Bakalar, N. (2014, March 4). Is breast-feeding really better? Retrieved from http://well.blogs.nytimes.com/2014/03/04/is-breast-feeding-really-better/.

Barber, E. W. (2013, November 11). Etsy's industrial revolution. *New York Times*. Retrieved from http://www.nytimes.com/2013/11/12/opinion/etsys-industrial-revolution.html.

Barboza, D. (2008, January 5). In Chinese factories, lost fingers and low pay. *New York Times*. Retrieved from http://www.nytimes.com/2008/01/05/business/worldbusiness/05sweatshop.html.

Barthes, R. (2012, originally 1957). *Mythologies*. Translated by Annette Lavers. New York: Hill and Wang.

Bee, A., Meyer, B., & Sullivan, J. The validity of consumption data: Are the Consumer Expenditure Interview and Diary Surveys informative? In *Improving the measurement of consumer expenditures*, edited by C. Carroll, T. Crossley, & J. Sabelhaus, 204–240. Chicago: University of Chicago Press, 2015.

Bell, D. (1973). *The coming of post-industrial society: A venture in social forecasting*. New York: Basic Books.

———. (1976). *The cultural contradictions of capitalism.* New York: Basic Books.

Bennhold, K. (2012, April 26). Class war returns in new guises. *New York Times.* Retrieved from http://www.nytimes.com/2012/04/27/world/europe/27iht-letter27.html.

Berridge, K. (2007). *Madame Tussaud: A life in wax.* New York: Harper Perennial.

Berry, C. R., & Glaeser, E. L. (2005). The divergence of human capital levels across cities. *Papers in Regional Science 84*(3): 407–444. doi:10.1111/j.1435-5957.2005.00047.x.

Bianchi, S. M. (2000). Maternal employment and time with children: Dramatic change or surprising continuity? *Demography 37*(4): 401–414. doi:10.1353/dem.2000.0001.

Bianchi, S. M., Milkie, M. A., Sayer, L. C., & Robinson, J. P. (2000). Is anyone doing the housework? Trends in the gender division of household labor. *Social Forces 79*(1): 191–228. doi:10.1093/sf/79.1.191.

Blaszczyk, R. L. (2005). Review of *Point of purchase: How shopping changed American culture,* by Sharon Zukin. *Enterprise and Society 6*(2): 339–341. doi:10.1093/es/khi047.

Bourdieu, P. (1984). *Distinction: A social critique of the judgment of taste.* Cambridge, MA: Harvard University Press.

Bremmer, I. (2016). These five facts explain the unstable global middle class. *Time Magazine,* January 29. Retrieved from http://time.com/4198164/these-5-facts-explain-the-unstable-global-middle-class/.

Brooks, D. (2000). *Bobos in paradise: The new upper class and how they got there.* New York: Simon & Schuster.

———. (2013). The humanist vocation. *New York Times,* June 13.

Browne, A. (2014, August 15). The great Chinese exodus. *Wall Street Journal.* Retrieved from http://online.wsj.com/articles/the-great-chinese-exodus-1408120906?mod=WSJ_hp_RightTopStories.

Burrows, M. (2015). The emerging global middle class—so what? *Washington Monthly 38*(1): 7–22.

Canning, R., Pereira, J., Frias, M., & Ibanga, I. (2008, November 14). Victoria's secret: Formaldehyde in bras? *ABC News.* Retrieved from http://abcnews.go.com/GMA/story?id=6225503&page=1.

CDFuneralNews. (2011, November 3). Cremation by the numbers, CANA Projections Are In.

Centers for Disease Control. (2013). Breastfeeding report card/United States. https://www.cdc.gov/breastfeeding/pdf/2013breastfeedingreportcard.pdf.

———. (2014). Breastfeeding report card/United States. Retrieved from https://www.cdc.gov/breastfeeding/pdf/2013breastfeedingreportcard.pdf.

Charles, K. K., Hurst, E., & Roussanov, N. (2009). Conspicuous consumption and race. *Quarterly Journal of Economics 124*(2): 425–467. doi:10.1162/qjec.2009.124.2.425.

Chin, N., & Dozier, A. (2012). The dangers of baring the breast: Structural violence and formula feeding among low income women. In *Beyond health, beyond choice: Breastfeeding constraints and realities,* edited by P. H. Smith, B. L. Hausman, & M. Labbok, 64–73. New Brunswick, NJ: Rutgers University Press.

Christopherson, S., & Storper, M. (1986). The city as studio; the world as back lot: The impact of vertical disintegration on the motion picture industry. *Environment and Planning D: Society and Space* 4, 3: 305–320.

Cisotti, C. (2013, September 11). Claire used £1 Nivea cream on half her face—and £105 Crème de la Mer on the other. The results are very revealing. *Mail Online.* Retrieved from http://www.dailymail.co.uk/femail/article-2418153/Claire-used-1-Nivea-cream -half-face--105-Cr-la-Mer-The-results-VERY-revealing.html.

Clifford, S. (2013a, September 19). U.S. textile plants return, with floors largely empty of people. *New York Times*. Retrieved from http://www.nytimes.com/2013/09/20 /business/us-textile-factories-return.html?pagewanted=all.

———. (2013b, September 29). A wave of sewing jobs as orders pile up at U.S. factories. *New York Times*. Retrieved from http://www.nytimes.com/2013/09/30/business/a -wave-of-sewing-jobs-as-orders-pile-up-at-us-factories.html.

———. (2013c, November 30). That "made in U.S.A." premium. *New York Times*. Retrieved from http://www.nytimes.com/2013/12/01/business/that-made-in-usa-pre mium.html.

Cohen, C. (2014, May 22). The politics of breastfeeding. *New York Times*. Retrieved from http://www.nytimes.com/roomfordebate/2014/05/22/the-politics-of-breastfeeding /most-women-cant-afford-to-breastfeed.

Colgate expands reach of quirky toothpaste. (2006, March 21). *USA Today*. Retrieved from http://usatoday30.usatoday.com/money/industries/retail/2006-03-21-colgate -toms_x.htm.

ConnectingDirectors.com. Retrieved from http://connectingdirectors.com/articles /3220-cremation-by-the-numbers-cana-projections-are-in#sthash.Ol9aUPLC.dpuf.

Cooke, R. (2012, April 21). Where does Francis Maude keep his condiments? *Guardian*. Retrieved from http://www.theguardian.com/lifeandstyle/2012/apr/22/kitchen-sup pers-francis-maude.

Coontz, S. (2014, July 26). The new instability. *New York Times*. Retrieved from http:// www.nytimes.com/2014/07/27/opinion/sunday/the-new-instability.html.

Corak, M. (2013). Income inequality, equality of opportunity, and intergenerational mo bility. *Journal of Economic Perspectives 27*(3): 79–102. doi:10.1257/jep.27.3.79.

Costa, D. L., & Kahn, M. E. (2000). Power couples: Changes in the locational choice of the college educated, 1940–1990. *Quarterly Journal of Economics 115*(4): 1287–1315.

Court, D., & Narasimhan, L. (2010, July). Capturing the world's emerging middle class. *McKinsey Quarterly*. Retrieved from http://www.mckinsey.com/insights/consumer _and_retail/capturing_the_worlds_emerging_middle_class.

Cowen, T. (2015, December 24). The marriages of power couples reinforce income in equality. *New York Times*. Retrieved from http://www.nytimes.com/2015/12/27 /upshot/marriages-of-power-couples-reinforce-income-inequality.html.

Crane, D. (2013, October 11). The high-end matchmaking service for tycoons. *New York Times*. Retrieved from http://www.nytimes.com/2013/10/13/fashion/the-high-end -matchmaking-service-for-tycoons.html.

Cunningham, M. (2008). Review of *Changing rhythms of American family life*, by Suzanne M. Bianchi, John P. Robinson, and Melissa A. Milkie. *Gender and Society 22*(4): 524–526. doi:10.1177/0891243208315383.

Currid, E. (2006). New York as a global creative hub: A competitive analysis of four theories on world cities. *Economic Development Quarterly 20*(4): 330–350. doi:10 .1177/0891242406292708.

Currid-Halkett, E, Lee, H., Painter, G. (2018). *Veblen Goods and Metropolitan Distinc tion: An Economic Geography of Conspicuous Consumption*. Working Paper: LUSK Center for Real Estate, University of Southern California.

Currid-Halkett, E., Lee, H., & Painter, G. (2016). Veblen goods and metropolitan distinction: An economic geography of conspicuous consumption. Working paper, University of Southern California.

Dale, S., Krueger, A. B., & National Bureau of Economic Research. (2011). *Estimating the return to college selectivity over the career using administrative earnings data.* National Bureau of Economic Research.

Dana, R. (2005, March 7). Battle of the butts. *Observer.* Retrieved from http://observer.com/2005/03/battle-of-the-butts/#ixzz3ftn8Qx9B.

———. (2005, April 25). Lotte Berk in last stretch? *Observer.* Retrieved from http://observer.com/2005/04/lotte-berk-in-last-stretch/#ixzz3fnrZvF13.

Daniel, C. (2016, February 16). A hidden cost to giving kids their vegetables. *New York Times.* Retrieved from http://www.nytimes.com/2016/02/16/opinion/why-poor-children-cant-be-picky-eaters.html?_r=0.

Dewan, S. (2014, April 14). In many cities, rent is rising out of reach of middle class. *New York Times.* Retrieved from http://www.nytimes.com/2014/04/15/business/more-renters-find-30-affordability-ratio-unattainable.html.

Diamond, J. (2012). *The world until yesterday: What can we learn from traditional societies?* New York: Penguin Press.

Diamond, R. (2016). The determinants and welfare implications of US workers' diverging location choices by skill: 1980–2000. *American Economic Review 106*(3): 479–524. doi:10.1257/aer.106.3.479.

Doherty, D., & Etzioni, A. (2003). *Voluntary simplicity: Responding to consumer culture.* Lanham, MD: Roman & Littlefield.

Douglas, M., & Isherwood, B. C. (1996). *The world of goods: Towards an anthropology of consumption: With a new introduction* ([Rev.] ed.). London; New York: Routledge.

Drucker, P. F. (1993). *Post-capitalist society.* New York: Routledge.

Druckerman, P. (2012). *Bringing up bébé: One American mother discovers the wisdom of French parenting.* New York: Penguin Press.

Easterlin, R. (2007). The escalation of material goods: Fingering the wrong culprit. *Psychological Inquiry 18*(1): 31–33.

Easterlin, R., Angelescu-McVey, L., Switek, M., Sawangfa, O., & Zweig, J. S. (2010). The happiness-income paradox revisited. Proceedings of National Academy of Sciences of the United States of America, 2010, 107(52), pp. 22463–22468.

Estabrook, B. (2012). *Tomatoland: How modern industrial agriculture destroyed our most alluring fruit.* Kansas City, MO: Andrews McMeel Publishing.

Engels, F. (1845). The conditions of the working class in England. Panther Edition, 1969, from text provided by the Institute of Marxism-Leninism, Moscow; First published: Leipzig, 1845. https://www.marxists.org/archive/marx/works/download/pdf/condition-working-class-england.pdf.

Etzioni, A. (2004). The post affluent society. *Review of Social Economy 62*(3): 407–420. doi:10.1080/0034676042000253990.

Ewing, J. (2014, March 7). Offering more than luxury, supercars draw a crowd of makers and buyers. *New York Times.* Retrieved from http://www.nytimes.com/2014/03/08/business/international/market-is-crowded-for-high-end-cars.html.

Farmers' market sales revenue in the UK 2002–2011. (2016). *Statista.* Retrieved from http://www.statista.com/statistics/282479/sales-revenue-of-farmers-markets-in-the-united-kingdom-uk/.

Farrell, A. (2007, October 31). Clorox to buy Burt's Bees. *Forbes*. Retrieved from http://www.forbes.com/2007/10/31/clorox-burts-bees-markets-equity-cx_af_1031markets15.html.

Florida, R. L. (2002). *The rise of the creative class: And how it's transforming work, leisure, community and everyday life*. New York: Basic Books.

Fortnum & Mason. (2014, February 27). How to make tea. *Fortnum & Mason*. Retrieved from http://www.fortnumandmason.com/c-77-the-perfect-cup-of-tea-fortnum-and-mason.aspx.

Frank, R. (2012, April 27). Do the wealthy work harder than the rest? *Wall Street Journal*. Retrieved from http://blogs.wsj.com/wealth/2012/04/27/do-the-wealthy-work-harder-than-the-rest/tab/video/.

———. (2015, June 20). For the new superrich, life is much more than a beach. *New York Times*. Retrieved from http://www.nytimes.com/2015/06/21/business/for-the-new-superrich-life-is-much-more-than-a-beach.html?_r=0.

Freeland, C. (2012). *Plutocrats: The rise of the new global super-rich and the fall of everyone else*. New York: Penguin Press.

Fussell, P. (1983). *Class: A guide through the American status system*. New York: Simon & Schuster.

Galbraith, J. K. (1958). *The affluent society*. New York: Houghton Mifflin Harcourt.

Garcia-Navarro, L. (2013, May 12). C-sections deliver cachet for wealthy Brazilian women. *NPR.org*. Retrieved from http://www.npr.org/2013/05/12/182915406/c-sections-deliver-cachet-for-wealthy-brazilian-women.

Gershuny, J. (2000). *Changing times: Work and leisure in postindustrial society*. Oxford; New York: Oxford University Press.

Ghertner, D. A. (2015). *Rule by aesthetics: World-class city making in Delhi*. New York: Oxford University Press.

Gibbons, F. (2011, April 1). In France, breast is definitely not best. *Guardian*. Retrieved from https://www.theguardian.com/commentisfree/2011/apr/01/france-breast-breastfed-baby-death.

Gill, A. A. (2014, May). Perfection anxiety. *Vanity Fair*. Retrieved from http://www.vanityfair.com/society/2014/05/super-rich-perfection-anxiety.

Gittleson, K. (2015, February 20). US manufacturing: The rise of the niche manufacturer. *BBC Business*. Retrieved from http://www.bbc.com/news/business-31527888.

Glaeser, E. L. (2005). Urban colossus: Why is New York America's largest city? *Economic Policy Review* (112): 7–24.

———. (2011). *Triumph of the city: How our greatest invention makes us richer, smarter, greener, healthier, and happier*. New York: Penguin Press.

Glaeser, E. L., Kolko, J., & Saiz, A. (2001). Consumer city. *Journal of Economic Geography* 1(1): 27–50.

Goldberg, C. (1999). Vermonters would keep a lid on Ben & Jerry's pint. *New York Times*, December 22.

Golden, J. (1996). *A social history of wet nursing in America: From breast to bottle*. Cambridge: Cambridge University Press.

González, M. C., Hidalgo, C. A., & Barabási, A.-L. (2008). Understanding individual human mobility patterns. *Nature* 453(7196): 779–782. doi:10.1038/nature06958.

Gould, J. B., Davey, B., & Stafford, R. S. (1989). Socioeconomic differences in rates of cesarean section. *New England Journal of Medicine* 321(4): 233–239. doi:10.1056/NEJM198907273210406.

Graham, C., & Pettinato, S. (2001). Frustrated achievers: Winners, losers and subjective well-being in new market economies. Brookings Institution Center on Social and Economic Dynamics, Working Paper No. 21. https://www.brookings.edu/wp-content/uploads/2016/06/frustrated.pdf.

Greenfeld, K. T. (2014, May 24). Faking cultural literacy. New York Times. Retrieved from http://www.nytimes.com/2014/05/25/opinion/sunday/faking-cultural-literacy.html.

Grigsby, M. (2004). *Buying time and getting by: The voluntary simplicity movement.* Albany: State University of New York Press.

Groskop, V. (2013, February 9). Breast is best – isn't it? Debate rages over the effect on mother and child. *Guardian.* Retrieved from https://www.theguardian.com/lifeandstyle/2013/feb/10/breastfeeding-best-debate.

Guendelman, S., Kosa, J. L., Pearl, M., Graham, S., Goodman, J., & Kharrazi, M. (2009). Juggling work and breastfeeding: Effects of maternity leave and occupational characteristics. *Pediatrics 123*(1): e38–e46. doi:10.1542/peds.2008-2244.

Gunderman, R. (2014, July 16). The case for concierge medicine. *Atlantic.* Retrieved from http://www.theatlantic.com/health/archive/2014/07/the-case-for-concierge-medicine/374296/.

Guryan, J., Hurst, E., & Kearney, M. (2008). Parental education and parental time with children. *Journal of Economic Perspectives 22*(3): 23–46. doi:10.1257/jep.22.3.23.

Handbury, J. (2012). *Are poor cities cheap for everyone? Non-homotheticity and the cost of living across U.S. cities* (Job Market Paper). Retrieved from www.princeton.edu/~reddings/cure2012/Handbury.pdf.

Haughney, C. (2013, September 17). A magazine for farm-to-table. *New York Times.* Retrieved from http://www.nytimes.com/2013/09/18/business/media/a-magazine-for-farm-to-table.html.

Heck, K. E., Braveman, P., Cubbin, C., Chávez, G. F., & Kiely, J. L. (2006). Socioeconomic status and breastfeeding initiation among California mothers. *Public Health Reports 121*(1): 51–59.

Heffetz, O. (2011). A test of conspicuous consumption: Visibility and income elasticities. *Review of Economics and Statistics 93*(4): 1101–1117. doi:10.1162/REST_a_00116.

Hills-Bonczyk, S. G., Tromiczak, K. R., Avery, M. D., Potter, S., Savik, K., & Duckett, L. J. (1994). Women's experiences with breastfeeding longer than 12 months. *Birth 21*(4): 206–212.

Holt, D. B. (1998). Does cultural capital structure American consumption? *Journal of Consumer Research 25*(1): 1–25. doi:10.1086/jcr.1998.25.issue-1.

Hutchinson, T. W. (1957, November 28). An economist outsider. *Listener.*

Hvistendahl, M. (2012, January 3). Why does China have the world's highest C-section rate? *Slate Magazine.* Retrieved from http://www.slate.com/articles/double_x/doublex/2012/01/cesarean_nation_why_do_nearly_half_of_chinese_women_deliver_babies_via_c_section_.html.

Industrial metamorphosis. (2005, September 29). *Economist.* Retrieved from http://www.economist.com/node/4462685.

Inglehart, R. (2000). Globalization and postmodern values. *Washington Quarterly 23*(1): 215–228.

Iritani, E. (2004). Great idea but don't quote him. *Los Angeles Times*, September 9. http://articles.latimes.com/2004/sep/09/business/fi-deng9.

Is college worth it? (2014, April 5). *Economist*. Retrieved from http://www.economist.com/news/united-states/21600131-too-many-degrees-are-waste-money-return-higher-education-would-be-much-better.

Jackson, K. T. (1985). *Crabgrass frontier: The suburbanization of the United States*. Oxford: Oxford University Press.

Jacobs, J. (1969). *The economy of cities*. New York: Random House.

Johnson, P. (1988). Conspicuous consumption and working-class culture in late-Victorian and Edwardian Britain. *Transactions of the Royal Historical Society 38*: 27–42. doi:10.2307/3678965.

Johnston, J. (2008). The citizen-consumer hybrid: Ideological tensions and the case of Whole Foods Market. *Theory and Society 37*(3): 229–270. doi:10.1007/s11186-007-9058-5.

Johnston, J., & Baumann, S. (2007). Democracy versus distinction: A study of omnivorousness in gourmet food writing. *American Journal of Sociology 113*(1): 165–204. doi:10.1086/518923.

Kahnemon, D. and Deaton, A. (2010). High income improves evaluation of life but not emotional well-being. *PNAS* vol. 107(38) pp. 16489–16493.

Keller, S. (2015). Straight talk on fair trade versus direct trade according to Brazilian coffee farmers. *Huffington Post*. Retrieved from http://www.huffingtonpost.com/stephanie-keller/straight-talk-on-fairtrad_b_8305090.html.

Kendall, M. (2013, September 23). The real mommy wars. *Salon.com*. Retrieved from http://www.salon.com/2013/09/23/the_real_mommy_wars/.

Kerr, W. (1962). *The decline of pleasure*. New York: Simon & Schuster.

Keynes, J. M. (1920). *The economic consequences of the peace*. Library of Economics and Liberty. Retrieved from http://www.econlib.org/library/YPDBooks/Keynes/kynsCP2.html.

Khan, S. (2012). The sociology of elites. *Annual Review of Sociology 38*(1): 361–377. doi:10.1146/annurev-soc-071811-145542.

———. (2015). The counter-cyclical character of the elite. In *Elites on trial: Research in the sociology of organizations*, vol. 43 (1st ed.), pp. 81–103. UK: Emerald Group Publishing.

Khan, S., & Jerolmack, C. (2013). Saying meritocracy and doing privilege. *Sociological Quarterly 54*(1): 9–19. doi:10.1111/tsq.12008.

Kharas, H. (2011). The emerging middle class in developing countries. OECD Development Centre Working Paper No. 285.

Kharas, H., & Gertz, G. (2010). "The new global middle class." A crossover from west to east. Brookings Institution Report. Retrieved from https://www.brookings.edu/research/the-new-global-middle-class-a-cross-over-from-west-to-east/.

Khazan, O. (2014, September 16). Wealthy L.A. schools' vaccination rates are as low as South Sudan's. *Atlantic*. Retrieved from http://www.theatlantic.com/health/archive/2014/09/wealthy-la-schools-vaccination-rates-are-as-low-as-south-sudans/380252/.

Kleinberg, E. (2012). One's a crowd. *Sunday Review: New York Times*, February 4. http://www.nytimes.com/2012/02/05/opinion/sunday/living-alone-means-being-social.html.

Klinkenborg, V. (2013). The decline and fall of the English major. *Sunday Review: New York Times*, June 22.

Kornrich, S., & Furstenberg, F. (2013). Investing in children: Changes in parental spending on children, 1972–2007. *Demography 50*(1): 1–23. doi:10.1007/s13524-012-0146-4.

Krugman, P. (2015, November 30). Inequality and the city. *New York Times*. Retrieved from http://www.nytimes.com/2015/11/30/opinion/inequality-and-the-city.html?_r=0.

Kunstler, J. (1993). *The geography of nowhere*. New York: Simon & Schuster.

Kurtzleben, D. (2013, October 23). Just how fast has college tuition grown? *US News & World Report*. Retrieved from http://www.usnews.com/news/articles/2013/10/23/charts-just-how-fast-has-college-tuition-grown.

Lamont, M. (1992). *Money, morals, and manners: The culture of the French and American upper-middle class*. Chicago: University of Chicago Press.

Landy, B. (2013, August 28). A tale of two recoveries: Wealth inequality after the Great Recession. *Century Foundation*. Retrieved from https://tcf.org/content/commentary/a-tale-of-two-recoveries-wealth-inequality-after-the-great-recession/.

Langellier, B., Chaparro, M. P., Wang, M., Koleilat, M., and Waley, S. E. (2014). The new food package and breastfeeding outcomes among women, infants and children participants in Los Angeles County. *American Journal of Public Health* 104: 2S.

Lee, H., and Painter, G. (2016). Consumption inequality in the Great Recession. *Journal of Economic and Social Measurement 41*, 2 (2016): 145–166.

Leher, J. (2010). A physicist solves the city. *New York Times Magazine*, December 17. Retrieved from http://www.nytimes.com/2010/12/19/magazine/19Urban_West-t.html.

Leibenstein, H. (1950). Bandwagon, snob, and Veblen effects in the theory of consumers' demand. *Quarterly Journal of Economics 64*(2): 183–207. doi:10.2307/1882692.

Leonhardt, D. (2014, April 26). Getting into the Ivies. *New York Times*. Retrieved from http://www.nytimes.com/2014/04/27/upshot/getting-into-the-ivies.html.

Lesnard, L. (2003). Review of *Changing times: Work and leisure in postindustrial society*, by Jonathan Gershuny. *European Sociological Review 19*(2): 235–239. doi:10.1093/esr/19.2.235.

Lewis, L. B., McMillan, T., & Bastani, R. (2015, July 29). *Is healthy living only for the rich?* Zócalo Public Square lecture presented at Museum of Contemporary Art, Los Angeles.

Lewis, M. (2010). *The big short: Inside the doomsday machine*. New York: W.W. Norton.

Lightfeldt, A. (2015, March 1). Bright lights, big rent burden: Understanding New York City's rent affordability problem. *StreetEasy Blog*. Retrieved from http://streeteasy.com/blog/new-york-city-rent-affordability/.

Linder, S. B. (1970). *The harried leisure class*. New York: Columbia University Press.

Livingston, G. (2014, May 7). Opting out? About 10% of highly educated moms are staying at home. *Pew Research Center*. Retrieved from http://www.pewresearch.org/fact-tank/2014/05/07/opting-out-about-10-of-highly-educated-moms-are-staying-at-home/.

Lloyd, R., & Clark, T. N. (2001). The city as an entertainment machine. *Research in Urban Sociology 6*: 357–378.

The lost decade of the middle class. (2012, August 22). *Pew Research Center*. Retrieved from http://www.pewsocialtrends.org/2012/08/22/the-lost-decade-of-the-middle-class/.

Lowrey, A. (2014, April 30). Changed life of the poor: Better off, but far behind. *New York Times*. Retrieved from http://www.nytimes.com/2014/05/01/business/economy/changed-life-of-the-poor-squeak-by-and-buy-a-lot.html.

Luce, E. (2010, July 30). The crisis of middle-class America. *Financial Times*. Retrieved from https://www.ft.com/content/1a8a5cb2-9ab2-11df-87e6-00144feab49a.

Luttmer, E. F. P. (2005). Neighbors as negatives: Relative earnings and well-being. *Quarterly Journal of Economics 120*(3): 963–1002.

"Made in the USA" matters to shoppers [press release]. (2012, September 13). Retrieved from https://www.greenbook.org/marketing-research/made-in-the-usa-matters-to-shoppers-00707.

Martin, J. (1982). *Miss Manners' guide to excruciatingly correct behavior.* New York: W. W. Norton.

McCann, M., Baydar, N. and Williams, R. (2007). Breastfeeding attitudes and report problems in a national sample of WIC participants. *Journal of Human Lactation 23*(4): 314–324.

McDowell, M. M., Wang, C.-Y., & Kennedy-Stephenson, J. (2008). *Breastfeeding in the United States: Findings from the National Health and Nutrition Examination Survey, 1999–2006.* Centers for Disease Control. NCHS Data Brief. Retrieved from http://www.cdc.gov/nchs/data/databriefs/db05.htm.

Mendoza, M. 2016. Federal officials are preparing to enforce an 86-year-old ban on importing goods made by children or slaves under new provisions of a law signed by President Barack Obama. *US News and World Report*, February 16. Retrieved from http://www.usnews.com/news/us/articles/2016-02-24/obama-bans-us-imports-of-slave-produced-goods.

Menken, H. L. (1920). *Prejudices: First series.* New York: Knopf.

Miller, C. C., & Bui, Q. (2016, February 27). Equality in marriages grows, and so does class divide. *New York Times.* Retrieved from http://www.nytimes.com/2016/02/23/upshot/rise-in-marriages-of-equals-and-in-division-by-class.html.

Miller, D. (2012). *Consumption and its consequences.* Cambridge: Polity.

Mills, C. W. (1956). *The power elite.* New York: Oxford University Press.

Molotch, H. (2002). Place in product. *International Journal of Urban and Regional Research 26*(4): 665–688. doi:10.1111/1468-2427.00410.

———. (2003). *Where stuff comes from: How toasters, toilets, cars, computers, and many others things come to be as they are.* New York: Routledge.

Moore, C. (2012, March 30). Even I'm starting to wonder: What does this lot know about anything? *Daily Telegraph.* Retrieved from http://www.telegraph.co.uk/news/politics/conservative/9176237/Even-Im-starting-to-wonder-what-do-this-lot-know-about-anything.html.

Murray, C. A. (2012). *Coming apart: The state of white America, 1960–2010* (1st ed.). New York: Crown Forum.

North, D. C. (1955). Location theory and regional economic growth. *Journal of Political Economy 63*(3): 243–258.

Obniski, M. (2008). The Arts and Crafts movement in America. Metropolitan Museum of Art. Retrieved from http://www.metmuseum.org/toah/hd/acam/hd_acam.htm.

O'Brien, M. (2014, July 29). The middle class is 20 percent poorer than it was in 1984. *Washington Post.* Retrieved from http://www.washingtonpost.com/blogs/wonkblog/wp/2014/07/29/the-middle-class-is-20-percent-poorer-than-it-was-in-1984/.

Oster, E. (2015, May 20). Everybody calm down about breastfeeding. *FiveThirtyEight.* Retrieved from http://fivethirtyeight.com/features/everybody-calm-down-about-breastfeeding/.

Packard, V. (1959). *The status seekers.* David McKay Publications.

PBS NewsHour. (2013, December 26). Tracking the breakdown of American social institutions in "The Unwinding." Retrieved from http://www.pbs.org/newshour/bb/business-july-dec13-packer_12-26/.

Pellow, D. (2005). Review of *Buying time and getting by: The voluntary simplicity movement*, by Mary Grigsby. *American Journal of Sociology 110*(5): 1520–1522. doi:10.1086/431619.

Percentage of the U.S. population with a college degree 1940–2014, by gender. (2016). *Statista*. Retrieved from http://www.statista.com/statistics/184272/educational-attainment-of-college-diploma-or-higher-by-gender/.

Pezinni, M. (2012). An emerging middle class. *OECD Observer*. http://oecdobserver.org/news/fullstory.php/aid/3681/An_emerging_middle_class.html.

Piketty, T. (2014). *Capital in the twenty-first century*. Cambridge, MA: Harvard University Press.

Piore, M. J., & Sabel, C. F. (1984). *The second industrial divide: Possibilities for prosperity*. New York: Basic Books.

Postrel, V. (2008, July 8). Inconspicuous consumption: A new theory of the leisure class. *Atlantic*. Retrieved from http://www.theatlantic.com/magazine/archive/2008/07/inconspicuous-consumption/306845/2/.

Price, Q. (2014). Capitalism for the many, not the few. Unpublished working paper.

Pugh, A. J. (2004). Windfall child rearing: Low-income care and consumption. *Journal of Consumer Culture 4*(2): 229–249. doi:10.1177/1469540504043683.

———. (2005). Selling compromise: Toys, motherhood, and the cultural deal. *Gender and Society 19*(6): 729–749. doi:10.1177/0891243205279286.

———. (2011). Distinction, boundaries or bridges?: Children, inequality and the uses of consumer culture. *Poetics 39*(1): 1–18. doi:10.1016/j.poetic.2010.10.002.

Raffaelli, R. (2015). *The re-emergence of an institutional field: Swiss watchmaking*. Harvard Business School working paper no. 16-003.

Ramey, G., & Ramey, V. A. (2010). The rug rat race. *Brookings Papers on Economic Activity 2010*(1): 129–176. doi:10.1353/eca.2010.0003.

Rampell, C. (2013, April 23). Who says New York is not affordable? *New York Times*. Retrieved from http://www.nytimes.com/2013/04/28/magazine/who-says-new-york-is-not-affordable.html.

Rapoza, K. (1999, December 16). Will big business gobble up Ben and Jerry's? *Salon*. Retrieved from http://www.salon.com/1999/12/16/ben_and_jerry/.

Reich, R. B. (1992). *The work of nations: Preparing ourselves for 21st-century capitalism* (1st ed.). New York: Knopf.

Rice, A. (2014, June 29). Stash pad. *New York Magazine*. Retrieved from http://nymag.com/news/features/foreigners-hiding-money-new-york-real-estate-2014-6.

Richards, T. (1991). *The commodity culture of Victorian England: Advertising and spectacle, 1851–1914*. Palo Alto, CA: Stanford University Press.

Riis, J. (2009, originally 1890). *How the other half lives*. New York: CreateSpace.

Roberts, G. (2010, November 16). Ben & Jerry's builds on its social-values approach. *New York Times*. Retrieved from http://www.nytimes.com/2010/11/17/business/global/17iht-rbofice.html.

Robinson, A. (2011). An A to Z of theories: Roland Barthes' mythologies: A critical theory of myths. *Cease Fire* magazine. Retrieved from https://ceasefiremagazine.co.uk/in-theory-barthes-2/.

Rogers, K. (2014, May 14). Median American savings: $0. *Fox Business*. Retrieved from http://www.foxbusiness.com/personal-finance/2014/05/14/median-american -savings-0/.

Rosenberg, R. (1999). Possibility of sale chills Ben & Jerry's ally. *Boston Globe*, December 10.

Rosin, H. (2009, April). The case against breast-feeding. *Atlantic*. Retrieved from http:// www.theatlantic.com/magazine/archive/2009/04/the-case-against-breast -feeding/307311/.

Roth, L. M., & Henley, M. M. (2012). Unequal motherhood: Racial-ethnic and socioeco- nomic disparities in cesarean sections in the United States. *Social Problems 59*(2): 207–227.

Sacker, A., Kelly, Y., Iacovou, M., Cable, N., & Bartley, M. (2013). Breast feeding and intergenerational social mobility: What are the mechanisms? *Archives of Disease in Childhood*, archdischild–2012–303199. doi:10.1136/archdischild-2012-303199.

Sadler, P. (2010; 2016). *Sustainable growth in a post-scarcity world: Consumption, de- mand, and the poverty penalty*. Burlington, VT: Gower.

Salkin, A. (Feb. 6 2009). You try to live on 500k in this town. *New York Times*.

Salsburg, D. (2002). *The lady tasting tea: How statistics revolutionized science in the twen- tieth century*. New York: Henry Holt.

Sandberg, S. (2013). *Lean in: Women, work, and the will to lead*. New York: Knopf.

Sassen, S. (1991; 2013). *The global city: New York, London, Tokyo* (2nd rev. ed.). Prince- ton: Princeton University Press.

———. (2012). *Cities in a world economy* (4th ed.). Thousand Oaks, CA: SAGE/Pine Forge.

Saxenian, A. L. (1994). *Regional advantage: Culture and competition in Silicon Valley and Route 128*. Cambridge, MA: Harvard University Press.

Sayer, L., Bianchi, S., & Robinson, J. (2004). Are parents investing less in children? Trends in mothers' and fathers' time with children. *American Journal of Sociology 110*(1): 1–43. doi:10.1086/386270.

Schor, J. (1991). *The overworked American: The unexpected decline of leisure*. New York: Basic Books.

———. (1998). *The overspent American: Upscaling, downshifting, and the new consumer* (1st ed.). New York: Basic Books.

Scott, A. (2005). *Hollywood: The place, the industry*. Princeton: Princeton University Press.

Seckler, D. W. (1975). *Thorstein Veblen and the institutionalists: A study in the social philosophy of economics*. Boulder: Colorado Associated University Press.

Second wind. (2014, June 14). *Economist: Schumpeter*. Retrieved from http://www .economist.com/news/business/21604156-some-traditional-businesses-are-thriving -age-disruptive-innovation-second-wind.

Segran, E. (2016, March 16). Why clothing startups are returning to American factories. *Fast Company*. Retrieved from https://www.fastcompany.com/3057738/most-creative -people/why-clothing-startups-are-returning-to-american-factories.

Shapiro, S. M. (2012, May 23). Mommy wars: The prequel. *New York Times Magazine*. Retrieved from http://www.nytimes.com/2012/05/27/magazine/ina-may-gaskin-and -the-battle-for-at-home-births.html.

Shaxson, N. (2013, April). A tale of two Londons. *Vanity Fair*. Retrieved from http:// www.vanityfair.com/society/2013/04/mysterious-residents-one-hyde-park-london.

Silver, D., Clark, T. N., & Yanez, C.J.N. (2010). Scenes: Social context in an age of contingency. *Social Forces* 88(5): 2293–2324. doi:10.1353/sof.2010.0041.

Simmel, G. (1903). The metropolis and mental Life. Taken from K. H. Wolff (1st Free Press paperback ed.). *The Sociology of Georg Simmel.* New York, London: Free Press; Collier Macmillan.

———. (1957). Fashion. *American Journal of Sociology* 62(6): 541–558.

Sirkin, H. L., Zinser, M., & Manfred, K. (2013, January 17). That "Made in USA" label may be worth more than you think. *BCG Perspectives.* Retrieved from https://www .bcgperspectives.com/content/commentary/consumer_products_retail_that_made _in_usa_label_may_be_worth_more_than_you_think/.

Smock, P. J. (2010). Review of *Longing and belonging: Parents, children, and consumer culture,* by Allison Pugh. *Contemporary Sociology* 39(2): 196–197.

Somerville, K. (2012). Not one of us: Four books that explore the implications of class in America. *Missouri Review* 35(3): 163–175.

Spin to separate: Sweating on purpose is becoming an elite phenomenon. (2015, August 1) *Economist.* Retrieved from http://www.economist.com/news/united-states /21660170-sweating-purpose-becoming-elite-phenomenon-spin-separate.

Steiner, I. (2011, January 11). Etsy sales increase 74% in 2010 as growth rate slows. *EcommerceBytes.* Retrieved from http://www.ecommercebytes.com/cab/abn/y11/m01 /i11/s01.

Storper, M. (1997). *The regional world: Territorial development in a global economy.* New York: Guilford Press.

———. (2013). *Keys to the city: How economics, institutions, social interactions, and politics shape the development.* Princeton: Princeton University Press.

Sullivan, P. (2014, July 11). Vacation experiences that only money can buy. *New York Times.* Retrieved from http://www.nytimes.com/2014/07/12/your-money/bespoke -luxury-travel-from-100000-and-up.html.

Summers, L. (2006, December 10). Only fairness will assuage the anxious middle. *Financial Times.* Retrieved from https://www.ft.com/content/06ab25e6-8869-11db-b485 -0000779e2340.

Surowiecki, J. (2014, May 19). Real estate goes global. *New Yorker.* Retrieved from http:// www.newyorker.com/magazine/2014/05/26/real-estate-goes-global.

Sussman, G. D. (1975). The wet-nursing business in nineteenth-century France. *French Historical Studies* 9(2): 304–328. doi:10.2307/286130.

Taylor-Gooby, P. (1998). Comments on Amitai Etzioni: Voluntary simplicity: Characterization, select psychological implications, and societal consequences. *Journal of Economic Psychology* 19(5): 645–650.

Tracking the breakdown of American social institutions in "The Unwinding." (2013, December 26). *PBS NewsHour.* Retrieved from http://www.pbs.org/newshour/bb /business-july-dec13-packer_12-26/.

Trebay, G. (2010, September 1). The tribes of San Francisco. *New York Times.* Retrieved from http://www.nytimes.com/2010/09/02/fashion/02Diary.html?pagewanted=all.

Trentmann, F. (2016). *Empire of things: How we became a world of consumers, from the fifteenth century to the twenty-first.* New York: Harper.

Tully, K. (2010, June 23). My liquidity moment. *Financial Times.*

Vaizey, J. (1975, May 29). The return of Veblen. *Listener.*

Wallace-Hadrill, A. (1990). The social spread of Roman luxury: Sampling Pompeii and Herculaneum. *Papers of the British School at Rome 58*: 145–192.

——. (1994). *Houses and society in Pompeii and Herculaneum*. Princeton: Princeton University Press.

Weber, M. (1905). *The Protestant ethic and the spirit of capitalism*. London and Boston: Unwin Hyman.

——. (1978). *Economy and society: An outline of interpretive sociology*. Berkeley: University of California Press.

Who's in the middle? (2009, February 12). *Economist*. Retrieved from http://www.econ omist.com/node/13063338.

Wilson, W. J. (1987). *The truly disadvantaged: The inner city, the underclass, and public policy*. Chicago: University of Chicago Press.

Wirth, L. (1938). Urbanism as a way of life. *American Journal of Sociology* 44(1): 1–24. doi:10.1086/217913.

World Wildlife Fund—endangered species conservation. (n.d.). Retrieved from http://www.worldwildlife.org/.

Wright, A. L., & Schanler, R. J. (2001). The resurgence of breastfeeding at the end of the second millennium. *Journal of Nutrition* 131(2): 421S–425S.

Yardley, J. (2013, May 22). Report on deadly factory collapse in Bangladesh finds widespread blame. *New York Times*. Retrieved from http://www.nytimes.com/2013/05/23/world/asia/report-on-bangladesh-building-collapse-finds-widespread-blame.html.

Yoon, H., & Currid-Halkett, E. (2014). Industrial gentrification in West Chelsea, New York: Who survived and who did not? Empirical evidence from discrete-time survival analysis. *Urban Studies* 52(1), 20–49. doi:10.1177/0042098014536785.

Young, M. (2014, March 9). SOMA: The stubborn uncoolness of San Francisco style. *New York Magazine*. Retrieved from http://nymag.com/news/features/san-francisco -style-2014-3/.

Yueh, L. (2013, June 18). The rise of the global middle class. *BBC News*. Retrieved from http://www.bbc.com/news/business-22956470.

Zukin, S. (1989). *Loft living: Culture and capital in urban change* (2nd ed.). New Brunswick, NJ: Rutgers University Press.

——. (1993). *Landscapes of power: From Detroit to Disney World*. Berkeley: University of California Press.

Zukin, S., & Kosta, E. (2004). Bourdieu off-Broadway: Managing distinction on a shopping block in the East Village. *City & Community* 3(2): 101–114. doi:10.1111/j.1535 -6841.2004.00071.x.

Zukin, S., & Maguire, J. S. (2004). Consumers and consumption. *Annual Review of Sociology* 30(1): 173–197. doi:10.1146/annurev.soc.30.012703.110553.

INTERVIEWS CONDUCTED

Eugene Ahn, Forage Restaurant, September 16, 2013
Kate Berridge, author, February 26, 2014
Elizabeth Bowen, Altadena Farmers Market, October 15, 2013
Kevin Carney, Mohawk Botique, September 16, 2013

Nancy Chin, professor, Department of Public Health and Sciences, University of Rochester Medical Center, May 29, 2014

Paula Daniels, Los Angeles Food Policy Council, February 24, 2016

Juan Gerscovich, Industry of All Nations, October 9, 2013

Andrew Wallace Hadrill, professor of Roman Studies, University of Cambridge, March 17, 2014

Corky Harvey, The Pump Station, November 30, 2012

Marian MacDorman, senior statistician, Centers for Disease Control and Prevention; editor-in-chief, *Birth: Issues in Perinatal Care*, May 28, 2014

Laura and Jason O'Dell, Bucks and Does, October 23, 2013

Geoff Watts, Intelligentsia, October 30, 2013

Essie Weingarten, founder, Essie Cosmetics Ltd, December 1, 2012

Jen Williams and Derec Williams, founders, Pop Physique, July 9, 2015

Mark Zambito, Intelligentsia, October 2, 2013

INDEX

Note: Page numbers followed by "f" or "t" indicate figures or tables, respectively.

248 • INDEX

Burberry's, 13–14
Bureau of Labor Statistics, 27
Burt's Bees, 144

California, food production in, 125–26
Cameron, David, 56
candles, 2–3
capitalism: conspicuous production and, 141;
    cultural contradictions of, 106–7; Marx's
    critique of, 141–42; reactions against,
    139–40
Capote, Truman, 10
Carlin, George, 182
Carney, Kevin, 137
car purchases/sales, 177, 193
Carson, Rachel, *Silent Spring*, 135
cash contributions, 29
Centers for Disease Control (CDC), 79–80
Century Foundation, 189
CES. *See* Consumer Expenditure Survey
Chanel, 194
Chappell, Kate, 144
Charles, Kerwin, 35–38
chavs, 13
Chemex manual coffee brewer, 184
Chez Panisse, 122
Chicago, 167–68, 170
child care, 64, 65t, 168
Chin, Nancy, 84–86
China, 94, 127, 132, 192–95
cities, 148–81; amenities of, 153–54, 157,
    172–75; aspirational class linked to, 148,
    151–52; clothing consumption in, 170, 176;
    conspicuous consumption in, 175–81;
    consumption in relation to, 152–58, 161,
    178; cost of living in, 156–57; decline and
    resurgence of, 149–53; desirability of,
    148–49, 151–57; drink in, 163–64; elites
    in, 174–75, 180–81; as extension of one's
    home, 169–70; food in, 162–63; growth of,
    151–53; household furnishings in, 169–70;
    housing costs in, 164–68; during Industrial
    Revolution, 149, 152; meaning of small
    things in, 161, 179; neighborhoods in,
    158; patterns of consumption in, 169–72;
    peculiarities of, 158–68, 178–80; reproduc-
    tion of, 155; similarities and connections of,
    158, 180–81, 231n58. *See also* global cities
citizen-consumer hybrid, 123–24
city size, consumption patterns by, 43–44, 43t
Clark, Terry, 158

class: consumption as informative about, 21;
    cultural divide based on, 185–86; current
    state of, 182–98; practicality in relation to,
    1–3; status markers linked to, 177–78
Clean Air Act, 135
Clean Water Act, 135
Cleveland, 165, 173
Clifford, Stephanie, 133
Clorox, 144
clothing and fashion: American-made,
    131–34; of city-dwellers, 170, 176; class as
    factor contributing to, 224n4; conspicuous
    consumption of, 126–30; democratization
    of conspicuous consumption of, 11–12
coffee, 111–16, 163–64
Cohen, Ben, 143–44
cohort crowding, 96–97
Colen, Cynthia, 83–84
Colgate-Palmolive, 144–45
college admissions, 69, 77, 96–97
college tuition, 70, 72f
Collins, Joan, 100
concerted cultivation, 97, 108
concierge medicine, 72
Connecticut suburbs, 168, 173, 230n38
conspicuous consumption: backlash to, 13–14;
    in cities, 175–81; by city size, 43–44, 43t;
    democratization of, 10–13; educational
    attainment as influence on, 40–41, 41t,
    42f; factors contributing to, 178–79; by
    geographic region, 42–43, 43t; income in
    relation to, 30–31, 31t; Industrial Revolu-
    tion and, 8–10; marketing aimed at, 10–13;
    of middle class, 26, 31, 62, 63f; online
    shopping as boon to, 12; pervasiveness of,
    9–10, 22, 44, 184; of the poor and low-
    income group, 31; in pre-industrial
    societies, 6–8; of the rich, 26, 30, 32, 35–36,
    38, 61, 63f; trends in, 26; in twenty-first
    century, 24–45; Veblen's concept of, 4–5.
    See also inconspicuous consumption;
    status
conspicuous leisure, 5, 22, 80, 96, 99–100;
    productive, 100–109
conspicuous production, 110–47; clothing
    and, 126–30; coffee as example of, 111–16;
    costs of, 133; Etsy as example of, 130–31;
    factors contributing to, 117; food as,
    117–26; inconspicuous consumption of,
    145–46; in mass market, 131–34, 145; rise
    of, 116–17, 184–85; roots of, 139–40